GOD, TIME,
and the INCARNATION

GOD, TIME,
and the INCARNATION

RICHARD A. HOLLAND JR.

WIPF & STOCK · Eugene, Oregon

GOD, TIME, AND THE INCARNATION

Wipf & Stock
An Imprint of Wipf and Stock Publishers
199 W. 8th Ave., Suite 3
Eugene, OR 97401

www.wipfandstock.com

ISBN 13: 978-1-61097-729-6

Manufactured in the U.S.A.

Contents

Acknowledgments

A PROJECT OF THIS scope bears the marks of many. On each page is found encouragement from friends and family, challenges from colleagues, and guidance from mentors. Without the contribution and influence of countless people in my life, I would not have even been able to begin this book, let alone bring it to completion. Although there are many who deserve recognition for the support they have provided for me, space here will not be sufficient to mention them all.

I owe a special word of thanks to my mentor and teacher Dr. Bruce Little. It was Dr. Little who first heightened my interest in Philosophy and Philosophical Theology when I was working on my MDiv degree; and it was his continued influence that eventually led me to study on the PhD level. As he does with all of his students, Dr. Little pushed me hard and demanded nothing but the best work from me. He was relentless and required far more than what the academic program required; and he gave far more to me than his job description required. He has devoted himself to making me a better student; and he has inspired me to become a better theologian, a better philosopher, and a better person.

I owe a word of thanks to Dr. Garrett J. DeWeese and Dr. Steven W. Ladd, who provided helpful advice and guidance as I developed earlier versions of the arguments presented in this book. I also must thank my faithful friends and colleagues Dr. John D. Wilsey and Dr. James K. Dew Jr. John has provided both encouragement and helpful advice—academic, personal, and professional—and has provided keen insights as I worked on this project. Jamie also has been a constant source of encouragement. He has continually provided trustworthy and reliable advice, and his insights into the substance of this book have been invaluable.

I also must thank my dear wife Larissa, without whose love, devotion, and extraordinary patience this project would not have been possible. Over the past fifteen years of marriage, she has put up with late nights, long commutes, difficult moves, inconvenient schedules, and uncertainty about the future; all the while displaying the grace and charm fitting a woman of God. She has sacrificed more than anyone should be asked to sacrifice, and has given more than anyone should be asked to give. She has provided for me a peaceful, loving home and four beautiful children, whom she has taught to love their father. She has encouraged me to accomplish much, and to dream for more; and many times it was her confidence in me that kept me going when I wanted to quit. And so I thank my wife for her unending love and affection, her encouragement, and her unwavering support.

Above all I give thanks and praise to God who rescued me many years ago, and whose grace and mercy have followed me ever since. It is through the natural abilities he has given me, and the supernatural grace he has lavished upon me that I have been able to complete this project.

Introduction

ROM THE EARLIEST DAYS of Christian history the consensus opinion
among theologians has been that God enjoys a *timelessly* eternal existence. Those comprising this majority have asserted that God is atemporal—that he does not experience temporal sequence or succession of
any kind. This assertion has been founded on theological and philosophical inquiry into the nature of God's existence—inquiry that was often
prompted by various challenges brought forth. Augustine's development
of God's relation to time, for example, arises from his consideration of
the question, "What was God doing before He made heaven and earth?"[1]
Augustine considers this question (which was presumably posed by a critic as a challenge against Christian doctrine) in the context of his discussion of God's creative activity. A hundred years later, Boethius developed
his model of God's relation to time as a solution to the apparent conflict
between God's foreknowledge and human freedom. In his *Consolation of
Philosophy* Boethius gives the now famous depiction of God's knowledge
as *spatial* rather than temporal. He writes that God's knowledge of future
human choices should be referred to as "*providentia* ('looking forward
spatially') rather than *praevidentia* ('looking forward in time'), for . . . it
gazes on everything as from one of the world's lofty peaks."[2]

The view held by Augustine and Boethius—that God's existence is
atemporal—quickly became the accepted model, with notable theologians from Anselm and Aquinas, to many of the Reformers, to Friedrich
Schleiermacher all defending the atemporal view.[3] Paul Helm emphasizes
that this became the "classical" view. He writes, "The classical Christian
theologians, Augustine . . . or Aquinas or John Calvin, each took it for

---

1. Augustine, Confessions, 11.10.12 (*NPNF*[1] 1:167).

2. Boethius, *Consolation of Philosophy*, 5.6 (112). The emphasis and parentheticals
are original to the edition cited.

3. See Padgett, *God, Eternity, and the Nature of Time*, 38–55 as an example of a brief
historical survey of the development of the idea of Divine timelessness, including a brief
outline of major figures holding to the atemporal view.

granted that God exists as a timelessly eternal being."[4] Standing in this tradition, contemporary authors who have defended Divine timelessness include Helm, Eleonore Stump and Norman Kretzmann, Richard Swinburne, and Brian Leftow.[5] In the works defending the classical atemporal view, the contemporary arguments typically follow those first made by Augustine and Boethius.

The arguments and definitions laid down by the two early proponents of the doctrine of God's timelessness share some common features. One key similarity is the emphasis on God experiencing the whole of his life at once, with no passage and no temporal relation of one part of his life to another. In Book XI of his *Confessions*, Augustine argues that the eternity of God is such that it has no temporal relations such that there is no past, no passage, and no future, but that all things are equally present. He writes that "in the Eternal nothing passeth away, but that the whole is present."[6] This, of course, is the main thrust of Boethius's definition of eternity as "the total and perfect possession of life without end."[7] In Book 5 of his *Consolation*, Boethius goes on to contrast that which is eternal from that which is in time; and he concludes that while time passes away, God's eternity is always wholly present.

4. Helm, *Eternal God*, xi.

5. Ibid., which has been recently appeared in a new edition, is his most exhaustive work on the subject. Another important defense of the classical atemporal view is found in Helm, "Divine Timeless Eternity," 28–68. One of the more significant works defending the atemporal view is Stump and Kretzmann, "Eternity," 429–58. Their essay defends the idea that a timelessly eternal being could interact in the temporal world by offering positing "E-T Simultaneity" as a model for how divine eternal (atemporal) actions could be simultaneous with temporal events. This article is quoted in most major contemporary works on the subject and has been reprinted as a component part of several anthologies and other books dealing with the topic. Swinburne's defense of the traditional model is found in Swinburne "Timelessness of God, I," 323–37; and "Timelessness of God, II," 472–86. In later works, Swinburne has reversed himself and rejected the classical atemporal view. Nevertheless, the two articles will be considered as an example of a well-formed defense of the atemporal view. Subsequent works in which Swinburne defends the alternative thesis include Swinburne, *Coherence of Theism*; and Swinburne, "God and Time." Leftow's main works defending the traditional view include "Why Didn't God Create the World Sooner?" 157–72; "Timelessness and Foreknowledge," 309–25; "Eternity and Simultaneity," 148–79; *Time and Eternity*; "Timeless God Incarnate," 273–99; and "The Eternal Present," 21–48.

6. Augustine, *Confessions*, 11.10.13 (*NPNF* [1] 1:167).

7. Boethius, *Consolation of Philosophy*, 5.6.4 (110).

Further, the idea of immutability also plays a key role in what is now known as the classical atemporal position. A strong sense of immutability is logically connected to Boethius's argument. If God experiences the fullness of his life at once, without passage of any kind, it would follow that God is necessarily immutable, by virtue of his timelessness. This connection is found also in Augustine's argument in *The Trinity*. He argues that to refer to God as "eternal" is the same as to refer to him as "unchangeable." Making the case, Augustine writes, "His immortality is genuine immortality, as in his nature there is no change. But that is also genuine eternity by which God is unchangeable, without beginning, without end, and consequently incorruptible. Therefore one and the same thing is being said, whether you say God is eternal or immortal or incorruptible or unchangeable."[8] So these two concepts—the fullness of the Divine life and God's immutability—are commonly tied together in atemporal models.

Contemporary defenders of the classical view generally invoke these main features in their arguments. Stump and Kretzmann, for example, use Boethius's definition of eternity to develop their model of divine interaction with the world. In their often quoted and highly influential article "Eternity," Stump and Kretzmann rely heavily on Boethius, and devote a significant portion of their essay to expounding Boethius's conception of eternity.[9] The two authors seek to defend the Boethian model by developing a framework for how an atemporal being can act within time. Brian Leftow addresses the topic in a similar manner, as he discusses the compatibility between God's foreknowledge and human freedom in his article "Eternity and Simultaneity."[10] Elsewhere, Leftow also connects timelessness with immutability. He concludes one argument by asserting that "a being is both maximally perfect and immutable only if it is not temporal."[11] Likewise, Helm argues that immutability entails timelessness. In his discussion, Helm argues for what he calls a "strong" sense of immutability, and concludes that "an individual who is immutable in the

---

8. Augustine, *The Trinity*, 15.2.7 (400). Nelson Pike quotes this same passage in his *God and Timelessness*, 39. Pike goes on to argue that a prominent feature of Augustine's thought is understanding God's immutability as a logical consequence of his atemporality.

9. See Stump and Kretzmann, "Eternity," 430–34.

10. Leftow, "Eternity and Simultaneity," 148–79.

11. Ibid., 65.

strong sense must be [timelessly] eternal."[12] These four authors are representative of the contemporary defense of the classical atemporal view.

Some contemporary arguments, however, have challenged the traditional view that God is timeless. During the past thirty years, a body of literature has developed among Christian philosophical theologians that challenges the classical formulation of God's relation to time. These authors have suggested, as an alternative, the thesis that God does experience a kind of temporal existence.[13] Typically, their arguments focus on two primary issues. First, some develop arguments for God's temporality based on the dynamic nature of time. Alan Padgett, for example, relies heavily on a dynamic theory of time to develop his model challenging the classical view.[14] Second, a prominent feature of many temporal arguments is God's action in and interaction with the created universe. These arguments tend to be multifaceted and include factors such as the acts of creation and sustenance of the universe, issues such as prophecy and prayer, as well as concerns about God's knowledge of tensed facts about the world. Nicholas Wolterstorff, for example, develops a robust argument for God's temporality founded on the Bible's representation of God acting within history. Wolterstorff argues that the Bible presents God as being an agent within the history of the world, dynamically interacting as events unfold. He writes that the biblical narrative presents "God as having a history, which then can be narrated."[15] This contemporary divergence from the classical position has spawned a debate on God's relation to time; and my intent in this work is to make a contribution to the ongoing discussion.

---

12. Helm, *Eternal God*, 94.

13. Gregory Ganssle argues that atemporal views were in the majority as of 1975, but that "[m]ost philosophers today disagree." See Ganssle, *God and Time: Four Views*, 13. See also Wolterstorff, "God Everlasting," 77, which Ganssle cites as a source for his statement. Characterizing the history of the debate, Wolterstorff writes, "Only a small minority have contended that God is *everlasting*, existing within time." In addition to this work, other notable examples of temporal arguments include Pike, *God and Timelessness*; Sturch, "Problem of Divine Eternity," 489–90; Padgett, *God, Eternity, and the Nature of Time*; and Feinberg, *No One Like Him: The Doctrine of God*.

14. See Padgett, *God, Eternity, and the Nature of Time*.

15. Wolterstorff, "Unqualified Divine Temporality," 188. See also Sontag, "Is God Really in History?" 379–90.

PURPOSE OF THIS WORK

The purpose of this work is twofold: to examine God's relation to time, and to offer a critical evaluation of traditional atemporal models and contemporary temporal models in light of the Christian doctrine of the Incarnation of Christ. I will argue that the Incarnation of Christ indicates that God experiences temporal sequence in his existence.

In order to accomplish this purpose, my argument is developed in three main points of focus. First, it reviews the history of the debate within Christianity from Augustine to the present, highlighting the development of various models consistent with the classical atemporal view. Second, it asserts the central importance of the Incarnation for Christian theology, and provides a theological evaluation of prominent temporal and atemporal models in light of this doctrine. Finally, it will provide a philosophical model for how God experiences temporal sequence in his existence based on the Incarnation of God the Son. In each phase of the presentation, special attention is given to how the various models of God's relation to time account for the Incarnation, both as Christ entered the world, and as he remains incarnate in a post-resurrection transformed state. Thus, I am attempting to offer a viable solution to the debate by using the Incarnation as the lens through which God's relation to time is properly viewed.

The topic of God's relation to time is certainly not uncommon within the field of philosophical theology. And in the available literature, several key authors mention the Incarnation and state that this doctrine is significant for the debate on God and time. What seems to be absent from this large body of literature, however, is a book-length treatment or other detailed examination of how the Incarnation impacts the debate. There have been a few short essays addressing the topic, most notably Thomas Senor[16] arguing for temporality and Brian Leftow[17] arguing for atemporality. These articles, however, are limited in scope and are not crafted for the purpose of detailed or comprehensive examination of the topic. According to Garrett DeWeese, arguments for divine temporality on the basis of the Incarnation are rare. He writes that such arguments have "not figured large in the literature."[18] Therefore, I am attempting to

---

16. Senor, "Incarnation and Timelessness," 149–64. Senor's essay presents a narrowly focused logical argument, which will be examined in a later chapter of this work.

17. Leftow, "Timeless God Incarnate."

18. DeWeese, *God and the Nature of Time*, 232.

fill a void by giving a more detailed and focused examination on how this essential core of Christian theology may shape the philosophical debate.

While arguments focusing on the Incarnation are rare; I am suggesting here that the Incarnation should be most prominently featured in discussions about God's relation to time, for it is this essential doctrine that is at the center of Christian Orthodoxy. Some have recognized the importance of such theological considerations. Nicholas Wolterstorff, for example, highlights the importance of considering the Incarnation. In his discussion of how the atemporal position can account for divine action in time he writes, "The most important question for the Christian to consider, in reflecting on [the classical, atemporal] understanding of divine action, is whether it is compatible with an orthodox understanding of what happens in the incarnation."[19] DeWeese recognizes that the argument from the Incarnation represents a significant challenge to the traditional atemporal view. He writes, "At the very least, the argument from the Incarnation raises a serious problem for the atemporalist, and the available responses to it are beset with significant difficulties."[20]

In this book, I will present an analysis of some of the difficulties that proponents of the atemporal view face when considering the Incarnation, and will argue that accounts of God's existence as being temporal are to be preferred in light of this vital doctrine.[21] This will be an argument *in favor of* God's existence as being (in some sense) temporal—that God experiences temporal sequence in his life and action—using the Incarnation as the standard by which all God-time models should be evaluated.

METHOD AND APPROACH TO THE TOPIC

In my examination of the topic, I will not seek primarily to argue against any particular feature of common atemporal arguments, although objections to some of the common features will be offered. Nor will I simply re-

19. Wolterstorff, "Unqualified Divine Temporality," 209.

20. DeWeese, *God and the Nature of Time*, 234.

21. Throughout this book, the term *timeless* (and its cognates) is used as an equivalent to *atemporal* (and its cognates); while the term *temporal* will be used as an antonym of both, indicating the passage of moments and temporal sequence in divine experience and action. The term *eternal* will not be used to indicate either timeless existence, temporally everlasting existence, or any other kind of time referent, for this is the very issue in question. Some authors discussed in this work use *eternal*, and I will attempt to preserve their meaning and bring clarity to the discussion.

count or strictly follow any one of the contemporary temporal arguments. Instead, I will attempt to highlight an *alternative approach to the question of God's relation to time*—an approach that will show the classical approach to be deficient, and many of the contemporary temporal models insufficient or improperly based. Further, the approach presented here will lead to a model of God's relation to time that suggests that he does experience temporal sequence. All along the way, the Incarnation will be used as the template demarcating the borders of philosophical inquiry that gives Christian orthodoxy its proper place.

In his book, *Reason within the Bounds of Religion*, Wolterstorff puts forward the concept of "control beliefs," referring to those beliefs that govern and control what further beliefs one is willing to adopt.[22] Wolterstorff's discussion is primarily concerned with the apparent conflict between religion and science; and he points out that both parties in the debate employ control beliefs in accepting or rejecting other beliefs. But I want to suggest that a similar model can and should be applied to the debate concerning God's relation to time. It is my contention that the Christian doctrine of the Incarnation ought to function as the primary control belief in the debate concerning God's relation to time. The assertion I am making is not that one ought to have a control belief, for when examining the literature it is clear that control beliefs are employed. For Augustine and Thomas Aquinas, the operative control belief is absolute Divine immutability; and for Boethius, the fullness of the Divine life and absolute Divine omniscience serve this function. Modern defenders of the classical view follow suit. For others, the dynamic nature of time holds priority; and for still others the dynamic nature of God's personality serves as the control belief.

Rather than argue that one ought to have a control belief concerning the present topic, I am making a suggestion as to *which belief* among the essential Christian doctrines ought to serve this function: namely, the doctrine of the Incarnation. The fundamental assumption I am making is that the Incarnation is an essential doctrine of Christianity and stands at the very heart of Trinitarian theism. In Jesus Christ, orthodoxy asserts, man is given a unique and direct revelation of God. As the Apostle Paul writes to the Colossians, "He is the image of the invisible God, the

22. Wolterstorff, *Reason within the Bounds of Religion*. While Wolterstorff uses this term in a context unrelated to God's relation to time, it nevertheless is useful here, and in any similar debate.

firstborn over all creation;" and, "For in Him dwells all the fullness of the Godhead bodily" (Col 1:15; 2:9).[23] As such, my argument follows the observation made by Thomas Senor, who, in his article, "Incarnation and Timelessness" argues for divine temporality. Senor writes, "[M]y argument . . . depends on the central distinguishing feature of Christian orthodoxy—the doctrine of the Incarnation."[24] In this work, I will go further than Senor, and take into account the full scope of the doctrine as outlined in both the Nicene and Chalcedonian Creeds.

Given the theological priority of the Incarnation for Christian theism, at least two important philosophical considerations must be made in an analysis of the debate on God's relation to time. First, the Incarnation can be considered as a special case—or perhaps a test-case—of God acting in time. The biblical data uniformly testifies that God acts within time—that is, God speaks, acts, and intervenes in the normal course of human history. Further, the Bible portrays God's interaction with the world as having normal temporal sequence. In the creation account, for example, this sequence is given textual demarcation with the phrase, "then God said" (Gen 1:3–26). When considering the Bible as a whole, God's interaction with the world also carries its temporal ordering: God spoke to the fathers by the prophets *before* he sent his son (Heb 1:1–2). Considered in the abstract, however, the classical atemporal view may still be able to account for this apparent temporal ordering of God's interactions with the world. One could construct (and many have attempted to construct) a philosophical model by which God performs just one atemporal act which then has its effects borne out in the temporal order of the world.[25]

Such models, however, are stretched to their philosophical limits when required to account for God's interaction with the created order in the Incarnation. Given what Christian theism has said about the Incarnation, it is not merely the *effects* of God's actions seen in a temporal order, but the actions themselves. If true, Christianity's assertion that Jesus is God who lived a temporal life on earth in human flesh requires that the actions of Jesus are in some sense the actions of God himself.

---

23. All scripture quotations, unless otherwise indicated, are taken from the New King James Version®. Copyright © 1982 by Thomas Nelson, Inc. Used by permission. All rights reserved.

24. Senor, "Incarnation and Timelessness," 149.

25 Stump and Kretzmann, "Eternity" represents one of the most important works that attempts to construct such a model.

The second philosophical consideration that must be made in this analysis is one that goes to the very heart of Christian claims about the Incarnation: In what sense does the Incarnation reveal God to man? The Old Testament prophet Isaiah proclaimed that the Messiah would be called "God with us" (Isa 7:14; Matt 1:23). According to the Gospel of John, Jesus himself asserted that to see him was to see the Father (John 14:9). These passages are reflected in the declaration of the council of Chalcedon that "Jesus Christ is one and the same God, perfect in divinity, and perfect in humanity, true God and true human."[26] But while orthodox Christianity is unanimous in its affirmation that Jesus is both God and man, it becomes more difficult to explain (with one voice) the philosophical implications of such a doctrine on the current debate. As God, common predicates of deity are properly applied to Jesus Christ: he is good and holy, he transcends creation, he is perfect and just. But if Jesus is God, then the application of predicates must move in the opposite direction: Jesus himself reveals to human beings what God is like. Indeed, the New Testament affirms that Jesus has "declared" the Father (John 1:18), and that "in him dwells all the fullness of the Godhead bodily" (Col 2:9).

These statements about Jesus must be considered to be something other than a theological paradox. Instead of thinking of this as some sort of mysterious theological puzzle, it seems more prudent and more consistent with the Biblical data to conclude that Jesus actually reveals God to man. In light of this, certain questions must be considered. If Jesus is the full revelation of God in bodily form, to what extent are properties essential to divinity apparent in the life of Jesus? It would be inappropriate to argue based on Jesus' embodiment that experiences such as hunger and thirst or physical dimensions apply to God, because these apply only to embodied persons. But more significant to the debate on God's relation to time is the question: What does Jesus' apparently ordinary life of temporal passage and temporal sequence reveal about the life of God? This question will be considered as my argument unfolds.

TERMINOLOGY

The present topic is one in which terminology employed can sometimes bring confusion. Various authors use different terms to identify the same concepts; and some words (like "eternity," for example) are sometimes

---

26. In Gonzalez, *Story of Christianity*, vol. 1, 257.

given contradictory meanings by different authors. So, defining terminology can serve to both clarify the position defended, and avoid criticism brought from misunderstanding. In this work, I will take great care in how I use certain relevant terms.

At least four key terms must be examined, the first and most obvious of which is "time." Discussing the possibility of arriving at an adequate definition of time Augustine famously quipped, "What, then, is time? If no one asks me, I know; if I wish to explain to him who asks, I know not."[27] This appropriately captures the difficulty in attempting to develop an adequate definition; and as with Augustine, the ideas presented here may seem less than adequate for accomplishing that task. Nevertheless, when considering the nature of time, it seems that at least three options are available. The first option—which is the one favored by Augustine and is required by the atemporal view of God's relation to time—is that time is a created aspect of the universe, just as light, or space, or physical objects in the cosmos are created. If God created time, it would be difficult to imagine how God's existence could be anything but purely atemporal. The second option available is similar: time can be considered part of the framework of created order—like causation or the observable regularity of the physical universe. If time is such an aspect of the created order, this also would suggest that the classical atemporal view is correct.

Both of these two options share in common the fact that they refer to physical time; and so it is important at this point to make the distinction between physical time and *metaphysical* time. Physical time is that which refers to the physical operations of material objects in the universe: the passage of days, months, and years (as well as our perception of their passage) depend solely on the movement of physical objects in space. But there is also a metaphysical time that applies to creation, but transcends the material realm. An analogy that compares time to God's moral law can be helpful in the discussion: The moral law applies to creation, yet is not itself part of creation. The moral law is not created; rather it owes its source to God's very being. God is, in a sense, perfectly obedient to the requirements of the moral law, yet God is not subject to the moral law; rather, it flows from who he is. Likewise, time—metaphysical time—can be something that finds its source in God's being, and therefore transcends creation, and is itself (in another sense) transcended by God.

27. Augustine, *Confessions*, 11.14.17 (*NPNF*[1] 1:168).

This leads naturally to another key idea that must be examined: God's *relation* to time. The view one has regarding the nature of time will shape the language used in discussing God's relation to it. If the classical atemporal view is correct, God can be spoken of as being "outside" of time, timeless, or simply atemporal, because time is seen as a feature of God's created universe. But if time is not created by God, but instead is seen as analogous in some way to the moral law (as discussed above, for example), the language would be different. It would seem inappropriate in this case to speak of God being "in" or "outside of" time. Further, it would also not be appropriate to suggest that if God experiences temporal passage this fact would somehow take away from his sovereignty, omnipotence, or immutability. Paul Helm suggests, for example, "To many, the idea that God is subject to the vicissitudes of temporal passage . . . is incompatible with divine sovereignty, with divine perfection and with that fullness of being that is essential to God."[28] If time transcends creation as I have suggested, then God could indeed experience temporal passage without being "subject" to time (any more than he is "subject" to the moral law). Further, if this is the case, "vicissitudes" are not to be associated with time so much as they are to the tumult and decay seen in the world brought by the fall of man (Rom 8:19–22).

Given the history of the debate, a third term should be examined: eternity. When found in the Bible, this term is used to refer to the nature or existence of God, as well as to the unending life granted to the believer in Christ. In the literature on the topic, eternity is often associated with time, and is employed often in the debate about God's relation to time—it is sometimes assumed that "eternity" is synonymous with "atemporal." Indeed, perhaps Boethius has set the precedent for using the term "eternity," for his definition of eternity is the centerpiece of much of the contemporary debate. Given the multiple usages of the term, however, it seems unwise to develop an argument on God's relation to time based solely on the use of the word "eternal" or its cognates. Further, in order to arrive at a working definition of the word, the debate seems to force a minimalist approach: at the least, when applied to God, the term "eternal" means that God has existed at every point in the temporal past, and will continue to exist at every point in the temporal future—that is, he never comes into or goes out of existence. Of course defenders of atemporal

28. Helm, "Divine Timeless Eternity," 30–31.

models will want to say much more than this about the nature of God; but since biblical examples of how the term is used are limited to temporal reference points, it seems wise to similarly limit the present discussion.

Finally—and most importantly for this work—it is important to consider what is meant by "Incarnation." As has been apparent thus far, this work is written from a *Christian* perspective: it takes for granted the traditional understanding that Jesus Christ is truly God and truly man—God Incarnate—who lived a genuine earthly existence and even now continues to exist as the God-man in a glorified state. The matters addressed by the ancient councils concerning Christology in general and the Incarnation in particular, the results of which were codified in the creeds of the early church, are not considered open for debate for the purposes of the discussion presented in this work.

As discussed above, I am asserting that the Incarnation is the most vital and most central distinguishing feature of Christian theism; and this fact cannot be overemphasized. The Bible not only affirms, but also seems to highlight that Jesus Christ is himself a direct revelation of God, "the express image of his person" (Heb 1:3); and the Christian church has focused its doctrine on Christ. Millard Erickson argues this as he writes, "Throughout its history, the Church has realized that Christology . . . is of the greatest importance."[29] Furthermore, in analyzing the prologue to John's Gospel, Erickson interprets John 1:14 as affirming that the Incarnation "is not some timeless occurrence, but a specific event at a definite point of history."[30] These two facts together are what lay at the foundation of my argument: (1) in the Incarnation, God himself took on human nature and flesh; and (2) this was (and is) a purely temporal activity. The implications of this perspective will (of course) be examined in great detail in the following chapters.

One idea that I will highlight is that the Incarnation was not a temporary condescension on God's part into the realm of humanity, but rather the coming about of a permanent state of affairs in the life of the Second Person of the Trinity. As J. I. Packer has written, "Without diminishing his divinity, he added to it all that is involved in being human."[31] This transformation began in the womb of Mary, was made visible in the

---

29. Erickson, *Word Became Flesh*, 9.

30. Ibid., 26.

31. Packer, "Eternally Incarnate," 72.

earthly life, sufferings, death, and bodily resurrection of Jesus; and even now the God-Man lives on fulfilling his role in a glorified state. Again, as Packer writes, "The work of the Kingdom—that is, the perfecting of the church—will finish, but 'the Man Christ Jesus' will be our beloved prophet, priest, and king forever."[32] This fact highlights that any model of God's relation to time must not be limited to distinct actions of God on earth, or even theories of how the whole earthly life of Jesus may be taken into account. Rather, in order to develop a solution to the God-time puzzle—a solution that is faithful to what Christians have long affirmed concerning the Incarnation—one must account for how the eternal God can become a temporal individual man, and then live on in perpetuity as such in the person of Jesus Christ.

SUMMARY AND CONTENT OUTLINE

The first chapter will begin the examination of the matter by focusing on a synopsis of the history of the debate on God's relation to time. The chapter will first frame the debate by highlighting the most important theological and philosophical concepts relating to the nature of time itself which have been employed in the debate, including a brief discussion of J. M. E. McTaggart's formulation of A-series and B-series distinctions,[33] as well as several insights from physical scientific investigation and philosophical inquiry. Following this, the chapter will highlight the most important contributions by key figures of early Christian theology, including that of Augustine, Boethius, Anselm, and Aquinas. Further, the chapter will survey several key modern arguments, for the purpose of illustrating how these arguments owe their heritage to the more ancient arguments. During the discussion of each argument, both ancient and modern, the chapter will highlight whether and how each attempted to account for the Incarnation.

Chapter two will focus on the Incarnation, as it has been historically understood by Christian theologians. Paramount in this analysis will be the Nicene formulation, which will be used as a template for what Christians mean when they say God is Incarnate in Jesus Christ. Further, the chapter will address the Chalcedonian concerns about "person" and "nature" and how these distinctions impact the debate. The chapter will

32. Ibid.
33. McTaggart, *Nature of Existence*, vol. 2.

focus specifically on the union of the two natures in the one person of Jesus Christ. It will highlight the fact that the Incarnation requires that there be no conflict or contradiction in the union of the natures in one person. The chapter will also focus on the Incarnation as an event in the life of God the Son, and will suggest that this event—as well as other ordinary temporal events in the life and work of Christ—indicates the temporal sequence in the Divine life.

The third chapter will be dedicated to a detailed analysis of several prominent examples of atemporal arguments. A significant portion of the chapter will be dedicated to analyzing Paul Helm's atemporal argument.[34] Helm is a prominent contributor to the current debate, therefore his argument will be considered as exemplary in understanding God's existence as atemporal. Additionally, the chapter will offer an analysis of the atemporal arguments offered by Brian Leftow[35] and Richard Swinburne.[36] The chapter will then highlight several philosophical and theological implications of considering God's existence as atemporal. The atemporal view will also be examined with regard to how these arguments are able to account for the Incarnation.

Chapter four will examine several prominent examples of arguments intended to show that God's existence is temporal. It will offer an analysis of the arguments made by Nicholas Wolterstorff,[37] Alan Padgett,[38] and Thomas Senor.[39] Additionally, a brief examination of God's relation to time as put forth by Open Theism will be given. Following the pattern of analysis from chapter three, several philosophical implications for temporal models will be considered, and several variations of the temporal view will be examined for their consistency with the doctrine of the Incarnation.

34. Two key sources for Helm's argument are Helm, *Eternal God*; and "Divine Timeless Eternity."

35. Primarily from Leftow, "Timeless God Incarnate;" but also from Leftow, "Eternity and Simultaneity," and Leftow, "Eternal Present," 21–48.

36. Primarily from Swinburne, "Timelessness of God, I," 323–37; and Swinburne, "Timelessness of God, II." Swinburne, *Space and Time*, will also be considered. Swinburne, "God and Time," Richard Swinburne, *Resurrection of God Incarnate* will be juxtaposed in the analysis because in these later works, Swinburne defends the opposite thesis.

37. Wolterstorff, "God Everlasting," and "Unqualified Divine Temporality," 187–225.

38. Padgett, "New Doctrine of Eternity," 559–78; Padgett, *God, Eternity, and the Nature of Time*; and Padgett, "Eternity as Relative Timelessness," 92–128.

39. Senor, "Incarnation and Timelessness."

Chapter five will conclude my argument by applying the work of the previous chapters to a model of God's mode of being as temporal. The chapter will focus on the priority of the Incarnation for philosophical theology, and will argue that when this doctrine is given priority, the classical atemporal model is far less tenable. The chapter will also give a brief discussion on the nature of time, as well as a brief discussion on how the two natures are united in the one person of Christ without contradiction. The three-fold pattern first introduced in chapter 2 will be revisited, for the purpose of highlighting how the Incarnation indicates that God experiences temporal sequence.

1

The Nature of Time and the History of the Debate

WHEN THE HISTORY OF the debate about God's relation to time is examined, the earliest voices have been nearly unanimous in their assertion that God lives an atemporal existence; and dissent from this view (with few exceptions) seems to have been expressed only recently. For each prominent contribution, slightly different reasons and arguments have been given to support the classical atemporal position. In this chapter, I want to highlight some of the most important contributions by key figures of early Christian history, including that of Augustine, Boethius, Anselm, and Aquinas; and I'll briefly survey one modern argument made by Friedrich Schleiermacher. It will be important to note what theological priorities are brought into the discussion, and what motivates each of these theologians to adopt the atemporal view—an emphasis on God's immutability is often seen, for example. These prominent figures have built what has become the foundation of the classical atemporal view. In order to move the debate forward, I want to challenge the ordering of the theological priorities; and so I will suggest that the doctrine of the Incarnation should be at the center of the discussion and the foundation of our understanding of God's relation to time.

The debate about the nature of time and the debate about God's relationship to time are inseparable, because the former (in many ways) has shaped the latter—especially with regard to the terminology and methodology employed. So before examining the historical contributions to the discussion of God's relation to time, I first want to frame the debate by highlighting several of the most important philosophical and theological concepts relating to the nature of time itself. This will include a brief synopsis of major philosophical contributions, and will highlight several insights from philosophical inquiry and physical scientific investigation, as well as J. M. E. McTaggart's formulation of A-series and B-series distinctions.[1] Additionally, some important methodological considerations will be discussed from a Christian perspective.

THE NATURE OF TIME

Important philosophical questions asked with regard to the nature of time include: What is time?, What is the relationship between time and "eternity"?, Is time part of the created universe only?, Is time real or merely an illusion of experience?, Is time static (tenseless) or dynamic (tensed)?, and What does the biblical evidence contribute to our understanding of the nature of time? Answers given to these and other related questions are a continuous matter of debate. When approaching the subject, however, any philosophical inquiry will be wise to follow the advice given by John Callahan in his *Four Views of Time in Ancient Philosophy*. Callahan argues that there are two sources of knowledge about time: first, common experience; and second, philosophical investigation. With regard to the first, he argues that "[t]his common knowledge of time is something that we must consider, and any detailed examination of time must not be out of harmony with it. Otherwise we should be explaining something other than that which men in general call time."[2] Additionally, whatever is said of the nature of time will have important implications for one's view of God's relationship to time. What follows is a brief survey of some of the more important philosophical contributions to understanding the nature of time, and an examination of how these contributions have left their mark in the debate on God and time.

Early Philosophy

As with most areas of the Western philosophical tradition, the ancient Greeks have laid down the foundations in the inquiry into the nature of time. As the pre-Socratics sought to define the fundamental nature of the universe, two opposing points of view emerged. For Heraclitus (540–480 BC), the universe was characterized primarily by change. He argued that everything in nature is in a continual state of flux, and that change is

1. McTaggart, *The Nature of Existence*, vol. 2.
2. Callahan, *Four Views of Time in Ancient Philosophy*, 97.

constant and pervasive, even if imperceptible. He writes, "Cold warms up, warm cools off, moist parches, dry dampens;"[3] and "One cannot step twice into the same river, nor can one grasp any mortal substance in a stable condition, but it scatters and again gathers; it forms and dissolves, it approaches and departs."[4] Contrasting this view, Parmenides (515–445 BC) taught that all plurality is an illusion and that change is impossible. The concept of non-existence is impossible, he argued, because if something can be spoken of, it must exist. He writes, "It must be that what is there for speaking and thinking of is; for, whereas nothing is not; that is what I bid you to consider."[5] But since change requires something coming in to existence from non-existence, change cannot be possible; and what exists must be unchanging and eternal. Zeno (490–430 BC) followed Parmenides, offering his famous paradoxes intended to prove that motion was impossible.

The work of Plato (427–347 BC) was perhaps (in part) an effort to unite the two seemingly contradictory notions put forward by the pre-Socratics. With his theory of Forms, he postulated a model of the universe divided between the unchanging ultimate reality and the ever changing and moving physical world. Plato's model of the universe along with his understanding of the nature of time has had great influence in Christian philosophical theology, from Augustine to the present day. For Plato, time belonged to the realm of the natural, physical world. Plato taught that time was a created image, modeled after the perfect Form of the eternal. He writes, "Now the nature of the intelligible being is eternal, and to bestow eternity on the creature was wholly impossible. But [the father and creator] resolved to make a moving image of eternity, and as he set in order the heaven he made this eternal image having a motion according to number, while eternity rested in unity; and this is what we call time."[6] This description of time as the "moving image of eternity" fits neatly into Plato's larger theory of Forms. The description of time as "moving" implies that eternity is in some sense static. As is the case with everything experienced in the natural world, so it is that when one

---

3. Heraclitus, *Fragments*, 49 (53).

4. Ibid., 51 (53).

5. Parmenides, *Parmenides of Elea: Fragments*, 28.

6. Plato, *Timaeus*, 37 (2:530).

experiences time, one is experiencing an imperfect moving image of an eternal, unchanging Form.

Implicit in the idea of time being the image of an eternal Form is the fact that time is a created part of the universe. Plato argued that in creation, time was not brought about from something that existed before the physical world, but rather came into being with the physical world. He writes, "For there were no days and nights and months and years before the heaven was created, but when he constructed the heaven he created them also."[7] To be sure, Plato was not saying that merely the *periods of time* known as "day," "month," and "year" came as a result of the creation of the physical universe. Rather, he was arguing that time itself came into existence with the physical universe. Lawrence Fagg agrees with this conclusion as he writes, "Thus Plato divided the cosmos into the temporal domain of the natural world and the nontemporal realm of an eternal Ideal."[8]

Not only did Plato argue that time was confined to the physical universe, he further argued that the two were inextricably connected. In the *Timaeus*, the protagonist makes two clear assertions that, first, the planets of the solar system were necessary for the creation of time, and, second, that the motion of the planets *is* time. He writes, "And in order to accomplish this creation [of time], he made the sun and the moon and five other stars, which are called planets, to distinguish and preserve the numbers of time, and when God made the bodies of these several stars he gave them orbits in the circle of the other."[9] Later in the same portion of the dialogue, he refers to the bodies as "all the stars which were needed to make time,"[10] arguing that day and night are created by one revolution of the earth, the month is created by the orbit of the moon, and the year by the orbit of the sun. Plato's belief that the motion of the bodies constituted time is made even more clear as he writes, "Thus, and to this end, came into existence such of the stars as moved and returned through the heaven, in order that the created heaven might be as like as possible to the perfect and intelligible animal, and imitate the eternal nature."[11]

7. Ibid.

8. Fagg, *The Becoming of Time*, 16. It seems clear that Fagg uses "nontemporal" as I have used "atemporal."

9. Plato, *Timaeus*, 38 (2:531).

10. Ibid.

11. Ibid., 39 (2:532).

John Callahan's analysis of the *Timaeus* brings the same conclusion. After pointing out the declaration of Timaeus that time itself is the movement of the planets, Callahan writes, "Time is a moving image and the motion of these bodies along with the motion of the sidereal equator is thought of as being the most fundamental motion in the universe."[12] Therefore, Plato made two significant contributions to the philosophical understanding of the nature of time: time is a created part of the physical universe, and time is constituted in the movement of the heavenly bodies.

The differences between how Plato described time and how Aristotle (384–322 BC) described it perhaps follows the caricature of the difference between the overarching philosophies of the two. Both linked time with motion; but while Plato had his eyes fixed on the heavenly bodies in order to define time, Aristotle marked it out in the motion of more earthly objects. Plato's time was in the motion of the planets in their orbits, but Aristotle saw time in Coriscus traveling between the Lyceum and the marketplace.[13] But both (along with the other ancients) contributed to the discussion on the nature of time by relating it to the change and motion of physical objects.

In book 4 of *Physics*, Aristotle's focus was how time relates to the functioning of the physical world. Considering the nature of time, Aristotle's views are contained in how he associates time with both change and motion. Beginning his discussion, and perhaps referring to the teaching of Plato, he considers a prevailing view: that time is "supposed to be motion and a kind of change."[14] He argues that time can be neither change nor motion, arguing that both of these are measured and defined by time. But since time cannot be measured or defined by itself, then time cannot be equated to motion or change. He writes, "Again, change is always faster or slower, whereas time is not; for fast and slow are defined by time—fast is what moves much in a short time, slow what moves little in a long time; but time is not defined by time, by being either a certain amount or a certain kind of it. Clearly then it is not movement."[15] So, time is not movement. Furthermore, Aristotle states that a similar argument could be constructed that would rule out the possibility that time is change.

12. Callahan, *Four Views of Time in Ancient Philosophy*, 20.

13. This is the first illustration Aristotle uses in book 4 of *Physics*.

14. Aristotle, *Physics*, 4.10 (1:370).

15. Ibid., 4.10 (1:371).

Having overturned the idea that time is to be equated with either movement or change, Aristotle argues that time does not exist independent of change and movement. He argues that change and movement are only perceived along with the perception of time, writing, "But neither does time exist without change; for when the state of our minds does not change at all, or we have not noticed its changing, we do not think that time has elapsed."[16] Therefore, in his view, the mind always associates time with change and movement. He further states that even if no movement is observed, movement in the mind is also associated with time. He states, "Now we perceive movement and time together; for even when it is dark and we are not being affected by the body, if any movement takes place in the mind we at once suppose that some time has indeed elapsed."[17] He goes on later to explain, "But we apprehend time only when we have marked motion, marking it before and after; and it is only when we have perceived before and after in motion that we say that time has elapsed."[18] So for Aristotle, human perception cannot separate time from motion and change.

If time is not to be equated with motion or change, and yet if human perception always links them together, then, Aristotle argues, time must be the marker of motion and change. Time is the measurement of—and itself is measured by—motion and change. He writes, "Not only do we measure the movement by the time, but also the time by the movement, because they define each other."[19] Aristotle then gives a series of brief illustrations that give insight into his view of the nature of time. Through these illustrations, he first argues that time is succession. He writes, "Just as motion is perpetual succession, so also is time."[20] Next, he argues that time is the measurement of movement. He writes, "And we measure both the distance by the movement and the movement by the distance; for we say that the road is long, if the journey is long, and that this is long, if the road is long—the time, too, if the movement, and the movement, if the time."[21] Finally, he argues that time is the cause of decay. In this

16. Ibid., 4.11 (1:371).
17. Ibid.
18. Ibid.
19. Ibid., 4.11 (1:373).
20. Ibid., 4.11 (1:372).
21. Ibid., 4.11 (1:374).

illustration, Aristotle points out that all things that are in time are subject to decay:

> A thing, then, will be affected by time, just as we are accustomed to say that time wastes things away, and that all things grow old through time, and that people forget owing to the lapse of time, but we do not say the same of getting to know or of becoming young or fair. For time is by its nature the cause rather of decay, since it is the number of change, and change removes what is. . . . Hence, plainly, things which are always are not, as such, in time; for they are not contained by time, nor is there being measured by time. An indication of this is that none of them is *affected* by time, which shows that they are not in time.[22]

This final illustration provides some point of contact with Plato's insistence on dividing the world into two realms, one temporal and one atemporal. Aristotle plainly states that everything in the physical world is subject to decay because it is in time (which is the cause of decay). By contrast, there exists an atemporal realm of eternal things, which are not affected by decay and do not experience temporal passage. Aristotle explains this by writing, "Thus none of the things which are neither moved nor at rest are in time; for to be in time is to be measured by time, while time is the measure of motion and rest."[23] Further, he states, "Those things therefore which . . . at one time exist, [and] at another do not are necessarily in time."[24] So as with Plato, Aristotle envisions a bifurcated universe, divided between that which experiences temporal passage and that which does not. What is "in time" changes and moves; and what is not, is eternally at rest.

Drawing from both Plato and Aristotle, Plotinus (204–270 AD) envisions a linkage between time and eternity. In his *Enneads*, Plotinus personalizes time. In contrast to Aristotle's argument that time is the measure of motion, for Plotinus time is equated with what calls "the Life of the Soul."[25] Plotinus takes Plato's definition and says that since the activity of the Soul cannot be measured within itself, then the planets and stars had to be created as a means of measurement. However, he differs from Plato's

22. Ibid., 4.11 (1:374–75).

23. Ibid.

24. Ibid.

25. For a detailed analysis of this concept, see Callahan, *Four Views of Time in Ancient Philosophy*, 88–148.

conclusion that the movement of the heavenly bodies constitutes time. Plotinus agrees that "the Movement, the orbit of the universe, may legitimately be said to measure Time since any definite stretch of that circuit occupies a certain quantity of Time."[26] Departing from Plato's conclusion, however, Plotinus makes the distinction that time is "manifested by the Movement but not brought into being by it."[27]

Analyzing the distinction between Plotinus and Plato, Callahan points out that for Plotinus the universe is in time; but no part of the universe is to be identified with time. He writes, "Plato says that time came into existence along with the universe. The reason for this [according to Plotinus] is that the soul generated time and the universe together. For in this activity of soul the universe was generated as well as time, and this activity is time, while the universe is in time."[28] Thus, for Plotinus time is identified as the activity of the soul.

In this definition, a distinction between time and eternity is seen, and is similar to the Platonic distinction. Plotinus argues that eternity is "life in repose," the absence of activity and complete changelessness. In a passage that foreshadows his influence on later Christian thinkers, Plotinus makes clear the difference between time and eternity, as he understands it:

> [T]hus we know Identity, a concept or, rather, a Life never varying, not becoming what previously it was not, the thing immutably itself, broken by no interval; and knowing this, we know Eternity.
>
> We know it as Life changelessly motionless and ever holding the Universal content . . . in actual presence; not this now and now that other, but always all; not existing now in one mode and now in another, but a consummation without part or interval. All its content is an immediate concentration as at one point; nothing in it ever knows development: all remains identical within itself, knowing nothing of change, for ever in a Now, since nothing of it has passed away or will come into being, but what it is now, that it is ever.[29]

So then Plotinus' *eternity* is the lack of differentiation, the lack of activity and progress, and the total without interval. By contrast, *time* is the

26. Plotinus, *The Enneads*, 3.7.12 (236).

27. Ibid.

28. Callahan, *Four Views of Time*, 135.

29. Plotinus, *The Enneads*, 3.7.3 (224).

differentiated activity of life, the activity when "[p]utting forth its energy in act after act, in a constant progress of novelty, the Soul produces succession as well as act; taking up new purposes added to the old it brings thus into being what had not existed."[30] In this distinction, the Platonic influence is clearly seen; and it illustrates the significance of Plotinus' influence on later Christian thinking about time, especially in the work of Augustine and Boethius.

Modern Science: Newton and Einstein

In the Ancients, almost every important category for understanding time has been addressed: change, motion, decay, changelessness, rest, and unity. The important contributions of the early Western philosophers paved the road upon which all philosophers and theologians of the Western tradition have since walked. In many ways, the contributions of later philosophers are merely adaptations or clarifications of principles first mentioned by Plato, Aristotle, or Plotinus. Some of these adaptations have resulted in new terminology and news ideas about time; and it is for these unique ways of thinking about time that the contributions of modern science, specifically Isaac Newton and Albert Einstein, become significant in the discussion.

Detailed analysis of the contribution made by Newton and Einstein could perhaps fill many volumes. The physical and mathematical principles necessary for such an analysis are complex and require understanding of both specialized terminology as well as recognition of commonly used symbols and illustrations. Any attempt here to engage in such analysis will be unsatisfying and inadequate. Instead, I want to merely summarize the contributions of these two figures by painting with a very broad brush; and I will offer some implications for the present topic.

Newton's most important work—and perhaps one of the most important works of science ever written—is his *Philosophiae Naturalis Principia Mathematica* (Mathematical Principles of Natural Philosophy, often *Principia*), which was published in July of 1687, with second and third editions appearing in 1713 and 1726. The *Principia* includes the statement of Newton's laws of motion, as well as the principles for gravitation and the motion of orbiting bodies.

---

30. Ibid., 3.7.12 (236).

For Newton, time could be categorized as either *absolute* or *relative*. Absolute time is given a metaphysical sense as uniformly flowing duration; while relative time is that which is measured physically, such as by clocks or the motion of planets. He writes, "Absolute, true, and mathematical time, in and of itself and of its own nature, without reference to anything external, flows uniformly and by another name is called duration. Relative, apparent, and common time is any sensible and external measure (precise or imprecise) of duration by means of motion; such measure—for example, an hour, a day, a month, a year—is commonly used instead of true time."[31] What is measured by clocks, then, is relative time, which may be more or less precise in its measurement. Relative time[32] belongs to the sphere of physical observation of moving objects, whether planets or pendulums. Absolute time, on the other hand, does not depend on any physical object, but flows independently and without reference to external objects.

Newton's view of absolute time seems to arise from his theological commitments. While the definition of absolute time given by Newton seems to indicate that time is utterly independent, Newton clarifies by stating that it arises from the attributes of God, namely, God's eternity. Newton writes, "He is not eternity and infinity, but eternal and infinite; he is not duration and space, but he endures and is present. He endures always and is present everywhere, and by existing always and everywhere he constitutes duration and space."[33] Therefore, the divine attribute of omnipresence constitutes space, and the divine attribute of eternity constitutes duration, or absolute time. Unlike the ancient Greek philosophers, and unlike later theologians, Newton does not anywhere describe eternity as timeless. Rather, God's eternity is the source or fountainhead of duration.

The criticisms of Newton's view of time are widely known, and are leveled not at his theological commitments, but on his supposed overstatement of absolute time at the expense of relativity. Craig, for example, argues that Newton had too much faith in physical measurement of time, and that some aspects of relativity were unknown to him. Characterizing Newton's position, Craig writes, "Unless a clock were at absolute rest, it

31. Newton, *The Principia: Mathematical Principles of Natural Philosophy*, 408. The passage quoted is from the Scholium to the Definitions.

32. The use of the term "relative time" in reference to Newton's discussion of physical time is not to be confused with Einstein's discussion of time and relativity.

33. Ibid., 941. The passage is from the general Scholium to the third edition.

would not accurately register the passage of absolute time. A clock moving relatively to oneself runs slowly. This truth, unknown to Newton . . . was finally grasped by Einstein."[34] Paul Davies also paints a less than flattering portrait of Newton's ideas. Davies writes, "Among other things, Newton's concept of time invites us to chop it up into past, present and future in an absolute and universal manner. Because the whole universe shares a common time and a common 'now,' then every observer everywhere . . . would concur with what has deemed to be past, and what is yet to be."[35]

These criticisms and characterizations may be overstated, however. In his discussion of absolute time, Newton seems to acknowledge the limitations of his system. Newton appears to disallow the possibility of ever finding an "ideal clock," and he fully admits that although absolute time exists, it may never be discovered using instruments of physical measurement. Days, for example, are thought commonly to be equal, although they are not. Astronomers may take more accurate measurements to correct for this fact in the representation of relative time, but even those measurements may need to be corrected. Newton writes, "It is possible that there is no uniform motion by which time may have an exact measure. All motions can be accelerated and retarded, but the flow of absolute time cannot be changed."[36] Further, Newton argues that while philosophers can make abstract judgments on the nature of absolute time, the practical matter of measuring relative time among bodies and motions within a local reference frame is sufficient for the activities of daily human life. Newton writes, "Thus, instead of absolute places and motions we use relative ones, which is not inappropriate in ordinary human affairs, although in philosophy abstraction from the senses is required. For it is possible that there is no body truly at rest to which places and motions may be referred."[37] So for Newton, absolute time is unobservable in practice; and while it is shared in common with all observers, is not measurable by those observers. This means that it is in the category of *meta*physical.

Nevertheless, Einstein is widely credited with undermining the system of Newtonian physics, and the notion of absolute time with it. Concerned partially over the puzzle of the constant speed of light through

34. Craig, "Elimination of Absolute Time by the Special Theory of Relativity," 131.
35. Davies, *About Time*, 32.
36. Newton, *The Principia: Mathematical Principles of Natural Philosophy*, 410.
37. Ibid., 411.

the relative motion of physical reference frames, Einstein offered a relativity theory that suggested that Newton's system was wrong. Davies argues that one of the results of Einstein's new system was the conclusion that "time and space are not, as Newton had proclaimed, simply *there*, fixed once and for all in an absolute and universal way for all observers to share. Instead, they are in some sense *malleable*, able to stretch and shrink according to the observer's motion."[38] Famously, Einstein's relativity models suggest that clocks in different inertial reference frames measure different "times." According to DeWeese, Einstein's relativity demonstrates that "simultaneity is relative to reference frames."[39] If this is true, it can easily be seen that absolute time is in trouble: if simultaneity is relative to reference frames, that means that some events which are observed by a particular reference frame as happening "now," are observed by another reference frame as being in the past. Therefore, there is no universal "now," no true simultaneity, and no absolute time.

But the existence of a privileged reference frame from which events can be observed is disallowed from the start in Einstein's system. Therefore, even if there were such a reference frame, it would not be detectible because the only instrumentation available for such detection is inextricably tied to a particular (non-universal) reference frame. What it seems that Einstein demonstrated, then, is not that absolute time as Newton defined it does not exist, but rather that it is not physically detectible. As Craig points out, Newton would have hardly been impressed by this proof.[40] Einstein's approach betrays a methodology which assumes that there is nothing to reality beyond the physical realm, which runs counter to Newton's metaphysical commitments. If the methodology employed assumes *a priori* that time is merely what clocks measure, then concepts such as absolute—metaphysical—time are disallowed from the start.

While Newton's notion of absolute time continues to be called into question by modern electrodynamics and Einstein's relativity theory, it must be remembered that absolute time is more metaphysical than physical. Such a concept is the direct result of theological reflection on the attributes of God: it owes its nature to divine attributes rather than

38. Davies, *About Time*, 53.
39. DeWeese, *God and the Nature of Time*, 66.
40. Craig, "Elimination of Absolute Time," 131.

clocks, whether such clocks are controlled by pendulums or the vibration of electrons in Cesium atoms, or the motion of any other physical object. Einstein's relativity seems to have dominion only in the realm of the observable physical universe, something that Newton specifically ruled out as having anything to do with absolute time. Thus, Davies comments that Einstein's work causes people to ask, "Is there a natural clock, or measure of time, for the universe as a whole?"[41] It would seem that Newton would answer with Einstein, "No." For both Newton and Einstein, there is no such clock because clocks are physical objects subject to the vacillations of motion. But Newton would clarify that there is no such *natural* clock because absolute time is not constituted in any physical object. Nevertheless, the debate on the physics of time made an important contribution by entering into the debate the notions of absolute and relative time.

Contemporary Philosophy: J. M. E. McTaggart's Distinctions

Ancient philosophy and modern science have laid the foundation for a meaningful discussion about the nature of time and the debate about God's relationship to time. But before proceeding to a history of the debate, one additional contributor will be surveyed. The work of J. M. E. McTaggart in his *The Nature of Existence* has produced a specific way of dealing with the nature of time that has impacted the theological debate. Specifically, McTaggart introduces the terminology used to differentiate between the tensed, or "dynamic," conception of time and the tenseless, or "static" conception.

It is worth noting that the chief feature of McTaggart's work is his attempt to prove that nothing is "in time," and that time is not a feature of reality.[42] Noting the paradoxical nature of his thesis, McTaggart writes, "But we have no experience which does not appear to be temporal. Even our judgments that time is unreal appear to be themselves in time."[43] So McTaggart's task seems to be a monumental undertaking, since by necessity the argument will run counter to all human observation and appearance. Anticipating some objections that might be based on observation,

41. Davies, *About Time*, 33.

42. McTaggart's most important work on the subject is found in chapter 33 of McTaggart, *The Nature of Existence*, vol. 2. As important source material for this work, McTaggart also published an article entitled "The Unreality of Time," which originally appeared in a 1908 issue of the journal *Mind*.

43. McTaggart, *Nature of Existence*, 2:9.

McTaggart writes, "But here again, our inability to know or imagine another solution might be due only to the limitations of our experience."[44] Nevertheless, he states flatly that time does not exist. He writes, "I believe that nothing that exists can be temporal, and that therefore time is unreal."[45] Of course, this approach also runs counter to Callahan's warning, noted above, that all philosophical examinations of the nature of time must be in harmony with the common human experience of time. Nevertheless, McTaggart makes a significant contribution to the discussion.

McTaggart begins by arguing that positions[46] in time can be distinguished in two ways: First, positions can be spoken of as earlier or later with respect to other positions. Second, positions can be said to be past, present, or future with respect to other positions. He argues that while the earlier/later distinction is permanent, the latter is not, for it is used from the perspective of a given temporal index. He writes, "If M is earlier than N, it is always earlier. But an event which is now present, was future, and will be past."[47] It is in this context that the now famous *A series* and *B series* distinctions arise. McTaggart assigns the name *A series* to the series of positions in time that are distinguished with past, present, and future; and the name *B series* to the series of positions distinguished using the earlier/later terminology.[48] Key to McTaggart's discussion is his assertion that "the A series is essential to the nature of time."[49] In fact he argues that all observation of events in time are in the form of A series designations.

His discussion then shifts to the main task of his thesis, and can be summarized as a two-step approach. First, McTaggart seeks to prove that the A series is essential to the nature of time. For this proof, he argues that change happens in time, but change is impossible unless there is an A series. Change, in its simplest form, requires that the universe, or a particular entity within the universe, possesses some feature at one time, but does not possess that feature at another. McTaggart concludes, "And, therefore, if there is any change, it must be looked for in the A series, and in the A series alone. If there is no real A series, there is no real change.

44. Ibid., 2:6.

45. Ibid., 2:9.

46. To clarify his terminology, McTaggart writes, "The contents of any position in time form an event." Ibid., 2:10.

47. Ibid.

48. Ibid.

49. Ibid., 2:11.

The *B* series, therefore, is not by itself sufficient to constitute time, since time involves change."[50] The conclusion, McTaggart argues, is unavoidable, because real change means that propositions are sometimes true and sometimes false; but B series distinctions are always true. He writes, "It follows from what we have said that there can be no change unless some propositions are sometimes true and sometimes false. This is the case of propositions which deal with the place of anything in the *A* series—'the battle of Waterloo is in the past,' 'it is now raining.' But it is not the case with any other propositions."[51]

Having demonstrated the necessity of the A series to the nature of time, McTaggart proceeds to the second step in his approach: he attempts to prove that the A series cannot exist. Reflecting on the purpose of this step in his argumentation, McTaggart writes, "I am endeavoring to base the unreality of time . . . on the fact that . . . the distinctions of past, present, and future are essential to time, and that, if the distinctions are never true of reality, then no reality is in time."[52] To accomplish this, McTaggart first argues that if anything is past, present, or future, it must be because it is in relation to something else. But, he continues, this relation must be to something outside the series, because the relation to things in the series is always the same. He proceeds by pointing out that past, present, and future are incompatible determinations. It is essential to time (and change) that if an event is past, it is not present or future. But, any event seems to have all three determinations. For example, there are moments of future time when an event E is future, other moments of future time when E is present, and still other moments of future time when E is past. One may attempt to explain this contradiction away by saying that an event has these distinctions successively, and not simultaneously (E is future, will be present, will be past); but this explanation assumes the desired conclusion (namely, the reality of time). Pointing out the apparent contradiction exposed in this argument, McTaggart writes, "Time must be pre-supposed to account for the A series. But we have already seen that the A series has to be assumed in order to account for time. Accordingly, the A series has to be pre-supposed in order to account for the A series. And this is clearly a vicious circle."[53]

50. Ibid., 2:13.
51. Ibid., 2:15.
52. McTaggart, "Unreality of Time," 101.
53. Ibid., 105.

If successful, then, McTaggart's argument demonstrates that a common feature of human observation, the A series distinction, is essential to the nature of time. But, as he points out, "[w]e have come to the conclusion that the application of the A series to reality involves a contradiction, and that consequently the A series cannot be true of reality. And since time involves the A series, it follows that time cannot be true of reality."[54] McTaggart points out that belief in the reality of the A series arises from experience and perception: at any moment I have certain perceptions, I remember others, and anticipate yet others. But since the A series cannot be a feature of reality, then McTaggart is led to the conclusion that the A series (and therefore time) is purely subjective, based on perception; it simply is not a feature of reality.

While McTaggart's conclusion, as he admits, seems eminently contrary to experience and quite paradoxical, his argument has played an important role in the unfolding of the debate on God and time. Specifically, the terminology and distinction between thinking of time as A series or B series have created categories that have shaped much of the contemporary debate. William Lane Craig points out, "Virtually no one agrees with McTaggart himself that time is unreal; rather the question has become the *nature* of time: Is it tensed or tenseless?"[55] McTaggart's distinctions of A series and B series have led to what has been called the "A Theory" and "B Theory" of time. Following the defining relations given by McTaggart, the A Theory (also called "dynamic" or "tensed") argues that events in the world are fundamentally linked with one another through tense relationships of past, present, and future. Some events will occur in the future, others are happening now, and still others have happened in the past. Conversely, the B Theory (also called "static" or "tenseless") argues that there is no privileged "present" standpoint from which past and future can be distinguished. This means that all events on the time continuum are ontologically on par with one another (none have passed by, none are yet to be, all are simply *there*). The only way the relationship between events can be accurately described is by saying that events occur earlier than, simultaneous with, or later than others.

While Craig's assessment of McTaggart's work seems to be generally correct—that most reject McTaggart's conclusions that time is not

---

54. Ibid., 107.

55. Craig, *Time and Eternity*, 144.

real—there is one sense in which McTaggart's "proof" seems to have fore-shadowed one portion of the contemporary debate. Some contributors to the debate on God's relation to time reject the B series, or static theory, of time on the basis that the A series is essential to the nature of time. There is much argumentation along these lines with which McTaggart may have agreed, based on the first step of his proof and his first conclusion that the A series is essential to time.

Nevertheless, the two theories of time first coined by McTaggart have been interjected into the debate on God's relation to time. If God is atemporal and lives his life in a timeless, atemporal eternity, and if time is a creation of God and limited to the physical universe, then the B Theory of time must be true. It must be true, because it describes things as they really are and not as human beings perceive them to be. On the other hand, if God lives his life in a sequence of events, and if he acts "in time" (performing some actions at certain times and other actions at other times), then the A Theory must be true. Reversing the order of argument, similar statements could be made: if the B Theory is true, then God is atemporal; if the A Theory is true, then God experiences time. How these two conceptions of time impact the debate on God's relationship to time will be discussed at length in chapters 3 and 4.

The Biblical Witness and Christian Theology

A theological-philosophical approach to the nature of time will have unique concerns that set it apart from ancient or modern philosophy and science. Christian theology, as well as the study of the Bible, brings with it both methodological questions, as well as important theological-philosophical questions. One particular methodology employed to arrive at a biblical understanding of the nature of time, for example, has been to study the words used in the Bible that refer to time. This method is one that is etymological and philological in nature: it studies the words used in various texts, including comment on both the statistical frequency of use in the Bible of key words. Authors such as Oscar Cullmann in his *Christ and Time*[56] have used this method. Cullmann's work includes a detailed analysis of the terminology found in the Greek New Testament used to refer to time. Cullmann then argues that the words themselves reveal what the early Christian conception of time was; and he argues that

---

56. Cullmann, *Christ and Time*.

all philosophical consideration must be excluded.[57] He concludes, "The *terminology* of the New Testament teaches us that . . . time in its unending extension as well as in its individual periods and moments is given by God and ruled by him."[58] The important item to note in this statement is not the conclusion Cullmann makes, but the basis for the conclusion: namely, the individual words of the New Testament.

This approach is certainly not unique to Cullmann.[59] In his article "The Biblical View of Time," James Muilenburg argues that the words used by the biblical writers reveals how those writers conceived of the nature of time. For example, when discussing the Hebrew conception of time, Muilenburg writes, "An examination of one or two of the words employed in Israel's extensive vocabulary of time affords us some further insight into the way in which it was apprehended in ancient Israel."[60] Another author, H. Wheeler Robinson, takes a similar approach. In his book, *Inspiration and Revelation in the Old Testament*, Robinson argues that the sense of time as apprehended by the ancient Hebrews is demonstrated in "the early vocabulary of time-measurement."[61] Concerning one particular word, he continues on to argue, "A more detailed and systematic knowledge of the Hebrew sense of time is best gained by an examination of the common term to denote 'time', which is *'eth*."[62] Robinson goes on to make similar statements are made concerning other Hebrew words.

The method employed by Cullmann, Muilenburg, and Robinson, however has been called rightly into question. DeVries, for example, argues that rather than focusing on the terminology employed, discovering

57. See, e.g., ibid., 48, where the author argues that in order to arrive at an understanding of the "Primitive Christian" understanding of a particular word, readers must first free themselves "completely from all philosophical concepts of time and eternity."

58. Emphasis added. Ibid., 49.

59. According to Barr, *Biblical Words for Time*, chapter 4; DeVries, *Yesterday, Today, and Tomorrow*, 31; and DeWeese, *God and the Nature of Time*, 95; the modern exponents of this methodology rely on the work done by Conrad von Orelli, *Die hebräishen Synonyma der Zeit und Ewigkeit genetisch und sprachvergleichend dargestellt*.

60. Muilenburg, "Biblical View of Time," 234. Analysis of the words used comprises only a small part of Muilenburg's article.

61. Robinson, *Inspiration and Revelation in the Old Testament*,106. Robinson makes similar statements with regard to several other Hebrew words appearing in the Old Testament. The chapter in which this analysis appears also contains an appendix listing the "Vocabulary of Time" in the Hebrew Old Testament.

62. Ibid., 109.

the biblical view of time requires the inclusion of a broader scope of data. He argues that "the only effective methodology is a comprehensive one."[63] Further, he states that the attempts to arrive at a biblical understanding of time through the study of language alone "have been . . . unsatisfying because the philologist has so often confined his analysis to the identification of cognates and the enumeration of statistics, without careful attention to the textual setting of the specific occurrences."[64] In other words, methodologies that rely on etymology and philology are inadequate to the task at hand. DeVries goes on to summarize succinctly that "words gain their full meaning only when put to use within a specific communicative context."[65] DeWeese has echoed the criticisms made by DeVries. He writes, "Attempts to derive 'the' biblical view of time from the vocabulary or the text of the Bible are doomed from the outset."[66]

Another significant criticism of methodologies that rely on the words employed by the biblical writers is found in Barr's work. Referring to Cullmann's statement that the terminology of the New Testament can reveal the Christian conception of time, Barr writes that such a position is "extremely precarious theologically."[67] He goes on to explain, "That some kind of authoritative value in teaching, similar in some respect to the authority of the statements . . . of the Bible, should be conceded to lexical structures of the terminology, must be very dubious doctrine within any currently accepted view of biblical authority."[68]

Barr's analysis highlights the main methodological problem in Cullmann's work; and it further offers a solution to that problem. One particular passage in Barr's work is of such great importance to the question of methodology that it will also be quoted here at length:[69]

> The position here developed means in effect that if such a thing as a Christian doctrine of time has to be developed, the work of discussing and developing it must belong not to biblical but to philosophical theology.

63. DeVries, *Yesterday, Today, and Tomorrow*, 335.

64. Ibid.

65. Ibid.

66. DeWeese, *God and the Nature of Time*, 109.

67. Barr, *Biblical Words for Time*, 143.

68. Ibid.

69. A portion of this section of Barr's work is also quoted in DeWeese, *God and the Nature of Time*, 109–10.

> In fact we may observe that the origin of the question lies in many ways within the philosophical rather than biblical material. We cannot take seriously Cullman's insistence that all philosophical considerations must be excluded, for the question asks, namely "What is the nature of time and eternity in biblical thought?," is a question for which the Bible itself gives no precedent, and one for the answering of which it affords so little material that his appeal has to be one to the lexical stock of the Bible rather than to its actual statements. . . . If, then, many or most of the modern discussions start out in fact from some problem or difficulty found in modern theological-philosophical discussion, we may regard it as probable that satisfactory results can be reached only by seeking clarification within that area, and not by expecting the Bible to answer the problem for us.[70]

Barr correctly points out that a successful study of the biblical view of time will not be etymological or philological in its methodology, nor ought it be confined to the field of biblical theology; but it will rather be systematic theological-philosophical. The development of a comprehensive Christian understanding of the nature of time must not be limited to the study of individual words or descriptive clauses used in the Bible. A theory of time consistent with the message of the Bible must be found in the field of philosophical theology: legitimate philosophical inquiry beginning with and preserving proper theological priorities.

These methodological conclusions lead naturally into a focus upon the important theological-philosophical questions found in Christian theology. It must be emphasized that the Bible simply speaks to its own concerns, and as Barr points out (and is the case for almost any topic) the questions asked by the philosopher often go unanswered in the biblical text. DeVries argues, for example, that the Hebrews were not concerned with abstract consideration on the nature of time, but rather with "describing and witnessing to an experience of time."[71] At the conclusion of his study of biblical evidence with regard to the nature of time, DeWeese writes that "there is no clear, univocal biblical view of time or eternity, or of God's relationship to time."[72] The primary concern of the biblical writers with regard to time seems to have been the religious experience of certain people, the temporal context of that experience, and the temporal

70. Barr, *Biblical Words for Time*, 156–57.

71. DeVries, *Yesterday, Today, and Tomorrow*, 336.

72. DeWeese, *God and the Nature of Time*, 110.

relation of that experience to theologically significant events happening at other times past or future. The Bible does not seem to contain any significant abstract consideration of the nature of time itself, or of God's relationship to time. Given this fact, however, four important insights can be gained from the biblical data.

First, it must be recognized that the Bible exclusively uses the language of temporality, and nowhere includes the Platonic concepts of timelessness to refer to a realm of existence outside the physical universe. This fact can be given one of at least three possible explanations: (1) The exclusive use of temporal language and the absence of abstract conceptual discussions from the text could mean that the biblical writers had no mental conceptions in their thinking of timelessness. (2) It could be interpreted to mean that while the biblical writers knew of timelessness and possessed the means to express such notions as atemporal eternity, they simply chose not to express any such conceptions. (3) The exclusive use of temporal language in reference to God's activity could have been meant to indicate that God's life and activity is temporal in nature,[73] whether or not the biblical writers were aware of such a concept. Given these three options, it seems as if (3) is the best explanation for a high view of biblical inspiration.

Second, the Bible also seems to use history as the primary objective parameter marking God's life and activity; and history is a temporal sequence. Throughout the Bible, religious significance is attached to the passage of time and to God acting in history. Ancient Israel, for example, is commanded to "remember" the activities of God in the past, to anticipate the fulfillment of God's promises for the future, and to conduct themselves (in the present) in a manner reflecting God's laws. As DeVries points out, "In ancient Israel, however, one God was Lord of history. History therefore was filled with positive potentiality. It had a goal and a meaning. Temporal event was seen as an ever renewed opportunity and challenge for bringing this goal to realization."[74] In recognition of the significance of history to ancient Israel, DeVries also notes the significance of historiography, "It has long been clear to biblical scholars that

73. It is important to note at this point that the term "temporal" is not used to indicate that a temporal being either *came into existence* or *will go out of existence*. Rather, it is simply a description indicating that the being in question exists through time and experiences temporal sequence.

74. DeVries, *Yesterday, Today, and Tomorrow*, 344–45.

the Hebrews took history seriously—that they were, in fact, the earliest people to produce any extensive historiography. If they took history seriously, it was because they understood time as meaningful. Time was for them the arena within which Yahweh acts purposefully; temporal event was the vehicle of his self-disclosure."[75]

DeVries goes on to argue that taking history seriously had significant religious implications in the daily lives of the people in ancient Israel. He argues that their taking history seriously was to "motivate their present." He writes, "Israel is anxious to understand its past and to anticipate its future in order to make a right choice in its present moment of responsible decision."[76] Moreover, even the modern reader of the text is constantly reminded to look both toward the past and toward the future along the timeline for personal religious meaning as well as motivation to act in a certain manner.

Third, the Bible indicates that sin is the cause of decay,[77] not time; therefore temporal sequence is not antithetical to divine existence. The Genesis account gives no indication that the processes of death, disease, or tumult were present in the world in the earliest days of mankind on earth. In fact, the account seems to make clear the point that the disease is a direct consequence of the sinful choice of the first two humans, and the subsequent divine curse. Given that six days (at the very least) passed before the introduction of these negative consequences, the conclusion is inescapable that, according to the Bible, decay of this kind is not an essential feature of time or of temporal passage.

Fourth, nowhere does the Bible indicate that time is a thing created as part of the material universe. One would be hard pressed to discover any statement in the Bible that even alludes to the idea that God created time, unless Platonic or Aristotelian presuppositions linking time to the motion of created objects are first brought to the text. In spite of this, a primary foundational assertion of Augustine and many later Christian theologians is that time is a created part of the material universe. The introduction of the assertions of ancient philosophy into the theological discussion is not *necessarily* imprudent; but inserting the thoughts and

75. Ibid., 34–35.

76. Ibid., 340.

77. The "decay" in view here is a reference to the digression of physical biological processes leading ultimately to death. Whether or not all processes of increasing entropy are the result of sin is not under consideration here.

concepts of ancient philosophy into Christian theology obviously must be taken with great care if importance is given to preserving sound biblical theology.

The examination of the nature of time from a theological-philosophical perspective must take into account these criteria; and so it is important once again to return to an examination of Cullmann's work. Despite the criticism leveled at Cullmann, his work does make some important contributions to the discussion. First, some of the conclusions drawn from his methodology do seem to be correct. After his examination of New Testament words for time and eternity, he argues that "[p]rimitive Christianity knows nothing of a timeless God"[78] In light of Barr's criticisms, perhaps Cullmann arrived at this conclusion through inappropriate means. However, Cullman's statement can be given a charitable reading. It can be read to mean simply that the writings of the New Testament always refer to God's life and activities in temporal terms. This is the case, regardless of how one explains it in light of other philosophical considerations. Further, Cullmann argues that the idea of a timeless eternity is a Platonic idea brought into Christianity. He writes that it is an "importation into Primitive Christian thinking of the Platonic contrast between time and timeless eternity."[79] This conclusion seems to be true, since, as has been already discussed, the New Testament writers did not engage in such a philosophical exercise. Whether the importation of the Platonic conception of eternity is advisable—and Cullmann thinks it is not—is a matter open to debate.

Second, and more importantly, Cullmann's work is also an example of using theological priorities to drive the conclusions about the nature of time. Cullmann suggests a model of time focused on the coming of Christ for redemption. He argues that the coming of Christ led the way for a new kind of division of time: there was the age past and the age to come, with Christ as the mid-point of the line. Cullmann proposes that the passage of time be considered as redemptive history, with the pinnacle, focusing event being the redemptive work of Christ on earth. From this, he rules out any notions of timeless eternity being found in the activity of Christ. He concludes his discussion, "It is not correct to say that in Christ '(timeless) eternity invades time,' 'conquers time.' We must rather say that

78. Cullmann, *Christ and Time*, 63.

79. Ibid., 65. In the passage in question, Cullmann characterizes this importation as "erroneous."

in Christ time has reached its mid-point, and that at the same time the moment has thereby come in which this is preached to men, so that with the establishment of the new division of time they are able to believe in it and in this faith to understand time 'in a Christian way,' that is, by taking Christ as the center."[80]

Whether or not Cullmann's model is philosophically adequate is only a secondary issue. The most important aspect of this model is that it is an effort to view time through the lens of theological commitments that are essential to Christianity. For Cullmann, the redemptive activity of Christ is paramount. So whether or not Christian philosophical theologians can accept Cullmann's conclusions, his methodology is to be commended and employed: theological priorities must be considered first, and should form the boundaries within which philosophical conclusions about time must be contained.

Preliminary Conclusions

For the purposes of the present discussion, the material surveyed thus far reveals that there are two, equally important concerns: the *content* of the philosophical matter of the debate, and the *methodology* employed in arriving at the content. If the methodology employed is not governed by important theological priorities, it may result in conclusions that violate—or rule out completely—certain theological commitments already held. So, a fine line must be walked. One might, after careful consideration of such priorities arrive at a Platonic conception of timeless eternity; but one ought not *begin* with such a conception. To do so is a matter of putting the philosophical cart before the theological horse. As has been demonstrated, the source data for Christian theology (the Bible) does not contain abstract consideration of the questions asked by philosophical theologians. So while the development of such theories is a philosophical matter, Christian theological commitments can and must be employed to adjudicate between competing theories of the nature of time and God's relationship to it. It will be demonstrated in the course of this work that when the theological notion of the Incarnation is given its proper weight, criteria will emerge that will be able to adjudicate between competing philosophical conceptions.

80. Ibid., 93.

At this early stage of discussion, a brief comment on the nature of time can be made, taking into account the above methodological concerns. It will be assumed—subject to further refinement as arguments are examined in the course of this work—that physical time is a dynamic feature of the material universe; and that it is not identical to metaphysical time. Additionally, the argument I am developing depends on the idea that "temporal becoming" is real; and that the past, present, and future are not on par with one another ontologically.

GOD'S RELATIONSHIP TO TIME: A HISTORY OF THE DEBATE

Key arguments in the history of the debate concerning God's relationship to time go back to some of the earliest days of Christian theological development. I will begin with Augustine, and then I will discuss several other key contributions up to the period of the Scholastics; and then one modern argument will be considered.

Augustine

Augustine of Hippo (354–430 AD) is undoubtedly one of the most influential figures in the history of the debate on God and time; and almost all who came after use his work as the foundation for their own. Augustine's discussion of time is found chiefly in book 11 of his *Confessions*,[81] which can be divided into three sections. In the first section (chapters 1–13), Augustine seeks to demonstrate that time is a created part of the physical universe, and gives insight into his understanding of God's relationship to time. In the second section (chapters 14–27), Augustine considers the nature of time itself, including discussion about whether and how time is measured, and whether the future and past exist objectively. Finally, (chapters 28–31) Augustine briefly discusses time as it is perceived in the human mind.

The immediate context of book 11 is Augustine's consideration of the doctrine of creation; and from this doctrine he begins his discussion of God's relationship to time. What appears to have sparked the consideration of the topic was a question posed by a critic intent on opposing the doctrine of creation: "What was God doing before He made heaven and earth?"[82] Before commenting on this question, however, Augustine

81. Augustine, *Confessions*, 11 (*NPNF*[1] 1:163–75).
82. Ibid., 11.10.12 (*NPNF*[1] 1:167).

lays out the first element of his argument: that God created time with the creation of the physical universe. He plainly refers to God as "the Creator of all times."[83] So for Augustine, time began with the creation of the universe.

Interestingly, having made the point that God created time with the creation of the universe, Augustine inserts into the discussion reflection on God's actions in time. Specifically, he considers how human beings can experience actions of God in time if God himself is atemporal. Using the example of Jesus' transfiguration on the mount, he reflects on the implications of his view of time on how his disciples heard the words from heaven, "This is my beloved son."[84] He argues that the words heard by the hearers were *not* the very words of God, but rather "the motion of a creature." He writes, "The syllables sounded and passed by, the second after the first. . . . Hence it is clear and plain that the motion of a creature expressed it, itself temporal, obeying Thy Eternal will. And these words formed at the time, the outer ear conveyed to the intelligent mind, whose inner ear lay attentive to Thy eternal word."[85] In other words, the reason that those present heard the words *at that time* is because they were of a mind to be cognizant of God's eternal—that is, atemporal—word; yet the words that they heard were only a creaturely manifestation of the timeless word of God.

After addressing this issue, Augustine extrapolates the example to explain the manner in which God creates by virtue of his word. Specifically, Augustine asserts that all of God's speaking takes place (tenselessly) in one eternal (timeless) act of speech. Otherwise, he argues, God would have to be in time and therefore experience change.[86] For Augustine, these are not acceptable possibilities. He writes, "For what was spoken was not finished, and another spoken . . . but all things at once and forever. For otherwise have we time and change, and not true eternity, nor a true immortality."[87] Therefore, Augustine concludes, God's word is "coeternal" with him, and

83. Ibid.
84. Matt 17:5.
85. Augustine, *Confessions*, 11.6.8 (*NPNF*[1] 1:165–66).
86. Exactly what kinds of change are admissible considering the doctrine of immutability is also a matter of debate. It will be shown in the discussion on Aquinas, below, that the classical atemporal model has settled on God's immutability excluding the possibility of change of any kind.
87. Augustine, *Confessions*, 11.7.9 (*NPNF*[1] 1:166).

that all his speaking is done in timeless eternity. Further, it is clear that Augustine believed that there was no temporal *before* creation, but that at the moment of creation, time came into existence. Therefore, to ask the question of what God was doing *before* creation is to ask an improper question. For Augustine, time, by which we judge before and after, did not exist until the moment of creation. He asks rhetorically, "For whence could innumerable ages pass by which Thou didst not make, since Thou art the Author and creator of all ages?"[88]

In these statements, what has been implied is now made specific: Augustine understands time and eternity to be opposite modes of being, with time being limited to the created physical universe and eternity being the timeless, tenseless abode of God. Further explaining his understanding of eternity, Augustine argues that times "never stand," but that "in the Eternal nothing passeth away, but the whole is present; but no time is wholly present."[89] And in contrasting God's life with human life, he writes, "Thy years neither go nor come; but ours both go and come, that all may come. All Thy years stand at once."[90] So clearly Augustine believes that God has a timeless, tenseless life; and that God created time along with all that exists. Remarking on God's life as it relates to time, he writes that God precedes all times in an "ever-present eternity."[91] Further, Augustine sees all of God's actions that are experienced in time by human beings to be a portion of the one timeless activity of God.

Having established the origin of time and God's relationship to it, Augustine engages in a lengthy discussion of the nature of time itself. He considers the notion that there are three times: past, present, and future; arguing that this is the most elementary view of time. He suggests that perhaps things that are future emerge from some secret place to become present, and then escape again into the secret place to become past. He considers that this must be the case if there can be such a thing as foretelling of the future, as in prophecy. But for Augustine, this elementary view does not stand well under scrutiny.

As a criticism of this elementary view, Augustine defends the alternative: that the past and the future do not exist objectively. In defending

88. Ibid., 11.13.15 (*NPNF*[1] 1:167).
89. Ibid., 11.11.13 (*NPNF*[1] 1:167).
90. Ibid., 11.13.16 (*NPNF*[1] 1:168).
91. Ibid.

this alternative, Augustine makes three key points. First, he argues that the present is a single, indivisible instant that exists without duration. He argues that for any time that is considered present, say a year, that time can be divided into past, present and future with a smaller division, as a month. This process can continue down to the most infinitesimal degree. He writes, "If any portion of time be conceived which can now be divided into even the minutest particles of moments, this only is that which may be called present; which, however, flies so rapidly from future to past, that it cannot be extended by any delay. For if it be extended, it is divided into the past and the future; but the present hath no space."[92] Therefore, the present moment exists, but is durationless. Second, Augustine argues that if the past and future could exist, they would exist as present moments. He writes, "wherever they are, that they are not there as future or past, but as present."[93] Explaining this, he argues that when someone speaks of the past, she speaks really of her present memories. He writes, "Although past things are related as true, they are drawn out from the memory,—not the things themselves, which have passed, but the words conceived from the images of the things which they have formed in the mind as footprints in their passage through the senses."[94] Similarly, on the future, he writes, "When, therefore, they say that things future are seen, it is not themselves, which as yet are not . . . but their causes or their signs perhaps are seen, they which already are."[95] So the past and the future exist only as present memories or expectations.

But Augustine's conclusion here creates a problem for his theory of how God knows the past or future; and he anticipates this problem in his discussion. Augustine resigns himself to the fact, however, that he is incapable of understanding how God could teach the future to the prophets if the future does not exist. He writes, "For what is not, of a certainty cannot be taught. Too far is this way from my view; it is too mighty for me, I cannot attain unto it."[96] But there are important implications to the question, and they must here be considered. Given Augustine's parameters, there seem to be at least two possibilities. The first possibility is that the more

92. Ibid., 11.14.20 (*NPNF*¹ 1:169).
93. Ibid., 11.18.23 (*NPNF*¹ 1:169).
94. Ibid.
95. Ibid., 11.18.24 (*NPNF*¹ 1:169).
96. Ibid., 11.19.25 (*NPNF*¹ 1:170).

elementary view of time is correct, and the past and future do exist objectively. This would seem to be consistent with Augustine's view of timeless creation, whereby God's creation is understood as creating all things in one timeless moment, even though humans experience them in temporal succession. A second possibility is that the past and future do not exist objectively, but God knows perfectly the "causes" and "signs" of things to come, and therefore knows the future comprehensively. This would be consistent with Augustine's assertion that the past and future do not exist, but would be problematic with his view of God's relation to time. The only solution Augustine attempts to offer is a change in wording of his initial statement: "[B]ut perchance it might be fitly said, 'There are three times; a present of things past, a present of things present, and a present of things future.'"[97] In any case, Augustine does not completely resolve this problem; and the reader is left to sort out any potential difficulties.

Having completed the bulk of his argumentation on the nature of time and God's relationship to it, Augustine concludes Book 11 with two brief discussions: one on how time is measured, and another on how the human mind experiences time. With regard to measurement of time, he rejects the Platonic notion that time is the motion of the heavenly bodies, and argues instead that times are measured in relative proportion to one another. With regard to the human experience of time, he argues that the mind expects the future, considers the present, and remembers the past. This leads to the possible conclusion that time is purely a matter of subjective experience.

While book 11 of the *Confessions* is Augustine's most complete discussion on God's relationship to time, it can be somewhat less than satisfying for the modern reader who might have concerns arising from the contemporary debate. For the topic I am addressing, for example, Augustine nowhere gives indication that the Incarnation has been taken into account in his view of God and time. However there are other doctrinal issues in the discussion that relate in a secondary way to the Incarnation. DeWeese suggests, for example, that one driving factor in the discussion about time is Augustine's view of God's immutability.[98] While there are certainly implications in Augustine's discussion for the doctrine of immutability, how the doctrine affects his view of God's relationship

---

97. Ibid, 11.20.26 (*NPNF*[1] 1:170).

98. DeWeese, *God and the Nature of Time*, 114–15.

to time is not made explicit, as DeWeese also points out.[99] The doctrine of immutability does bear significance on both the Incarnation and the impact it has on the debate on God's relationship to time. Nevertheless, Augustine laid a foundation that later arguments build upon: God is understood to have timelessly created time along with the rest of the material universe; therefore God's life and actions are atemporal.

Boethius

With Augustine, Anicius Manlius Severinus Boethius (480–524 AD) is one of the two most significant figures of early Christianity when it comes to the debate regarding God's relationship to time. His definition of eternity is most often quoted by those defending what has become the classical position: that God enjoys a timelessly eternal existence. The context of this definition is not often quoted, however, and it will be important to examine the source material in order to gain a more complete understanding of Boethius's view.

The main source of material for this comes from book 5 of his *Consolation of Philosophy.*[100] The main topic for this section of the *Consolation* is God's providence, which (for Boethius) has more to do with God's *knowledge* of future events than it does God's sovereign direction of future events. Throughout the course of the six chapters of book 5, Boethius develops his argument and defends the notion that human freedom is compatible with the fact that God has knowledge of future events before they take place.

Boethius begins his argument by posing the problem. After first stating definitively that humans do have freedom, he asserts that this fact seems to be contradictory with the idea that God sees or directs all things that come to pass. He writes, "If God foresees all things and cannot be in any way mistaken, then what Providence has foreseen will happen must

---

99. Augustine's discussion on immutability that DeWeese highlights in his analysis is from Augustine, *The Trinity*, 5.1.3. Augustine writes, "But God cannot be modified in any way, and therefore the substance or being which is God is alone unchangeable, and therefore it pertains to it most truly and supremely to be, from which comes the name 'being.' Anything that changes does not keep its being, and anything that can change even though it does not, is able to not be what it was; and thus only that which not only does not but also absolutely cannot change deserves without qualification to be said really and truly to be."

100. Boethius, *Consolation of Philosophy*, 5 (97–114).

inevitably come to pass."[101] This seems to indicate, according to the argument, that human beings do not possess freedom of the will; and the actions of human beings become necessary in one of at least two ways. First, human actions can be seen as necessary because God knows them: that which he sees occurring in the future will come about by necessity. Or, second, even if God's knowledge of future actions does not impart necessity to them, the fact that God knows them and the fact that they will come to pass indicates that the actions could not be otherwise. Boethius explains that "necessity lies either in that the future events are foreseen by God, or that things foreseen happen because they are foreseen." He concludes, "This alone is sufficient to eliminate the freedom of the will."[102] Furthermore, he argues, this indicates that God is the author of the evil actions of human beings; and that future punishment for evil and reward for good is an injustice because the evil and good that humans do are done of necessity and not by choice.

Having stated the problem as the apparent contradiction between human freedom and divine foreknowledge, Boethius goes on to present his solution. The reason that there appears to be a conflict between foreknowledge and freedom, Boethius argues, is that humans generally believe that the sole source of knowledge is the nature of things known. But this is incorrect. Knowledge comes not only from the nature of things known, but from the nature and capabilities of the knower. This can be seen in the how human beings gain knowledge: The sense organs first receive data, and then the understanding then grasps the whole form of the thing perceived by the sense organs. The imagination can then consider (in a more abstract way) the form of the object observed; and then the reason can consider the universals pertaining to the form. This creates a hierarchy of knowledge, and whenever there is conflict between some aspects, then the higher wins out. To illustrate Boethius's argument, if someone is in a fun house and his senses are deceived by warped mirrors or unnatural lighting, the person must let reason rule over sense perception, because reason is able to apprehend knowledge masked from the senses. At each step in the hierarchy, knowledge is gained not from the object observed, but in the capabilities of the powers of sense, understanding, imagination, and reason.

---

101. Ibid., 5.3 (100).
102. Ibid., 5.3 (101).

After demonstrating that knowledge arises from the abilities of the knower, Boethius goes on to describe the nature of God as a way to solve the conflict. Here, Boethius gives his famous definition of eternity, categorizing it as the mode of God's existence. He argues that eternity is the full and simultaneous possession of all of life at once. Even things that endure through time, even if they have no beginning and no end, could not be called eternal because they do not have this full possession of life. He writes, "So what does rightly claim the title of eternal is that which grasps and possesses simultaneously the entire fullness of life without end; no part of the future is lacking to it, and no part of the past has escaped it."[103] He explains that it is better to picture God's knowledge, then, not as foresight, but as a timelessly present observation. He writes, "For this reason it is better to term [God's foreknowledge] as *providentia* ('looking forward spatially') rather than *praevidentia* ('looking forward in time'), for . . . it gazes out on everything as from one of the world's lofty peaks."[104] So then God's knowledge of the future is not foreknowledge, but is rather present knowledge, likened to someone standing on a high hill observing a multitude of activity below.

Based on this understanding of God's knowledge, Boethius concludes that while humans experience events as present at some times, past at other times, and future at still other times, God always witnesses the events as present. For Boethius, this changes how the term "necessity" is applied to human actions. If you are aware of a person taking a walk, Boethius says, then it is conditionally necessary that the person is walking. But, he argues, there is no necessity forcing the person to walk, but the walking came about by a voluntary choice. And this changes what was said before about necessity that seemed to indicate a conflict between foreknowledge and freedom. Boethius explains, "So the things become necessary as related to God's observation of them, through the condition of his divine knowledge; but considered in themselves, they do not forfeit the total freedom of their nature."[105] So while some things come to pass out of necessity, others, although they will certainly come about, arise from free choices. Any necessity belonging to free actions is only conditional necessity arising from God's knowledge of them.

103. Ibid., 5.6 (111).

104. Ibid., 5.6 (112). The parenthetical definitions of *providentia* and *praevidentia* are original to this edition.

105. Ibid., 5.6 (113).

In the contemporary debate on God's relationship to time, the question of God's knowledge is sometimes introduced. When it comes to Boethius, however, authors seem to quote his definition of eternity more often than his argument about foreknowledge and freedom. But his definition of eternity is hardly unique. Writing some 200 years earlier, Plotinus defined eternity in almost exactly the same manner as Boethius. Plotinus writes, "Thus a close enough definition of Eternity would be that it is a life limitless in the full sense of being all the life there is and a life which, knowing nothing of past or future to shatter its completeness, possesses itself intact for ever."[106] Plotinus goes on to describe the divine life as a "Life instantaneously infinite."[107] The similarities between these two definitions suggest either a direct influence of Plotinus on Boethius, or a common philosophical outlook based on Platonism. Since Boethius is one of the more widely quoted figures among contemporary defenders of the classical atemporal view, it is significant to note that Boethius contribution owes its heritage to non-Christian sources. While this fact does not indicate that Boethius's definition is incompatible with Christian theology or the doctrine of the Incarnation, it does appear as though *logical* concerns were more important in the formulation of the definition than *theological* concerns. While these two ultimately will not be in conflict, the methodology seems inadvisable if one is to preserve a view of time consistent with Christian theological priorities.

Anselm

While Augustine and Boethius form the foundational influence for many contemporary Christian theological-philosophical arguments about God and time; later thinkers also have left their mark on the debate. Anselm of Canterbury (1033–1109) is one such figure, in whose work the influence of Boethius is clearly seen. The two works in which Anselm gives the clearest statements on the relationship of God and time are his *De Concordia* and *Monologion*.[108] In these two works is found an emphasis on God's simplicity and the compatibility between foreknowledge and

---

106. Plotinus, *Enneads*, 3.7.5 (227).

107. Ibid.

108. While the *Proslogion* does speak to the relationship, it does so primarily for clarification of the definitive statements in the *Monologion*.

human freedom. In the course of these two arguments, it seems apparent that Anselm holds to a static, tenseless view of time.[109]

In *Monologion*, Anselm's arguments about God's relationship to time come in the context of his discussion on God's simplicity.[110] For Anselm, God is simple, and everything that can be said of God is one and the same thing. God's eternity, for example, is identical to himself. From this Anselm argues that the divine life cannot have had a beginning and does not have an end, and thus begins his discussion on time. He argues that there can be nothing before and nothing after God, and that he exists everywhere and at all times, otherwise there would be no sustaining power over the universe. But, it cannot be the case that God exists at particular times—that is, contained by them, or living through a series of them—and in that sense is in no time. If God were to exist across a time span, that would violate his simplicity. Describing the consequence if God were to exist across a time span, Anselm writes that God's life would be "stretched out in parts through the parts of time. But its time span is its eternity and its eternity is precisely itself. The supreme essence, therefore, would be cut up into parts along the divisions of time."[111] The only acceptable conclusion, then, is that God's essence is *with* rather than *in* time. God is not contained by time (and therefore is in no time); but he is present to every time. And as a conclusion to his argument, Anselm arrives at a Boethian-like definition: "It would seem that [God's] eternity is life unending, simultaneous, whole, and perfectly existing."[112]

---

109. For a more detailed analysis of Anselm's views on the nature of time, see, e.g., Rogers, "Anselm on Eternity as the Fifth Dimension." Rogers states that Anselm was the first philosopher in history to adopt the tenseless view of time. Both DeWeese, *God and the Nature of Time*, 150; as well as Brian Leftow, *Time and Eternity*, 184, conclude the opposite, saying that Anselm held to a dynamic (tensed) view of time. Leftow cites as the basis for this conclusion certain phrases used by Anselm to describe time, phrases which suggest a dynamic view. Leftow goes on, however, to cite contradictions between Anselm's conclusions and the dynamic language he employed. It seems simpler to solve the apparent contradiction by noting that Anselm did not intend to communicate the difference between the static and dynamic views of time, and therefore that a definitive statement one way or the other should not be expected in his writing. It seems reasonable to follow Rogers in concluding that since many of Anselm's conclusions *require* a tenseless view of time that this is the view that he had.

110. Anselm, *Monologion*, 17–25 (30–42).

111. Ibid., 21 (36).

112. Ibid., 24 (41).

While the *Monologion* begins from God's simplicity, *De Concordia* approaches the topic as Boethius did: searching for a harmony between God's foreknowledge and man's free will. The first step Anselm takes in his argument is to say that since God can only foreknow what will be the case, and people act by their free choice, then God knows that they act freely. He writes, "But if something is going to occur freely, God, who foreknows all that shall be, foreknows this very fact."[113] If God knows what is going to occur, and "going to occur" can only be said of things that are in fact going to occur, then God's knowledge of them imparts no necessity and therefore is no threat to freedom. The second step in the argument reveals Anselm's tenseless view of time. While humans experience the passage of time from future, to present, to past, God experiences all times as equally present and contained within eternity. For God, various temporal events—no matter the interval between them—are all equally present at once; and God sees all of time as a tenseless whole. God's knowledge, then, is present knowledge rather than *fore*knowledge. Even things which have a past and future in time, are only present in eternity. He explains, "And when we say that something which has a past and future existence in time does not have a past or future existence in eternity, we are [saying] . . . that it does not exist there in a past or future fashion since it exists there unceasingly in its eternal-present fashion."[114] Therefore, human free actions which are seen as future from a particular reference point in time, are seen as simply present to God; and therefore Anselm sees no contradiction between God's knowledge of future events and human free choice.

From these two major works, it can be seen that Anselm's primary concern with regard to God's relationship to time was God's simplicity. According to Anselm, God's simplicity requires that God's life be an all-encompassing singular, with no temporal division whatsoever. While God's creative and sustaining power is present with every event in time, God's life is not contained by any time. God's eternity is seen as a simultaneous present, and all events in time are contained within that present. Time, then, must be a tenseless, static whole, since all parts are equally present to God.

---

113. Anselm, *De Concordia*, 1.1 (435).
114. Ibid., 1.5 (444).

Aquinas

Standing in the tradition of those who came before, Thomas Aquinas's view on God's relationship to time is unique, but quite similar to Anselm's approach. Like Anselm, Aquinas places a high priority on the simplicity of God; but Aquinas is somewhat unique in that he places the discussion in the immediate context of God's immutability. Also like Anselm, the influence of Boethius is obvious. Because of his emphasis on immutability and the influence of Boethius and Anselm, Aquinas seems to have held to a tenseless, static view of time.[115]

The main source of Aquinas's views on God and time is part 1 of his *Summa Theologiae*,[116] in which discusses at length the nature of God. Question 10 of this work begins by defending Boethius's concept of eternity, and in doing so links the concept to God's immutability. Adopting the Boethian definition of eternity, Aquinas argues that the notion of time arises from change; but since God is completely free of change, then God is atemporal. He writes that "just as numbering the antecedent and the consequent in change produces the notion of time, awareness of invariability in something altogether free from change produces the notion of eternity."[117] Aquinas continues this emphasis on immutability throughout his discussion, arguing that God is eternal—that is, in the Boethian sense, timeless—because he is unchangeable, possessing the whole of his life in one instant. He concludes, "Eternity, in the true and proper sense, belongs only to God, for eternity follows upon unchangeableness, as I have made clear. And, as I have also shown, God alone is altogether unchangeable."[118] So for Aquinas, the root of God's atemporality is his immutability.

Aquinas's concept of immutability seems to begin with his acceptance of the ancients. In Aquinas's *Summa Contra Gentiles*, he accepts as a presupposition the Aristotelian conception of time as "the number of motion."[119] After stating Aristotle's definition of time, Aquinas develops an argument harkening back to Parmenides and Zeno. Aquinas writes that since there does not exist within God any motion; and because God

115. DeWeese concludes the same. See DeWeese, *God and the Nature of Time*, 151. See also the detailed examination of the question in Craig, "Was Thomas Aquinas a B-Theorist of Time?" 475–83.

116. Aquinas, *Summa Theologiae: Questions on God.*

117. Ibid., 1a.10.1 (93).

118. Ibid., 1a.10.3 (96).

119. Aquinas, *Summa Contra Gentiles*, 1.15.3 (98).

does not have any movement from non-being to being, then God must be completely changeless. What follows from this conclusion is that God must be timeless, existing in a Boethian-like eternity where the whole of his life is immediately present. Aquinas describes this, saying, "But God, as has been proved, is absolutely without motion, and is consequently not measured by time. There is, therefore, no *before* and *after* in Him; He does not have being after non-being, or non-being after being, nor can any succession be found in His being. For none of these characteristics can be understood without time. God, therefore, is without beginning and end, having His whole being at once. In this consists the nature of eternity."[120]

Important to note in this definition is Aquinas's exclusion of the possibility of succession in God. Not only does God's existence lack before and after, but also there is no before or after in any of God's activity or experience. Because of his utter immutability, all of God's life, according to Aquinas, is an instantaneous whole, completely devoid of any passage or succession whatsoever. This argument is perhaps made most clear in Aquinas's *Compendium of Theology*, in which he draws as a direct consequent of God's immobility and immutability the absence of succession in the divine life. Aquinas argues that motion causes the succession of time; but God, since he is not subject to motion, possesses no temporal succession in his life. Therefore, his existence must be simultaneous. Aquinas states that if this were not the case, then there could be additions and losses in God's life, which would violate his immutability. Aquinas concludes, "That which passes is lost, and what is expected in the future can be acquired. But nothing is lost to God or accrues to Him, since He is immutable. Therefore His existence is simultaneously whole."[121] Aquinas's understanding of God's relationship to time can be summarized as follows: God is thought of as utterly immutable, not subject to any succession or sequence in his life, and therefore must live an atemporal existence, experiencing the whole of his life in one simultaneous instant, and relating to all temporal events in the physical universe in one timeless instant.

120. Ibid.
121. Aquinas, *Compendium of Theology*, 1.8 (13).

A Modern Argument: Schleiermacher

With few exceptions,[122] the predominant Christian figures of the Middle Ages—from Augustine to Aquinas—believed that God's existence is atemporal: all events are instantaneously simultaneous and immediately present to him; and he experiences no temporal succession in his life. But in the eighteenth century, Enlightenment thought began to influence the debate on God and time; and one of the key figures in this category was Friedrich Schleiermacher (1768–1834). Undeniably one of the most influential Protestant theologians of modernism, Schleiermacher's work on time was a modern reflection on the concepts laid down in the Middle Ages.

Schleiermacher begins his explanation of God's relation to time in *The Christian Faith* by linking together the concepts of eternity and omnipotence. He argues that "instead . . . of saying God is eternal and almighty, we should rather say He is almighty-eternal and eternal-almighty."[123] Schleiermacher goes on to argue that if the eternity of God were considered apart from his omnipotence, it would be merely an "inactive attribute,"[124] not really *affirming* anything at all about God. In this case, eternity could not be related to anything in the world; and descriptions of God's eternity would be reduced to ideas of infinity or immeasurability. But these negative concepts do not do justice to the religious consciousness of God, Schleiermacher argues, because they "encourage representation of God apart from the manifestation of His power."[125] On the other hand, if eternity is properly considered in relation to God's power, then it is also properly thought of as related to God's causal activity in creating and sustaining the world. Since God is the cause of everything, then this causality must extend to time itself; and therefore eternity must be "thought of as utterly timeless."[126] For Schleiermacher, this means that

---

122. DeWeese names three figures who seemed to argue for a dynamic conception of time, and whose arguments seem to have laid a foundation for later temporal arguments: John Duns Scotus (1266–1308), William of Ockham (1285–1347), and Luis de Molina (1535–1600). See DeWeese, *God and the Nature of Time*, 185–208. As has been argued above, temporal arguments remained in the minority until the latter part of the twentieth century. Additionally, temporal arguments do not seem to possess the unified heritage enjoyed by atemporal arguments.

123. Schleiermacher, *Christian Faith*, 51.1 (202).

124. Ibid., 52.1 (203).

125. Ibid., 52.1 (204).

126. Ibid.

eternity is the very antithesis of time. He concludes, then, that "[w]e must therefore reject as inadequate all those explanations which abrogate for God only the limits of time and not time itself, and would form eternity from time by the removal of its limits, while in fact these are opposites."[127]

Schleiermacher realizes, however, that if temporal descriptions of God are to be rejected, a problem of biblical interpretation arises. The Bible, after all, uniformly uses temporal language in describing God's eternity, the very thing that Schleiermacher wants to reject as inadequate. The solution to this problem is to characterize the primary biblical descriptions of God in temporal terms as "poetical," and therefore not appropriate for developing a doctrine with regard to eternity. Referring specifically to Psalm 90:2, he writes that temporal descriptions "cannot be taken up into didactic language without harm."[128] To solve the problem, Schleiermacher argues that these poetical representations must be supplemented. He writes, "Even if poetical passages cannot describe eternity except by pictures of unending time, the New Testament itself teaches us how for didactic purposes these must be supplemented."[129] In the footnote to the passage just quoted, Schleiermacher encourages the comparison of Psalm 90:2 ("from everlasting to everlasting, you are God"), which he takes to be a temporal description, to 1 Peter 3:8 ("for the Lord, one day is as a thousand years, and a thousand years as one day"). Whether the supplements Schleiermacher has in mind are limited to other biblical texts, or should include exercises in philosophical consideration as Schleiermacher has done, is not eminently clear. However, one element that does shed light on his concerns for methodology is his characterization of the arguments of Augustine and Boethius as "perfectly scriptural statements."[130]

While Schleiermacher made a unique contribution by pointing out the connection between God's eternity and his power, and by addressing concerns for biblical interpretation, he also stands firm with the theologians of the middle ages in linking eternity with immutability. Since God is completely timeless, Schleiermacher argues, there are no parts contained in his being. If eternity is deduced as a feature of immutabil-

127. Ibid., 52.2 (205).
128. Ibid., 52.1 (204).
129. Ibid., 52.2 (204).
130. Ibid., 52.2 (205).

ity, on the other hand, then eternity is reduced to "an inactive attribute which expresses nothing actually present in the religious consciousness."[131] Instead, he argues, immutability is seen as forming a boundary within which God's being can be considered. He explains, "We may do better, therefore, to take the principle, that God is unchangeable, merely as a cautionary rule to ensure that no religious emotion shall be so interpreted, and no statement about God so understood, as to make it necessary to assume an alteration in God of any kind."[132] So while his theological predecessors began with immutability and ended with timelessness, Schleiermacher starts with timelessness and argues that immutability is contained within the idea. While the priorities are reversed, he nevertheless stands in concert with the philosophical theologians of the Middle Ages in his staunch affirmation that God lives an atemporal existence.

SOME CONCLUSIONS

This chapter began by addressing the philosophical question of the nature of time, and then brought theological concerns to bear on that question. The most ancient philosophers seemed to have laid down the most fundamental and important concepts relating to the nature of time. In their struggle to understand the fundamental nature of the universe, the main distinction between Heraclitus and Parmenides was *change* versus *changelessness*. Plato, with his theory of Forms, united these two concepts in a broader picture of the universe: The universal, eternal, timeless Forms are unchanging, while the temporal particulars are in a constant state of change. In this model of the universe, the concept of "timeless eternity" is first introduced, and "time" is constituted in the motion of the heavenly bodies. While Plato focused on the heavens, Aristotle brought consideration of the nature of time back down to earth. Retaining the idea of timeless eternity, Aristotle focused on the measure of motion of particular physical objects as the key to understanding the nature of time. Plotinus, while influenced by both Plato and Aristotle, sought to refine the Platonic model by focusing on the activity of the "life of the Soul." Additionally, Plotinus is the first to describe what has become the classical Christian definition of eternity.

131. Ibid., 52 Postscript (206).
132. Ibid.

In examining the more modern science of time in Newton, it becomes clear that metaphysical commitments are of great importance, even when studying and interpreting the data from observations of the physical universe. Newton held fast to an *absolute* time—and rejected the idea of timeless eternity—that was constituted in the divine nature. Einstein's focus on relativity is credited with undermining Newtonian physics, but I suggested above that the paramount difference between the two scientists was methodological and theological. The modern philosophy of time as seen in McTaggart introduced the contemporary terminology of "dynamic" versus "static" time. In his A series / B series distinctions, McTaggart contributes the unique language of time employed by contemporary Christian theologians in their debate on God's relation to time.

When the debate about God's relation to time is examined, it seems clear that in the history of the discussion, there really was not much debate at all. All of the most influential theologians from Christianity's earliest days to the modern period held to one particular view of God's relationship to time: God exists atemporally in a timeless eternity. But each of these figures held their viewpoint for slightly different reasons. Augustine sought to preserve an idea of God as the all-powerful creator, and therefore believed that time was a part of the physical universe. If time is created, of course God must be atemporal in his existence. Boethius's main concern seems to have been solving the apparent conflict between divine foreknowledge and human freedom. If God is atemporal, then foreknowledge is really just *present* knowledge, and so no conflict exists. Anselm began with God's simplicity, and therefore could not escape the conclusion that God exists in a Boethian-like eternity. Aquinas also focuses on God's simplicity, but seems to have been more concerned with immutability. If God is immutable (as Aquinas defines immutability), then there must be no succession in God's life. If there is no succession, no sequence of events, then there is no *time* in God's life; so he must live an atemporal existence. Highly influential for modern Protestant thought, Schleiermacher focuses on the world's dependence on God for its existence. Therefore, "eternity" and "power" go hand-in-hand. Schleiermacher assumes an atemporal eternity, and then, working in the opposite direction from Aquinas, concludes that God is also immutable.

Each of these influential Christian thinkers employed certain theological priorities in their statements of God's relationship to time: God's creative power, his foreknowledge compatible with human freedom, his simplicity and immutability. It seems that there is a fundamental error in these approaches. Rather than develop a model of God's relationship to time based on these theological-philosophical concepts, I will argue that the Christian doctrine of the Incarnation should function as the centerpiece in the debate and the lens through which the topic ought to be examined. As I suggested earlier, the doctrine of the Incarnation should serve as a "control belief" in the development of a model of God's relationship to time. The Christian philosophical theologian has far more at stake in the Incarnation than in various formulations of immutability or simplicity. In what follows, I will attempt to demonstrate that the Incarnation indicates succession and a sequence of events in the divine life. Contrary to Aquinas, this indicates that God experiences *temporal* sequence in his existence. The following chapter, then, will examine the doctrine of the Incarnation as it has been traditionally understood in Christianity. From this foundation, a model of God's relationship to time that prioritizes this central doctrine can be developed.

2

The Doctrine of the Incarnation

THE DOCTRINE OF THE Incarnation is the very centerpiece of the Christian faith; it is what defines Christianity and sets it apart from alternative religious systems and other forms of theism. It also tends to be the area where division occurs among competing theological systems that share the self-designation "Christian." So important is the doctrine of the Incarnation that two of the most foundational creeds of the church have centered on its exposition. As Brian Hebblethwaite has said, "The Christian doctrine of the incarnation is one of the two central doctrines [with the doctrine of the Trinity] which set out the *unique* features of Christian faith in God."[1] By "Incarnation" Christian theology has intended to communicate the belief that at a particular point in human history, a member of the Trinitarian God became, or took on, flesh and a genuine human existence in Jesus of Nazareth. Therefore, Jesus is said to be God *incarnate*. It is this doctrine that defines the very nature of Christianity.

One of the clearest biblical passages that serve as a warrant for the belief that Jesus is God incarnate is the prologue to the fourth Gospel. In an obvious allusion to the opening verse of the book of Genesis, the first phrase of John's Gospel establishes the primary subject under consideration as "the Word." In John 1:1, the Gospel writer asserts that the Word was "in the beginning," "was with God," and "was God." The third verse then identifies this Word as the creator of all things, as it states, "All things were made through Him, and without him nothing was made that was made." In verses 6–13, the Gospel begins to identify this Word with the man Jesus Christ; and verse 14 states clearly the idea contained within the doctrine of the Incarnation: the Word "became flesh and dwelt among

---

1. Hebblethwaite, "Jesus, God Incarnate," 101.

us." It is this "becoming flesh" that lies at the root of the Christian under-standing of the Incarnation. Both the Nicene[2] and Chalcedonian Creeds have addressed the doctrine of the Incarnation by affirming that Jesus is true God—of one substance with the Father—and true man, existing in one person who, at a particular point in the past lived a genuine earthly existence. Summarizing the Christian perspective on the Incarnation, Wayne Grudem writes, "Jesus Christ was fully God and fully man in one person, and will be so forever."[3] Grudem's definition is exemplary of the traditional understanding of the doctrine of the Incarnation.

The purpose of this chapter is to examine the doctrine of the Incarnation, highlighting the theological and philosophical implications that this doctrine has for the debate on God's relationship to time. I will examine the doctrine as stated in the historic creeds of the church in or-der to define clearly what Christians mean when they say Jesus is God incarnate. Particular points of focus will be the Nicene formulation of the doctrine, and how this creedal statement can serve as a template for un-derstanding the Incarnation. Additionally, I will discuss the Chalcedonian concerns of "person" and "nature," and how these distinctions impact the present debate. Finally, I will describe the foundation for the argument concerning how Doctrine of the Incarnation informs the debate concern-ing God's relationship to time.

THE NICENE CREED

The Nicene Creed came about as the early church sought to resolve a conflict on the nature of Christ. The statements in the creed regarding Christ's nature were designed specifically to refute false teaching and settle the controversy. The debate leading up to Nicaea began between the Bishop of Alexandria, Alexander, and one of the elders in the same city, Arius.[4] The main issue between them was the question as to whether the Word of God, identified with Christ, was coeternal with God. Arius ar-gued that Christ was not eternal, but rather was the first creature, through

2. Specifically, the Nicene-Constantinopolitan creed of 381. See the detailed discus-sion, below.

3. Grudem, *Systematic Theology*, 529.

4. The historical information is presented here as common knowledge, but relies heavily on Gonzales, *The Story of Christianity*, vol. 1, 158–67, 251–65. See also chapter 11 of McGrath, *Christian Theology*, 345–79; chapters 2 and 3 of Erickson, *The Word Became Flesh*, 41–88; and Kelly, *Early Christian Doctrines*.

whom God made all other things. The Arian position was that there was once a time when he did not exist. This, of course, did not refer to a belief that there was once a time when *the man Jesus* did not exist, for all parties seemed to be in agreement about that fact. Rather, the Arians intended to communicate their belief that the Word was a creature, and was not eternal[5] with God.

This denial of the eternality of the Word called into question the deity of Jesus, which also cast doubt on the aptness of the Church's worship of Jesus, a practice well established by the time of the controversy. Arius argued that his opponents were threatening monotheism. Others recognized that if Arius was right, the Church must either cease its worship of Jesus or be willing to admit that it was worshipping a creature,[6] neither of which seemed to be an acceptable option. This debate resulted in the formation of two competing perspectives on Christology, and threatened to divide Christianity. In 325, bishops from churches all over Christendom gathered at Nicaea to settle the debate. Having been removed from his post by Alexander, Arius was not permitted to be in attendance; but his supporters were vocal in their defense of his position. Unwilling to accept the notion that Christ was merely a creature, the council overwhelmingly adopted a statement condemning Arius: "As for those who say that 'there was when he was not,' and 'before being born he was not,' and 'he came into existence out of nothing,' or who declare that the Son of God is of a different substance or nature, or is subject to alteration or change—the catholic and apostolic church condemns these."[7] This was an unequivocal assertion that the Son, or Word of God, was not a creature, but was the "same substance" with God.

This decisive action, however, did not end the debate. Politically, the Roman Empire became increasingly friendly to Arianism. After Alexander died, a new defender of Nicene orthodoxy took his place: Athanasius of Alexandria. Athanasius struggled under political attack, being falsely accused of criminal activity, and spending years in and

---

5. Because of the contemporary understanding of certain arguments, it is important to remind the reader that the word "eternal" is not used here to indicate either an ever-lasting or an atemporal existence, for that is the matter under debate. Many authors use the words "eternal" and "atemporal" as synonyms, but there is no adequately established basis for doing so.

6. Gonzales, *The Story of Christianity*, 161.

7. In McGrath, *Christian Theology*, 21.

out of exile. Athanasius eventually came to understand that much of the opposition to the Nicene formula was based on a concern that the statement did not allow for sufficient distinction between the Father and the Son. Eventually, Athanasius declared that referring to the Father and Son as one substance was appropriate, as long as this did not mean there was no distinction between the two. A second council was called in Constantinople in 381, which affirmed the original Nicene statement. The resulting Nicene-Constantinopolitan Creed made clear the church's convictions about the Incarnation:

> And [we believe] in one Lord Jesus Christ, the only-begotten Son of God, begotten of the Father before all worlds, God of God, Light of Light, very God of very God, begotten, not made, being of one substance with the Father; by whom all things were made; who, for us men and for our salvation, came down from heaven, and was incarnate by the Holy Spirit of the Virgin Mary, and was made man; and was crucified also for us under Pontius Pilate; he suffered and was buried; and the third day he rose again, according to the Scriptures; and ascended into heaven, and sitteth on the right hand of the Father; and he shall come again, with glory, to judge both the quick and the dead; whose kingdom shall have no end.[8]

The wording of this creed lacked some of the more specific anti-Arian statements found in the first Nicene statement, but it nevertheless elucidates the council's belief that Jesus Christ is the Son of God incarnate, existing as both God and man.

Some Implications of Nicaea for the Present Topic

The Christological statement from Constantinople in 381 presents a clear statement on the Incarnation. This statement contains at least three important theological concepts that have philosophical implications for the current topic: (1) the creed affirms that the Word existed before the Incarnation; (2) the redundant statements in the Nicene formula make clear the council's belief that in Jesus Christ, God himself was made man and lived a human life on earth; and (3) the formula also makes clear the council's belief that the Incarnation was not a temporary state, but rather God the Son continues to live a human existence as Jesus Christ.

---

8. Quoted in Grudem, *Systematic Theology*, 1169.

The Pre-Incarnate Existence of Christ

The first of these theological concepts is perhaps most directly related to the Arian controversy, for it is an answer to the Arian slogan: "There once a time was when he was not." Although some of specifically anti-Arian statements present in the first Nicene statement were left out of the creed, it nevertheless affirms that the divine Son of God—the Word—pre-existed the earthly life of Jesus. This is indicated in its describing the Son as "begotten . . . before all worlds," and as the maker of all things. Biblical support for this creedal statement is abundant, and is evident in the fourth Gospel, as highlighted above. Elsewhere in the same Gospel, Jesus himself asserts his own pre-existence in the so-called "I am" statements,[9] such as in John 8:58: "Before Abraham was, I am." Additionally, the Gospel writer records Jesus' statement in John 17:5, where Jesus prays to the Father about his glory before the world, "And now, O Father, glorify Me together with Yourself, with the glory which I had with You before the world was." In other words, the Son enjoyed the glory of the Father before the creation of the physical universe.

In his *Discourses Against the Arians* Athanasius refers to these and other important Scriptural statements to affirm of the pre-existence of the Word, and to refute the Arian position. Athanasius argues that statements about Christ in Scripture "forbid any one to imagine any interval at all in which the Word did not exist."[10] Referring specifically to the "I am" statements in the fourth Gospel, Athanasius writes, "And whereas the Lord himself says, 'I am the Truth' . . . who, hearing such language from God, . . . will any longer hesitate about the truth, and not forthwith believe that in the phrase 'I am,' is signified that the Son is eternal and without beginning?"[11] In his discussion, Athanasius also mentions other passages in the Bible that refer to the pre-existence of the Word, and concludes with a clear statement against the Arian position saying, "Thus it appears that the phrases 'once was not,' . . . and the like, belong to things originate in creatures, which come out of nothing, but are alien to the Word. But if such terms are ever used in Scripture of things originate, but 'ever' used of the Word, it follows, O ye enemies of God, that the Son did not come out of nothing, nor is in the number of originate things at all, but is the

---

9. John 6:35, 48, 51; 8:12, 58; 9:5; 10:7, 9, 11, 14; 11:25; 14:6; 15:1.

10. Athanasius, *Four Discourses Against the Arians*, 1.4.12 (*NPNF*[2] 4:313).

11. Ibid.

Father's Image and Word eternal, never having not been, but being ever, as the eternal Radiance of a Light which is eternal."[12]

Athanasius's position was affirmed at Nicaea and became recognized as the position that accurately represents the Scriptural data—and therefore the official doctrine of the early Church. The doctrine asserts that the Word existed eternally with God; and there was an event in the life of the Word in which he emptied himself of his position in glory[13] and "became flesh."[14] These ideas clearly have implications for God's relationship to time. The affirmations made by the creed indicate the council's belief that God the Son has temporally ordered events in his life. Specifically, there was a state of affairs of God the Son living in a pre-incarnate state. This is made explicit in biblical passages such as John 17:5, which clearly indicate a temporal sequence in the life of the Son, who lived in glory with the Father before the world was. This state of affairs was terminated at the occurrence of an event: the moment at which the Son took on human nature and entered into an incarnate existence on earth.

God Incarnate: Revelation and Salvation

This leads directly to the second element of the Nicene formula with philosophical implications for the present topic: Jesus himself is *God incarnate*, having become incarnate for the purpose of salvation.[15] To avoid any possible confusion or misunderstanding, the Nicene formula is repetitive in its assertion: Christ is "God of God," and "very God of very God," being of "one substance with the Father." Additionally, the formula makes clear that this "God of God" was made man in Jesus Christ; and it is God who lived the earthly life as Jesus of Nazareth. This of course is also the main theme of the prologue to John's Gospel, as noted above; and Jesus makes the same claim of himself when later in the Gospel account (John 14:9) he says, "[H]e who has seen me has seen the Father." Scriptural data of this kind is not limited to the fourth Gospel; and there are many key passages of the New Testament that strongly indicate that Jesus himself was God living a human existence. Two of the strongest of such statements are found in the book of Colossians, in which Paul writes (in Col 1:15) that

12. Ibid., 1.4.13 (*NPNF*[2] 4:314).

13. Phil 2:7, NKJV: "made Himself of no reputation."

14. John 1:14.

15. This point will be emphasized further in the examination of the Chalcedonian creed below.

Jesus "is the image of the invisible God," and (Col 2:9) that in Jesus "dwells all the fullness of the Godhead bodily." Echoing these sentiments, Heb 1:3 makes the bold claim that Jesus Christ is "the brightness of [God's] glory and the express image of His person." Thus the creed seems to be in perfect accord with several strong biblical statements that in Jesus, God lived an earthly, human life.

One key aspect of this idea becomes clear from examining such biblical passages, and is worth noting at this point. Implicit in the idea that Jesus is God Incarnate—and explicit in much of the relevant Scriptural data—is the idea that the Incarnation is a *revelation* of God by which human beings can come to know God. Expressing this fact, Erickson writes, "We can have real knowledge of God. Jesus said, 'He who has seen me has seen the Father' (John 14:9). Whereas the prophets came bearing a message from God, Jesus was God. If we would know the love of God, the holiness of God, the power of God are like, we need only look at Christ."[16] In his analysis of this concept, Wolfhart Pannenberg places a great deal of emphasis on the necessity of Jesus' divinity in the process of this revelation of God in Christ, as he writes, "God is as much the subject, the author of his self-revelation, as he is its content. Thus to speak of a self-revelation of God in the Christ event means that the Christ event, that Jesus, belongs to the essence of God himself. If this were not so, then the human event of Jesus' life would veil the God who is active therein and thus exclude his full revelation."[17] Statements such as these highlight the extent to which Jesus' divinity is connected to the idea of the Incarnation as a direct revelation of God.

In light of both biblical and historical theology, it has become a cornerstone of the Christian faith that the Incarnation is God's self-disclosure to mankind. Thomas Torrance, in his discussion of the Incarnation, also emphasizes this fact as he writes, "Thus it is the faith and understanding of the Christian Church that in Jesus Christ God Himself in His own Being has come into our world and is actively present as personal Agent within our physical and historical existence."[18] McGrath also argues that this idea is central to the Christian faith, as he writes, "A central element of Christian theology centers upon the idea of a *revelatory presence of God*

16. Erickson, *Christian Theology*, 703.
17. Pannenberg, *Jesus–God and Man*, 129.
18. Torrance, *Space, Time, and Incarnation*, 52.

in Christ. . . . Jesus Christ is regarded as making God known in a particular and specific manner, distinctive to Christianity."[19] Thus, the revelatory nature of the Incarnation is one of the *unique* features of Christianity. Concluding his discussion on the revelatory nature of the Incarnation, McGrath notes that "[t]his conviction has been central to mainstream Christianity down the ages."[20] That God reveals himself directly to mankind in Jesus Christ is now taken for granted in Christian theology.

Along with this understanding that the Incarnation is a *revelation* of God, Christian theology has also tightly joined Jesus' full divinity with the *soteriological purpose* of the Incarnation. Christianity has historically asserted that only a person who is both God and man could accomplish the redemptive purpose of Jesus Christ's coming to the world. Athanasius states as much, arguing "that it was in the power of none other to turn the corruptible into incorruption, except the Saviour Himself, that had at the beginning also made all things out of naught: and that none other could create anew the likeness of God's image for men, save the Image of the Father."[21] In other words, Athanasius asserts that restoring humanity to an incorruptible state, and rescuing men from sin, required the work of a person who identified with mankind in his humanity and with God in his divinity. Athanasius writes that "[Christ] came among us: to this intent, after the proofs of His Godhead from His works, He next offered up His sacrifice also on behalf of all, yielding His Temple to death in the stead of all. . . ."[22] Athanasius understood that if the atoning work of Christ were to be both efficient (truly atoning), and sufficient (truly substitutionary), Christ must be both God and man. Commenting on Athanasius' writings, Alister McGrath notes the following:

> What are the soteriological implications of this ontological affirmation [that Jesus is God]? Athanasius makes the point that it is only God who can save. . . . No creature can save another creature. Only the creator can redeem the creation. Having emphasized that it is God alone who can save, Athanasius makes the logical move which the Arians found difficult to counter. The New Testament and the Christian liturgical tradition alike regard Jesus Christ as Savior. Yet as Athanasius emphasized, only God can save.

19. McGrath, *Christian Theology*, 349.

20. Ibid., 349.

21. Athanasius, *The Incarnation of the Word* 20.1 (*NPNF*² 4:47).

22. Ibid.

So how are we to make sense of this? The only possible solution, Athanasius argues, is to accept that Jesus is God incarnate.[23]

Athanasius' position became standard in Christian theology. Writing in the eleventh century, Anselm followed Athanasius by arguing that salvation required the personal intervention of mankind's creator. In his monumental *Why God Became Man*, Anselm argues that "it was not fitting that what God had planned for mankind should be utterly nullified, and the plan in question could not be brought into effect unless the human race were set free by its Creator in person."[24] In other words, Christ was the same God who created mankind, and therefore could act as its redeemer. He concludes that if any other attempted the work of redemption, salvation would not be affected, asking, "Do you not understand that, supposing any other person were to rescue man from eternal death, man would rightly be judged his bondslave? If he were this, he would in no way have been restored to that dignity which he would have had in the future, if he had not sinned. For man, who had the prospect of being the bondsman of no one except God and the equal of the good angels in all respects, would be the bondslave of someone who was not God and to whom the angels were not in bondage."[25]

Contemporary theologians have continued the emphasis on the necessity of Christ's divinity for the purposes of salvation. Erickson comments that it is because Jesus is fully God that "[r]edemption is available to us. The death of Christ is sufficient for all sinners who have ever lived, for it was not merely a finite human, but an infinite God who died."[26] Grudem asserts that "only someone who is infinite God could bear the full penalty for all the sins of those who would believe in him—any finite creature would have been incapable of bearing that penalty."[27] Continuing later, Grudem offers an apt summary of the soteriological significance in the doctrine of the Incarnation: "Thus, if Jesus is not fully God, we have no salvation and ultimately no Christianity."[28]

---

23. McGrath, *The Christian Theology Reader*, 256–57.

24. Anselm, *Why God Became Man*, 1.4 (269).

25. Ibid., 1.5 (270).

26. Erickson, *Christian Theology*, 703.

27. Grudem, *Systematic Theology*, 553.

28. Ibid., 554.

These two ideas—the revelatory nature and soteriological purpose of the Incarnation—have important implications with regard to the debate concerning God's relationship to time. It means, for example, that the earthly temporal existence of Jesus reveals something about the kind of life lived by God the Son, since the life being lived in Jesus is the life of the person of God the Son. Further, God the Son entered human existence to *accomplish* his work. The very idea of accomplishment hints at the presence of temporal sequence: there was a state of affairs in the life of God the Son in which the work of salvation had not yet been accomplished; and this state of affairs came to an end at a later moment when the work was accomplished.

Christ's Session: Perpetual Existence as the God-Man

The Nicene Creed also affirms the continued and perpetual existence of Christ as both God and man. This highlights the fact that the Incarnation is not a temporary state, but rather it represents the beginning of a new and permanent state of affairs in the life of the Son of God. The creed states that Christ "ascended into heaven, and sitteth on the right hand of the Father; and he shall come again, with glory, to judge both the quick and the dead; whose kingdom shall have no end." In other words, after completing his earthly mission, Christ continues to live as the God-Man in the presence of the Father; and this continued existence will have no end. The Scriptural basis for this lies in passages such as Mark 16:19, which states, "So then, after the Lord had spoken to them, He was received up into heaven, and sat down at the right hand of God;" and Col 3:1, which says that Christ is "sitting at the right hand of God." It is important to note that the creed affirms at least three facts about the post-resurrection activity of Christ: after his bodily resurrection Christ ascended to the immediate presence of the Father; Christ will again return for judgment; and Christ will rule over his kingdom forever. These elements make clear the council's belief that the Incarnation was not temporary, but rather brought about a permanent state of affairs in the life of God the Son.

Bernard Ramm provides an analysis of the significance of the Christ's continued session, and gives four theological topics that are both framed by and understood through the concept of Christ's session.[29] First, Ramm notes that the concept of Christ's *intercessory role* hinges on the concept

29. Ramm, *Evangelical Christology*, 99–103.

of his continued session,[30] pointing to the evidence in the New Testament that Christ continues to intercede on behalf of believers before the Father.[31] Second, Ramm highlights the traditional concept of the *Christus Praesens*, or *presence of Christ*, which has been affirmed by both Catholic and Protestant traditions in their belief that the risen Christ continues to be present in his power among his followers.[32] Third, Ramm follows the creed in pointing out that "[i]n his session at the right hand of the Father, Christ begins his reign,"[33] thus demonstrating that Christ's kingdom is being established and his *reign* over it will not come to an end. Finally, and also following Nicaea, Ramm highlights the *eschatological* significance of the session of Christ: there is a day approaching in which Christ will return to the earth to reign, and there will be universal affirmation of Christ's lordship over all of creation. Ramm's analysis highlights what was affirmed in the creed: the Incarnation did not end at Christ's ascension, rather Jesus continues to live as both God and man in the presence of the Father, awaiting the final inauguration of his everlasting kingdom.

In light of the clarity of Ramm's analysis, the implications of the permanence of the Incarnation for the debate on God and time should be obvious. The fact that God the Son continues to live a temporal life in Jesus Christ, combined with the fact that Christ's rule over his kingdom will have no end indicates that time itself will have no end—that is, the temporally ordered states in the life of God the Son are unbound in the future direction. Jesus' temporal life is not bound by some future "final moment" of time, but rather his life will go on forever—in a temporally unending way. When considering the permanence of the Incarnation, the temporal sequence in the life of God the Son seems unavoidable.

Preliminary Summary from the Nicene Creed

Given the above analysis of the Nicene Creed and its theological context, I can now offer a brief summary of the creed's impact on the debate concerning God's relationship to time. The emphasis in the statement seems to have been that Christ, who is fully human and lived a genuine human existence, is also fully God. The Incarnation event was one

30. Ibid., 100.
31. Ibid., 103.
32. Ibid., 100–101.
33. Ibid., 100.

in which the pre-existing Word—God the Son—took on flesh, entered human history for the purposes of salvation, and now lives on awaiting the coming of his everlasting kingdom. At least three applications of this theological paradigm can be made in the debate. First, the brute fact of the Incarnation—the fact that God himself entered human existence in a personal way—indicates that all models of Divine-temporal interaction must account for God being a first-person participant in the temporal order. Second, the redemptive and ruling work of Christ has temporal implications, and therefore implications on our understanding of God's mode of existence with respect to time. Finally, insofar as Christ is God, and considering that the Incarnation is a revelation of God, God's relationship to time must in some way be revealed in Christ's relationship to time. Each of these three applications will be discussed toward the end of this chapter.

Having examined Nicaea, it is now beneficial to examine the Chalcedonian Creed; which gives insight into how Christ is both God and man existing as one person. This will shed further light on how the doctrine of the Incarnation can inform the debate on God's relationship to time.

The Chalcedonian Creed: Person and Nature

Christological controversies did not come to an end after the publication of the Nicene-Constantinopolitan Creed in 381; rather new challenges arose which eventually led to another council meeting at Chalcedon in 451. Central to the newer concerns was the question of how divinity and humanity were united together in the person of Jesus Christ. While the church was in basic agreement on the fact that Jesus Christ was both truly human and truly God, two different schools of thought emerged in the East—differing on their understanding of *how* he could be both God and man—which have been referred to as the Alexandrian and the Antiochene schools.[34]

---

34. These are labels used by historians for convenient classification. Their use is not to suggest the presence of actual institutions of learning, nor does it indicate monolithic thought in the two geographical areas. In addition to the other sources mentioned that discuss the history of the topic, see also Pannenberg, *Jesus: God and Man*, 287–93; and Sellars, *Doctrine of Chalcedon*, 132–206, both of which is contain helpful discussion of the relationship between the Alexandrian and Antiochene perspectives on the Incarnation.

The Alexandrian school of thought, motivated by soteriological concerns, emphasized that the divine Word, or Logos, took on human flesh and human nature. This led to a general trajectory that seemed to point in the direction of the presence of only one nature in Christ: namely, the human nature assumed by the divine. According to McGrath, John 1:4 became a central verse emphasized by this school of thought. Characterizing the Alexandrians, McGrath writes: "The Logos existed 'without flesh' before its union with human nature; after that union, there is only one nature, in that the Logos united human nature to itself."[35] Gonzales points out that this led to an under-emphasized humanity in Jesus. Gonzales characterizes this position as he writes, "His divinity must be asserted, even if this had to be done at the expense of his humanity."[36] This line of thinking led to the understanding that the Logos assumed human nature in general, rather than a specific human being.

The Antiochene school, on the other hand, seemed to stress the idea that in the Incarnation, the Logos assumed human nature *specifically*. According to Gonzales, the Antiochenes emphasized "that for Jesus to be the Savior of human beings he had to be fully human."[37] In other words, people are in need of redemption on account of sin; and redemption requires the obedience of a particular human being. Thus, emphasis is placed on the Logos becoming an individual human being, uniting both divine and human natures in one person. McGrath describes the Antiochene emphasis, "Christ is at one and the same time both God and a real individual human being."[38] Therefore, while the Antiochenes agreed with their Alexandrian counterparts that Jesus was fully divine, they emphasized this in a way to avoid a diminished view of Jesus' humanity.

Two extremes of these two schools of thought can be seen in the viewpoints of Apollinarius of Laodicea and Nestorius of Constantinople. Apollinarius took the Alexandrian perspective to the extreme. He emphasized the divinity of Christ so much so that he argued that Christ could not be fully human; arguing that in the Incarnation the Word assumed *flesh*. Apollinarius believed that if he were to possess a human mind, along with the human flesh, Christ could not be completely sinless. In his

35. McGrath, *Christian Theology*, 361.
36. Gonzales, *Story of Christianity*, 252.
37. Ibid.
38. McGrath, *Christian Theology*, 362.

understanding, then, the divine Word took the place of the human mind or rational soul, acting as the animating force of the flesh. Christ was seen as having but one nature, not two. Characterizing Apollinarius' position, Erickson writes, "Thus we have in Jesus a single entity compounded of the Logos and the flesh, not a duality, nor two complete, self-moving principles."[39] Apollinarius sought to avoid an extreme dualism in Christ, and in emphasizing the unity of the person of Christ, he denied the full humanity of Christ.

Nestorius, on the other hand, sought to preserve the duality of natures in Christ, and represents the extreme of the Antiochene school of thought. The main controversy concerning Nestorius' perspective was on the propriety of using the term *theotokos*—or, "God-bearer"—to describe Mary. Nestorius argued that rather than "God-bearer," Mary ought to be referred to as "Christ-bearer." The question was not so much one of what title should be given to Mary as it was a question of the nature of the Incarnation. Nestorius sought to avoid the errors of both Arius and Apollinarius; and so he drew a sharp distinction between Christ's humanity and his divinity. After all, he argued, God cannot be contained within the womb of a woman; so then Mary bore the flesh, the human vessel of the Incarnation. The result of this debate was a characterization that Nestorius was teaching Christ as being two natures *and two persons.*

The teachings of both Nestorius and Apollinarius were condemned by councils of the church. The council that met at Chalcedon in 451 developed a definition of the Incarnation that sought to both reject the false teachings concerning Christ's two natures, as well as affirm the previous statements made at Nicaea:

> Following, then, the holy Fathers, we all with one voice teach that it is to be confessed that our Lord Jesus Christ is one and the same God, perfect in divinity, and perfect in humanity, true God and true human, with a rational soul and a body, of one substance with the Father in his divinity, and of one substance with us in his humanity, in every way like us, with the only exception of sin, begotten of the Father before all time in his divinity, and also begotten in the latter days, in his humanity, of Mary the virgin bearer of God.
>
> This one and the same Christ, Son, Lord, Only-begotten, manifested in two natures without any confusion, change, division or

39. Erickson, *Word Became Flesh*, 60.

separation. The union does not destroy the difference of the two natures, but on the contrary the properties of each are kept, and both are joined in one person and *hypostasis*. They are not divided into two persons, but belong to the one Only-begotten Son, the Word of God, the Lord Jesus Christ. All this, as the prophets of old said of him, and as he himself has taught us, and as the Creed of the Fathers has passed on to us.[40]

The wording of this definition clearly reveals a desire to repudiate specific ideas that the council believed to be in direct contradiction to the biblical testimony. Responding to the Nestorian errors, the definition emphasizes that the two natures were united in "one person and *hypostasis*," and that they are "not divided into two persons." Speaking directly to the vocabulary of the Nestorian controversy, the definition refers to Mary as the "bearer of God." Addressing Apollinarianism, the definition emphasizes that Christ is "perfect in divinity, and perfect in humanity . . . with a rational soul and a body," and that he is "in every way like" other human beings, with the exception of sin.

Despite its heavy emphasis on rejecting specific error, the importance of the Chalcedonian definition (especially for the present debate) lies in its affirmation that Christ exists in two perfect and complete natures united in one individual person: the natures not in any way confused or diminished, and the person not in any way split or fragmented. Both the divine and human natures are *truly* present, so that it is correct to affirm (and incorrect to deny) that Christ is truly God and truly man. As in the debate surrounding Nicaea, the motivation for crafting such a strong statement lies at least partially in soteriological concerns. This can be seen in the writings of one contemporary to the controversy, Gregory of Nazianzus. In responding to Apollinarianism, Gregory emphasized the soteriological importance of the two natures in Christ. He writes, "If anyone has put his trust in Him as a Man without a human mind, he is really bereft of mind and quite unworthy of salvation. For that which He has not assumed He has not healed; but that which is united to His Godhead is also saved. . . . Let them not, then, begrudge us our complete salvation, or clothe the Saviour only with bones and nerves and the portraiture of humanity."[41] In other words, Gregory took for granted that Christ was

---

40. In Gonzales, *Story of Christianity*, 1:257.

41. Gregory of Nazianzus, "To Cledonius the Priest Against Apollinarius," letter 101 (*NPNF*[2], 7:440).

God, and then defended the idea that he was also human; for salvation can only be found when the human is united to the divine in the person of Christ.

Writing some 800 years after Chalcedon, Anselm discusses the issue in his *On the Incarnation of the Word*. In this work, Anselm emphasizes in detail the Chalcedonian affirmation of two natures in one person in Christ. He writes, "Therefore, as Christ is God and a human being, so there seems to be two persons in him. . . . But such is not the case. For as there is one nature and several persons in God, and the several persons are one nature, so there is one person and several natures in Christ, and the several natures are one person. . . . For there is not in Christ one who is God, another one who is the human being . . . rather, the very same one who is also the human being is God. For the 'Word made flesh' (John 1:14) assumed another nature, not another person."[42]

Anselm's statement reveals the connection between Chalcedon and Nicaea. Chalcedon's expression of concern over the concepts of *nature* and *person*—specifically as they relate to Christ—is a natural outworking of the theological struggle to understand Christ that began before Nicaea. While it was important to the council meeting at Chalcedon to refute certain specific false teachings, it can also be seen as an elaboration on what was already affirmed by the Nicene formulation, and therefore a continuation along the same Christological trajectory. While Nicaea affirmed that Christ was "very God of very God" who "was incarnate . . . [and] made man;" Chalcedon explains that Christ was God by virtue of the presence of the divine nature, and was man by virtue of the presence of human nature.

So when "the life of Christ" is discussed, it is imperative to bear in mind this cohesive theological foundation. While there was struggle to understand the Incarnation and put words to concepts, early Christianity spoke with one voice in its affirmation that Christ is—in every sense of the word—God. Thomas Morris, in his *The Logic of God Incarnate*[43] defends the position taken by the early church and explains the meaning behind the Chalcedonian definition. He writes, "An individual will count as human only if it has all the properties essential to being human, the joint satisfaction of which will be sufficient for exemplifying human

42. Anselm, *On the Incarnation of the Word*, 11 (252–53).
43. Morris, *Logic of God Incarnate*.

nature. Likewise, an individual will count as divine only if it has all the properties essential to being God, the joint satisfaction of which will suffice for having the nature of deity."[44] In other words, Christ possessed not only full humanity, but also all that was necessary in order for him to be properly called "God." Morris continues in his discussion as he writes, "It is the claim of orthodoxy that Jesus had all the kind-essential properties of humanity, and all the kind-essential properties of divinity; and thus existed (and continues still to exist) in two natures."[45] Indeed, it is the claim of historic Christian orthodoxy that Jesus is fully human, and at the same time possessed all the properties necessary for him to be referred to rightly as God.

The Creeds in Context: Time and the Unity of Christ

Foremost among the immediately relevant questions that arise when considering how Nicaea and Chalcedon relate to the topic is this: If Jesus is God (in the same way and to the same extent as the Father) in what way is the life of Jesus also the life of God the Son? Since the biblical data seem to indicate that Christ lived an ordinary life of temporal sequence, is this a revelation of something about God and his relationship to time? Writing on the implications of the Doctrine of the Incarnation, Anselm argues that the unity of the person of Christ serves as a guiding principle in understanding the two natures in Christ. He writes, "For when we designate Jesus, we understand the one whom the angel announced, the one who is God and the human being, the Son of God and the Son of the Virgin, and not any human being. And we truly predicate everything, whether regarding God or regarding the human being, of him. For we cannot designate or name the divine Son apart from the human son, nor the human son as a person apart from the divine Son, and the combination of proper characteristics of the Word and the assumed human being is the same."[46] Here, Anselm was arguing that in Christ, the "human son" cannot be divided from the "divine son" in the way his life is described. This clearly

---

44. Ibid., 40. It must be highlighted that a person's "nature" is not defined as "the set of properties or attributes possessed by the person." If it were, then it would be concluded that Christ only possesses one nature, because in him exist a singularly unique set of attributes. It must be emphasized that in the person of Christ are two distinct natures, united together so that both are preserved and neither diminished.

45. Ibid.

46. Anselm, *On the Incarnation of the Word*, 11 (253).

has implications for the present topic, because there is no doubt that Jesus lived on earth—and continues to live in the presence of the Father—a life of temporal sequence. So based on the unity of the natures in the person, it would seem that the ordinary temporal life of Jesus is an immediate indicator that the life of God the Son is also one in which he experiences ordinary temporal sequence.

When examining the life of Christ in light of his dual natures, authors often struggle to communicate how the two natures can be united in one person. Torrance, for example, speaks of the Incarnation as if it were a *paradoxical* doctrine. In relating the doctrine to the concepts of space and time, Torrance immediately goes to the question of the language used to discuss the Incarnation; and asks, "How then can we speak about the Incarnation as an act of God in this way without illegitimately projecting our creaturely time into God?"[47] Seeking to avoid the apparent paradox when viewing the Incarnation from a classical atemporal view, Torrance spends the rest of his discussion on the topic attempting to find a solution to that question. Ultimately, Torrance settles (rather unsatisfactorily) on the use of symbolic language, describing the Incarnation in part as "a coordinate system of vertical and horizontal dimensions."[48] Pannenberg also reveals the difficulties in explaining a dual-nature Christology:

> The formula about two natures [in the statement of Chalcedon] . . . does not take the concrete unity of the man Jesus as its given point of departure, but rather the difference between the divine and the human. . . . Throughout, the contradiction between God and creature is the logical starting point for thought; from this perspective the attempt was made to understand the unity of the two in Jesus, the relation between divinity and humanity in him. The pattern of thought thus moves in the opposite direction from the formula *vere deus, vere homo*. Jesus now appears as a being bearing and uniting two opposed substances in himself. From this conception all the insoluble problems of the doctrine of the two natures result.[49]

Pannenberg's comments are indeed indicative of the challenges faced when a theologian attempts to go beyond the mere statement of Chalcedon to an explanation of how the natures can be united.

47. Torrance, *Space, Time, and Incarnation*, 53.

48. Ibid., 86.

49. Pannenberg, *Jesus: God and Man*, 284.

This theological struggle, however, is at its maximal difficulty when an idea or doctrine other than the Incarnation is taken as the starting point in consideration of the Divine nature. If the Incarnation is to be seen as truly *revelatory*, then it should be the centerpiece in considering both the divine and human natures. At this point, a discussion by Colin Gunton in his examination of Chalcedonian Christology is extremely helpful. Gunton comments that the apparent paradox in the union of the natures in Christ has caused some to dismiss the statements of Chalcedon "as being unable to do anything more than simply juxtapose, in a dualistic manner, the divine and the human in Christ."[50] It is here that Gunton's analysis of this perspective of Christology has immediate application for the present topic. For this reason, the argument will be quoted at length:

> As a matter of fact, one might ask why, if they were so dualistic, the members of the Council of Chalcedon were *able* to juxtapose (if that is the correct word) the human and the divine in the "one and the same Christ." But if they were able to do no more than state a case without explaining it, it was surely partly because in their Platonic background there lay a conception of eternity derived from some such definition as Plato's. If time is the moving image, the implication appears to be that eternity is unmoving. And if eternity is by definition motionless, what is it doing in the very temporal figure of Jesus of Nazareth? It is no wonder that he tended to be crowded out. The wonder is, rather, that so often the Fathers were able to break through the axioms of their world to produce what, as orthodox Christology, came to assert the co-presence of both eternity and time in this one historical figure. Against this background it is possible to see orthodox Christology as not the slave but the critic of Hellenistic philosophy.[51]

While Gunton does not arrive at the same conclusions that I draw, his argument does indicate a trajectory that leads directly to the main point of emphasis being suggested here: Given the strong Scriptural statements about the revelatory nature of the Incarnation, and given the necessity of Chalcedonian and Nicene orthodoxy to the Christian faith, the Incarnation ought to be the theological starting point for examining such philosophical topics as God's relationship to time. It ought to govern both

---

50. Gunton, *Yesterday and Today*, 104. Gunton specifically addresses the discussion of Pannenberg, a portion of which was quoted above.

51. Ibid., 104–5.

method and conclusions about whether God experiences temporal sequence in his existence.

As Gunton has suggested, the Incarnation seems most paradoxical when viewed from a philosophical perspective that presumes a Platonic conception of time and eternity. But it seems inadvisable to allow the doctrine of the Incarnation—which is most central to the Christian faith—to be considered a paradox, for to do so risks emptying it of anything beyond myth or symbolism. It seems more advisable to follow Gunton's advice and allow the Incarnation to be the critic of the Platonic worldview and not the other way around. There is no doubt that when one begins with a Platonic view of eternity, the Incarnation will seem paradoxical (if not contradictory) because the Divine is so separated from the material world as to rule out anything like what was stated in the creeds of the church. On the contrary, what I am suggesting here is that *the Incarnation is not at all paradoxical,* for there is no real conflict between the human and divine that would create a paradox when the two are united in Christ. For all of Schleiermacher's faults, he seems to have been correct in his assertion that "one individual cannot share in two quite different [i.e., contradictory or incompatible] natures."[52] But what conclusion can be drawn from this observation? Clearly there is a difference between the natures; but this is not to say that the Incarnation was impossible. Rather, Schleiermacher's observation speaks to the discordance between the classical atemporal view of God and what Christians have long said about the Incarnation. Human nature, as exemplified in Christ, is essentially temporal. Rather than assert that divinity is essentially atemporal, and that therefore there is a contradiction in the Incarnation (the one person is both essentially temporal and essentially non-temporal), it seems more in keeping with Nicene and Chalcedonian orthodoxy to hold that there is no contradiction or conflict in the affirmation that in Christ are united both human and divine natures.

It seems clear that the difficulty arises when one first adopts the classical atemporal view, and then attempts to account for the Incarnation—and defenders of the view, with few exceptions,[53] have not produced significant consideration of the Incarnation. It would seem, however, that Jesus' earthly life of normal temporal sequence can be consistent with the

52. Schleiermacher, *Christian Faith*, 393.

53. The most significant is Leftow, "A Timeless God Incarnate," whose argument will be examined in chapter 3.

presence in him of the divine nature only if there is harmony between such a nature and normal temporal sequence. Gerald O'Collins speaks to this in his discussion:

> This claim [of the union of divinity and humanity in Christ] goes far beyond the general action and presence of God in creating and maintaining in existence all non-divine realities. The claim also leaves far behind such special divine actions as God's "taking possession" of a piece of ground, "being enthroned" on Zion, "filling" the Temple with his glory, "speaking through" the prophets, "guiding" the people across the desert, or working miracles. . . . Through the incarnation God, who is pure Spirit, assumes (and not merely creates and conserves) matter; the eternal God personally enters time.[54]

O'Collins is correct in his assertion that God entered the material world; and therefore the life of Jesus should be seen as God's personal (first-person) participation in the temporal world. If the life of Jesus is—at least in some meaningful way—the life of God the Son, then the conclusion that God himself *experiences* the temporal sequence in the life of Jesus seems unavoidable.[55] When a priority is placed on preserving a robust Chalcedonian Christology, the classical atemporal view appears at its weakest in its ability to account for ordinary temporal sequence in the life of Christ.

THE INCARNATION AND TIME: PARADIGM FOR AN ARGUMENT

When placed into the context of the debate on God's relationship to time, it is obvious that the statements of the creeds, as well as the statements of Scripture upon which the creeds are based, have direct implications on the debate. The question under consideration is: Can the Incarnation be a defeater for the classical atemporal view of God's relationship to time? Placing the doctrine of the Incarnation into this context, certain indicators emerge. Recall, for example, Aquinas's argument regarding succession in the life of God. In his *Compendium of Theology*, Aquinas draws as a direct consequent of God's immutability the absence of succession

---

54. O'Collins, "The Incarnation: The Critical Issues," 6.

55. Notably, Helm, "Divine Timeless Eternity," and Leftow, "A Timeless God Incarnate" have used various means to avoid this conclusion; the merits of which will be examined in chapter 3.

in the divine life. Aquinas argues that since God is not subject to motion or change, he possesses no temporal succession in his life. Therefore, his existence must be simultaneous. Concerning the possibility of the contrary, Aquinas writes, "That which passes is lost, and what is expected in the future can be acquired. But nothing is lost to God or accrues to Him, since He is immutable. Therefore His existence is simultaneously whole."[56] This argument is a direct descendant of the Boethian model of eternity, in which God is said to "[grasp and possess] simultaneously the entire fullness of life without end; no part of the future is lacking to it, and no part of the past has escaped it."[57] Considering these and other foundational statements of the classical view, it would seem that the absence of succession in God's life is a necessary element of the atemporal view.

Succession, in the context of the atemporal view, is nothing more than temporal sequence; as is obvious from both the Thomistic and Boethian descriptions of God. The term "simultaneous" is designed to rule out the notion of temporal sequence in the Divine life. Therefore, if an argument based on the Incarnation is to be constructed that defeats the classical atemporal view it will be one that demonstrates *succession*— the passage of temporal sequence—in the life of God. There are at least three ideas present in the doctrine of the Incarnation (as defined by the creedal formulae, above) that can together form a paradigm for an argument demonstrating the presence of temporal sequence in the divine life: (1) The Incarnation event itself indicates sequence, both in its occurrence and its permanence. (2) The earthly life of Christ demonstrates temporal sequence. (3) The salvific work of Christ—in its completion—indicates the necessity of sequence in the divine life. While the final argument will be developed in more detail in chapter 5, each of these indicators will now be given a brief description, because their relevance is directly connected to the creedal statements discussed in this chapter. This three-fold paradigm will begin to demonstrate the theological inadequacies of the classical view, as well as lay the framework for a suggested alternative perspective.

56. Aquinas, *Compendium*, 1.8 (13).
57. Boethius, *Consolation*, 5.6 (111).

Temporal Sequence in the Incarnation Event

Consistent in Scripture and in Christian theology is the use of the language of *transformation* or *becoming* employed to describe the Incarnation event. As indicated above, the Bible speaks of the Incarnation as a defining event (John 1:14, Phil 2:7). The idea is also highlighted and contained implicitly in the Nicene understanding of the preexistence of Christ. This means that Christ existed, as the divine Word of God, and then at a particular point became incarnate in Jesus—who, being man, did not exist prior to the Incarnation event. Describing this event, Packer has written, "Without diminishing his divinity, he added to it all that is involved in being human."[58] Thus the Incarnation can be said to be an *event* in the life experience of God.

Additionally, this event did not bring about a temporary result; but rather the Incarnation continues in the life and work of Christ in his Session and future reign over his kingdom. In the debate on God and time, this notion of the continued Session of Christ is often overlooked. As was suggested in the discussion of Ramm's analysis, the Incarnation cannot be dismissed as a temporary, mysterious condescension of God into human affairs. Rather, the becoming of flesh was an event with permanent results: the God-Man Jesus Christ was bodily resurrected, ascended into heaven, and continues to live his life, as both God and man, sitting "on the right hand of the Father" as the sole mediator between God and man. Even at the end of the age, as the creed states, Christ will continue this existence as the God-Man, ruling over his kingdom, which will never come to an end. Addressing this idea, Gregory of Nazianzus wrote, "If any assert that He has now put off His holy flesh, and that His Godhead is stripped of the body, and deny that He is now with His body and will come again with it, let him not see the glory of His Coming. For where is His body now, if not with Him Who assumed it?"[59] Therefore, the Incarnation event brought about a permanent state of affairs in the life of God.

The manifestation of an event immediately indicates temporal sequence, for an "event" generally is something that acts as a point of division in—or a marker of—temporal sequence. The Incarnation indicates an event in the divine life that brought about a state of affairs differenti-

58. Packer, "Eternally Incarnate," 72.

59. Gregory of Nazianzus, "To Cledonius the Priest Against Apollinarius," letter 101 (*NPNF*[2], 7:440).

ated from that prior to the event. The primary implication of the event as it relates to the present topic is that it indicates *sequence* in the divine life. The Incarnation was an event, serving as the dividing line between two consecutive states of affairs in the life of God: *before* the Incarnation and *after* the Incarnation. God the Son existed pre-incarnate, and the event of the Incarnation was an event in his life, after which he existed incarnate in Jesus Christ. To conclude otherwise would be to interpret biblical descriptions of the Incarnation as *purely* symbolic and figurative, with no application in concrete reality, thus calling into question long-employed hermeneutical methodologies.

Temporal Sequence in the Earthly Life of Christ

One element in particular that seems to be an important feature of the classical atemporal view of God's relationship to time is a strong emphasis on God's transcendence. God is seen as wholly distinct and separate from the sphere of creation. There is a sense in which Christian theology shares the concerns of Platonism at this point. We must say that God is *ontologically other* than the physical realm of the universe, for to say otherwise risks suggesting that God might also share in the corruption of the physical world. Clearly this would be unacceptable. Scripture indicates in such passages as Isa 6:1 that God is "high and lifted up." God is further quoted in Isa 55:9, "For as the heavens are higher than the earth, so are My ways higher than your ways, and My thoughts than your thoughts." Indeed, right theology places due emphasis on God's transcendence. However, the Incarnation reminds us that a robust statement of God's transcendence must be balanced with an equally robust statement of God's immanence. Christ is also "Immanuel . . . God with us."[60] But these two are by no means contrary to one another, and do not form a paradox. If it were not possible for the transcendent God to become immanent in Christ, then the Incarnation itself would not have been possible.

The affirmation of the Chalcedonian Creed is that the two natures are united in a singular person. This person is none other than God the Son, Incarnate in Jesus Christ. Therefore, it must be admitted that the life being lived by Jesus Christ is the life of that one person: God the Son. Scriptural statements about the life of Jesus indicate clearly that it was an ordinary earthly life, composed of temporally sequenced events. The

60. Matt 1:23.

most immediately obvious example of such an event is the conception and birth of Jesus Christ. The council at Chalcedon sought to affirm that Mary was not simply the bearer of flesh, but was the bearer of God. To suggest that Mary bore in her body something other than the person who is God the Son is to commit the error of Nestorianism. The life that was lived by Jesus Christ, from the event of his conception onward was the life of God the Son. It will be shown in chapter 3 that even defenders of the classical atemporal view of God's relationship to time admit this fact.

The consequence of Nicene and Chalcedonian orthodoxy when viewed in this light is that the ordinary temporal events in the life of Jesus Christ are also events in the life of God the Son. The creedal statements emphasize that there is only one person in view; and therefore, the life being lived by Jesus is the life of God the Son, and indeed, God the Son's life is Jesus' life. The argument could be restated as follows: Jesus' life contains temporally sequenced events. Since the life of God the Son is the life of Jesus (that is, only one life is being lived), the life of God the Son contains temporally sequenced events. The details of this kind of argument will be examined in chapter 4 in the discussion of Thomas Senor's argument.[61] Also included in this discussion will be some brief comments on Senor's attempt to defend his views against some challenges. Important conclusions about such argumentation will be made in chapter 4, as well as in chapter 5, where I will present my final argument.

Temporal Sequence in the Finished Work of Christ

One particular element of the life of Christ that must be highlighted—distinct from the mere fact that his life was ordinarily temporal—is the work that he accomplished through the Incarnation. As indicated above, a central element in the doctrine of the Incarnation is its *soteriological purpose.* Recall, for example, the statement made by Athanasius that "[Christ] came among us: to this intent, after the proofs of His Godhead from His works, He next offered up His sacrifice also on behalf of all, yielding His Temple to death in the stead of all. . . ."[62] It has been an indispensible element of the Christian faith that the work accomplished by Christ was an atoning work making salvation available to men. This idea has at its root passages such as Luke 19:10, "for the Son of Man has come to seek and to save that

---

61. Thomas Senor, "Incarnation and Timelessness," 149–64.

62. Ibid.

which was lost." The atoning work of Christ has the result that those who are found in him are transformed into new creatures, the consequences of sin having been disposed of, as in 2 Cor 5:19–21, which emphasizes the idea that Christ accomplished his intended work. This idea is further conveyed in Heb 9:26, which states that "[Christ] has appeared to put away sin by the sacrifice of Himself." These passages communicate the idea that Christ came to earth to accomplish the work of atonement; and this work was indeed accomplished. As is communicated in the passages such as Heb 10:12–14; Christ's earthly mission was accomplished and is now finished, offering the image of Christ sitting down as a sign that his work is complete. The Scriptural witness is clear in that Christ's work of atonement is now finished and accomplished.

But the very notion of being *complete and accomplished* can be seen as an indicator of sequence in the divine life. The passages in question describe people who *were* lost, but are *now* saved; who *were* in sin, but are *now* the righteousness of God. Such descriptions are not limited to creatures, for Christ himself was the one who *put away sin*, which at one time was not put away, but was present and active. Grudem describes this in terms of sufficiency, saying, "But when Christ's sufferings at last came to an end on the cross, it showed that he had borne the full measure of God's wrath against sin and there was no penalty left to pay. It also showed that he was himself righteous before God. In this way the fact that Christ suffered for a limited time rather than eternally shows that his suffering was a sufficient payment for sins."[63]

Each of these descriptions suggest a relational change between God and the one whose sins Christ paid for in his atoning work. But on the classical view God is atemporal; and such change in God is inadmissible. In what sense, then, can sin be thought of as having been put away? In the atemporal view, every event in the temporal order is equally real and present before God: Christ hanging on the cross to pay for sin, and the sin itself, are always equally real and present before God. Therefore, if the atonement is more than purely symbolic, it seems that sequence in the divine life must be accommodated: sin must really be put away; and Christ, having finished his work, has sat down because his payment for sin was a completed event in the life of God.

63. Grudem, *Systematic Theology*, 578.

PRELIMINARY CONCLUSIONS

What has been suggested above is a theological paradigm for both evaluating currently offered models of God's relationship to time, as well as for formulating an alternative argument. But *methodological* considerations must again be given brief consideration. The classical atemporal model has been formulated out of two primary sources of thought: (1) Platonic notions of a dichotomy between static eternity and dynamic time; and (2) a strong emphasis on God's transcendence and immutability within Christian theology. Undoubtedly, these two have played significant roles in the shaping of the philosophical debate, and have helped shape the arguments of Christian theologians, such as Augustine and Boethius, who argued fervently in favor of the atemporal view. Augustine believed that God's immutability (understood in a particular sense) and his timelessness entailed one another. Boethius tackled the issue as it relates to God's knowledge. Seeking to account for the apparent conflict between God's foreknowledge and human freedom, Boethius suggested that when God is seen as timeless—so that his knowledge of the future free actions of his creatures are known all at once, in a flash—the conflict is removed. God, then, must be seen as possessing all the fullness of his life in one, eternal "now," which cannot be divided into parts or sequence.

It is my contention, however, that the Christian doctrine of the Incarnation ought to function as a control belief in the debate, and ought to have priority over the concerns raised by defenders of the atemporal view. The Incarnation is the central indispensible element of Christian theology, and should therefore be placed at the very center of the philosophical debate; it should serve as the lens through which the debate itself should be viewed, and the theological standard by which the philosophical arguments should be judged. Christian theology has much—perhaps everything—at stake in the doctrine of the Incarnation. As Wolterstorff has said, "The most important question for the Christian to consider, in reflecting on [the classical] understanding of divine action, is whether it is compatible with an orthodox understanding of what happens in the incarnation."[64] In what follows, both atemporal and some contemporary temporal arguments will be evaluated in light of the Incarnation. In each case, the arguments will be evaluated as to how they account for a robust Chalcedonian and Nicene orthodox Christology regarding the

---

64. Wolterstorff, "Unqualified Divine Temporality," 209.

Incarnation. After this examination takes place, I will be able to develop and defend an argument using the three-fold paradigm of temporal sequence I have suggested.

3

Analysis of the Atemporal View

I WANT TO ANALYZE and comment on three prominent contemporary contributions to the debate that adopt the classical atemporal perspective. Richard Swinburne's work is included because it is rooted in the history of the classical atemporal perspective, and reveals important elements common to all versions of the atemporal argument. Although Swinburne later abandoned the atemporal view, his earlier work is exemplary of a well-formed defense; therefore, analysis of his earlier arguments is beneficial. Also, a significant portion of the chapter will be dedicated to Brian Leftow's defense of the atemporal view. Leftow's work is included because he makes a direct attempt to reconcile the notion of God's timelessness with the doctrine of the Incarnation. Finally, Paul Helm's atemporal argument will be considered. Helm's contribution is prominent in the contemporary debate; and several key elements of Helm's work reveal important implications of the atemporal view for the doctrine of the Incarnation. After surveying these three authors, I will highlight several philosophical and theological implications from the atemporal view, including whether and how it is able to account for the Incarnation.

RICHARD SWINBURNE

Swinburne's exposition and defense of the atemporal view appear in two essays published in 1965 in *Church Quarterly Review*, entitled "The Timelessness of God, I," and "The Timelessness of God, II." Swinburne now denies the thesis defended in these two essays; and it is difficult to trace the transformation of his belief by following his published works. Unfortunately, Swinburne does not tell his readers exactly why he abandoned the atemporal view. Nevertheless, Swinburne's atemporal argument is exemplary in that it reveals some important and essential elements to the classical view. Swinburne's argument is composed of three parts: The first essay consists of a brief historical account of the atemporal view, in which the view is anchored firmly in the ideas of Boethius. As the second element in his argument Swinburne seeks to explain the Boethian position in terms of God's timelessness being analogous to a timeless law of nature. The final element of the argument, which is given in the second essay, consists in Swinburne's addressing five objections that may be offered against the atemporal view.

At the outset, Swinburne states that the atemporal view of God's relationship to time is best expressed in the work of Boethius. He writes, "The *locus classicus* of the doctrine is the last section of the *Consolation of Philosophy* of the sixth-century Christian philosopher Boethius."[1] Describing Boethius's position, Swinburne interprets it using spatial concepts similar to those offered by Boethius himself: "The obvious analogy is to men traveling along a road; at each time they can see only the neighbourhood on the road where they are. But God is above the road and can see the whole road at once."[2] After giving this brief statement of the position, Swinburne goes on to trace its history.

Swinburne argues that the atemporal view originates from secular Greek philosophy, specifically in the influence of Parmenides and Plato.[3] In making its way into Christianity, Swinburne points out that the first clear statement of the idea in Christian theology is in Ambrose, whom Swinburne also indicates was the source of influence on Augustine.[4] Swinburne further comments that Augustine's eventual answer to the question about God's activity before the creation of the world became the standard Christian position. He writes that Augustine's view "became the orthodoxy of those theologians of the next nine centuries deep enough to discourse on these matters."[5] In how Augustine relates to Boethius's later writings, Swinburne remarks that Augustine's views on God's relation to time are "identical with those of Boethius"[6] Swinburne further states that

1. Swinburne, "Timelessness of God, I," 324.

2. Ibid.

3. Ibid., 325.

4. Ibid.

5. Ibid., 326.

6. Ibid.

the doctrine as defined by Boethius was later defended by Anselm and Aquinas, both of whom "quote and expound Boethius as giving the true doctrine of God and time."[7] Swinburne points out that in more modern times Paul Tillich and Karl Barth both opposed the classical view; but, he asserts, "these two sources of opposition to Boethian doctrine are the only ones which I know within Christian Theology [of the modern era]."[8] While much dissent from the Boethian position has appeared since the 1965 publication of the essay, Swinburne's historical analysis is quite similar to what I offered in chapter 1. He places his defense of the atemporal argument within the context of near unanimity among Christian theologians to the time of his writing. So, for Swinburne, although the rudiments of the classical atemporal view originate in Greek thinking, the fully developed doctrine of God's timelessness in Christian theology (including the modern expressions of the idea) is centered around and depends on the work of Boethius. After this historical analysis and critique, Swinburne goes on to make his case for why he believes that the atemporal view is correct.

Swinburne's argument in defense of the Boethian view can be summarized as follows: In order to be an adequate foundation that explains the existence and operation of the universe—like a natural law—God must be a timeless principle. Swinburne begins his argument by drawing as an example how the occurrence of any event can be explained by natural means. He asserts that any event has two causes: the efficient cause and a natural or scientific law.[9] The efficient cause is that which immediately causes the event, like a lit match igniting an explosion of gunpowder. In order to have the explosion (as in this case) a scientific or natural law is also required, which governs the behavior of gunpowder when it comes in contact with a lit match. Swinburne writes, "Only if both are in fact the case (or other events and laws with the same consequences hold) will the explosion occur."[10] Further, he argues, such laws as those governing the behavior of gunpowder are explained by higher laws of nature; and scientists continually seek for higher governing principles that can serve as a foundation for many classes of events. Swinburne points out that

7. Ibid., 327.
8. Ibid., 330.
9. Swinburne does not differentiate between "scientific" and "natural" laws.
10. Ibid., 332.

these natural or scientific laws not only describe what does happen, but they are of such explanatory power that they indicate what *would* happen in any given set of circumstances, and thus serve as "physical principles limiting the possible."[11]

Swinburne's argument then makes a critical turn leading directly to his conclusion. He argues that such scientific laws must be *outside of time* in order for them to be truly laws. Swinburne writes that while events themselves take place within the temporal order, the law that governs an event "does not have any temporal location," for "if a law be cited in explanation which is limited to some finite period of time, then the law cannot be a true law of nature and ultimate explanation is sought in terms of a true law."[12] He argues that such laws should not be thought of as everlasting, because this would then make them in need of explanation. Rather, he argues that true laws of nature do not merely exist forever, but are *timeless*. He writes that such laws "form the framework and not the content of the changing universe."[13] This leads directly to Swinburne's statements about God. He writes, "Now if God is fully to explain the existence and behavior of the universe, he must be a timeless principle."[14] He argues that if God is the creator and governor of the universe, it must be the case that things are the way they are because He brought them about. But, each event in the universe also has an immediate efficient cause to which it owes its explanation. Therefore, God is the overarching principle, the higher law that provides the ultimate explanation. Repeating his conclusion, Swinburne writes, "So, if God is to fully explain the laws which govern the order of things in the world, God must be a timeless principle."[15] Swinburne concludes that God, "like the laws of Nature, must be outside time, an entity to which temporal predicates are not properly ascribed."[16]

But Swinburne's conclusions do not stop here. He also asserts that the atemporal view is *essential* to the Christian faith. Therefore, in defending the atemporal view, he intends to show how the idea must be compatible with other doctrines. He writes, "This reason for the timeless-

11. Ibid., 333.
12. Ibid.
13. Ibid.
14. Ibid.
15. Ibid.
16. Ibid., 334.

ness of God is, I hope, adequate to show why this doctrine must be an integral part of Christian doctrine. It safeguards the omnipotence and necessity of God."[17] Swinburne admits that even if the atemporal view does preserve omnipotence and necessity, it becomes more difficult to defend when it is compared to other doctrines also essential to the Christian faith. Nevertheless, he believes that in comparing the atemporal view to these other essential doctrines, that the atemporal view can be clarified with greater precision. He states that "the true meaning of the [atemporal view] emerges in reconciling it with other doctrines essential to the Christian theistic system."[18] His second essay goes on to address the difficulties that arise in this effort.

In his "The Timelessness of God, II," Swinburne raises and offers an answer for five difficulties that come from an attempt to reconcile the atemporal view with other Christian doctrines: the notion of God's free will, the idea that the universe had a beginning point, that God acts in history, God's awareness of history, and the idea that God is able to have personal relationships. While acknowledging that other objections might be raised, it seems that Swinburne has chosen these five because they illustrate the fundamental nature of the atemporal view. He writes, "I hope that the meaning of the doctrine of the timelessness of God may become clear as I deal with objections to it. Indicating how a view can be attacked and is to be defended shows the meaning of that view."[19] In each example, Swinburne offers a doctrine about God which is usually accepted but which appears to be in conflict with the idea of God's timelessness. For each of these examples, he offers an explanation intended to show that there is no real conflict. These objections from which Swinburne defends the atemporal view will be summarized, with extra attention devoted to the third objection mentioned.

The first idea mentioned that appears to conflict with the atemporal view is the idea that God has free will. But, Swinburne argues, this difficulty can be resolved by an appeal to analogy: ascribing freedom of will to God is only analogous to the ascription of freedom to human beings. God's will does not change, and therefore his freedom in his actions is also timeless, and contains within itself the entire framework necessary to

---

17. Ibid., 335.
18. Ibid.
19. Swinburne, "Timelessness of God, II," 472.

account for events in time. The second difficulty mentioned is that of the doctrine of creation *ex nihilo*.[20] What seems to be missing in the coming about of the initial stages of creation, in Swinburne's scheme, is the efficient cause, which occurs in time, bringing about the series. Swinburne here also appeals to analogy: normally laws state what will occur *given a certain set of conditions*, but God also decrees that some things *will be the case*. Further, even though God's decree brought about the initial temporal creation event, his decree is still timeless because it is a decree governing the very existence of the universe and it applies at all times. The fourth objection listed is that if timeless, God seems either to lack knowledge or else his knowledge of tensed facts would create a contradiction. Swinburne deflects the force of the objection through a simple clarification: God is not aware *at one time* of many events happening at various times; rather he is aware *timelessly* of these various events. The fifth and final objection addressed in the essay is that the conception of God as timeless seems to make him so immovable and lifeless as to think that genuine relationships between humans and him would be impossible. Swinburne counters this objection simply by asserting that it is spurious, and therefore not really demanding a solution.

The objection listed third in Swinburne's essay is of central importance to the present topic: that God acts in history seems to be in conflict with the assertion that he is timeless. Since the Incarnation is a special case of God acting directly in history as a first-person participant, how Swinburne counters this objection is important to consider. Swinburne handles this objection by means of further clarifying what is meant when it is said that a timeless God "acts in history." He argues that while the acts of God have their effects within the temporal order, and are perceived by humans as temporal, the acts themselves remain timeless. Swinburne points out that "God, as the supreme ordering principle of the universe and . . . the initiator of the causal chains, is ultimately responsible for everything that happens."[21] He explains that even though humans perceive certain events as special acts of God (such as the call of Abraham and the Exodus), these are only to be considered special acts of God for their significance in human history. As acts of God, they are no more

20. See also Ladd, "Theological Indicators Supporting an Evangelical Conception of Eternity." Ladd offers an extensive analysis of this concept, and uses it to argue the inadequacy of the atemporal view for the doctrine of creation.

21. Swinburne, "Timelessness of God, II," 478–79.

special than any other act, and they fall within the idea of God ordering the laws of nature and the universe. He argues, "But all that such an event shows is that the laws of nature, which are derivable from the supreme law which is God, are more complicated than we originally supposed them to be."[22] Therefore, God's actions are not actually acts of intervention in human history, but are rather evidences of God's having set down the laws of nature such that the things that come about appear to be acts of intervention.

At this point of the essay Swinburne avoids dealing directly with the Incarnation. He argues that the topic of the Incarnation is so specific to Christian doctrine that it is outside the immediate purpose of his essay. He writes, "Problems arising from the acts of God Incarnate in history I do not discuss, because they are peculiar to revealed Christianity."[23] This seems to be in direct contradiction to the stated purpose of the essay to "consider . . . difficulties in our doctrine [of God's timelessness] arising from . . . other doctrines of Christian theism."[24] Swinburne may avoid this charge if his emphasis in the quoted passage is on *revealed* Christianity as opposed to Christian theism in general; but such a distinction seems arbitrary at this point.

But Swinburne does not avoid the topic of the Incarnation entirely, for he returns again to it at the end of the essay. Swinburne admits that the Incarnation poses a serious problem for the position he defends in the essay. He writes, "The spiritual omnipotent being took a body to himself and concentrated his existence. But if God is a timeless ordering principle, then how can he be part of what he orders? There are very awkward problems here which have sometimes not been taken sufficiently seriously by those who theologize on the Incarnation."[25] In other words, Swinburne seems to acknowledge that there is a *prima facie* conflict between the claims that God is timeless and that God became Incarnate. His solution to this apparent inconsistency is that the Incarnation is to be considered a mystery. He argues that properties[26] such as omnipotence

22. Ibid., 479.

23. Ibid.

24. Ibid., 472.

25. Ibid., 486.

26. The terms "property" and "attribute" could be used here interchangeably. To distinguish the essential from the accidental, I use "non-essential property" elsewhere in this work.

and omniscience were taken for granted by the church Fathers and how God possessed these properties was not considered a mystery. But, he says, "That God became incarnate among us and redeemed us from our sins was a mystery indeed."[27] He then asserts that in making claims about God, one must choose what remains a mystery and what is explained. If God is atemporal, then omnipotence is not a mystery but the Incarnation is. On the other hand if God is temporal, the Incarnation is no longer a mystery, but omnipotence is. Given the choice between those two, he argues that since the church Fathers saw the Incarnation as a mystery, so ought we. He writes, "If we find mysterious what the New Testament authors and the Fathers found mysterious, this suggests that their God is the same as our God. The doctrine of the timelessness of God preserves the mystery in the right place. It secures as fundamental those properties of God which the first believers held unquestioningly to belong to him."[28] In other words, Swinburne is saying a choice must be made between mutually exclusive mysteries. Either God is timeless and the Incarnation is a mystery, or God is temporal and omnipotence is a mystery. Given the choice, in this essay, Swinburne chooses the former.

Analysis of Swinburne's Argument

Swinburne's work on God and time represents one of the rare occasions where a philosopher reverses his position in print; and his subsequent publications can—to some extent—serve as a point of analysis for his previous work on the subject. One example is his 1993 essay "God and Time," which appeared in a book edited by Eleonore Stump.[29] In the opening paragraph of the essay, Swinburne writes that the more recent article is one in which he offers "a rebuttal of a thesis that I had previously defended in print."[30] Unfortunately, however, the author does not offer points of continuity between this essay and the earlier two; thus he fails to clarify on what specific points he thinks his previous argument to be in error. Rather, the arguments in the more recent essay and that

27. Swinburne, "Timelessness of God, II," 486.

28. Ibid.

29. Swinburne, "God and Time." The first published work in which Swinburne reverses himself is the 1977 work Swinburne, *Coherence of Theism*. The 1993 essay, however is a more refined version of the arguments presented there, therefore the it will be given priority here as more accurate version of the author's views on God's relationship to time.

30. Swinburne, "God and Time," 204.

in the earlier two stand as independent arguments with little contextual overlap. Nevertheless, the more recent essay is instructive for what factors contributed to the reversal of position. Therefore, this article will be examined briefly for how Swinburne defends his newly adopted thesis.

At the outset, Swinburne remarks that the "simple, naive, initial"[31] answer to the question of God's relationship to time is to say that he is everlasting—that is, temporal. But this view, Swinburne points out, has historically been rejected by philosophers because it seems to make time something by which God is bound. In other words, if God is merely everlasting, it would seem that time is something that stands outside of God, something to which God is subject; and God would then have a past ever receding from him and a future ever looming before him, neither being within his control. Swinburne refers to this view as "the view of God as time's prisoner."[32] Swinburne's strategy in this essay is twofold: first, he seeks to demonstrate the incoherence of the atemporal view; and then he seeks to defend the idea of God being everlasting against the charge that it makes God "time's prisoner."

In accomplishing this purpose, Swinburne first seeks to establish four principles about the nature of time. These principles are: (a) everything that happens in time happens over a period of time and never at an instant;[33] (b) time has a topology independent of whether there are laws of nature, but only has a metric if there are laws of nature;[34] (c) the past is logically contingent, and it is logically impossible for any agent to now affect the past;[35] and (d) there are truths about what happens at specific periods of time that can only be known during those periods of time.[36] After establishing these principles[37] Swinburne argues that the atemporal view is incoherent based on the principles (a) and (b): The view that God is timeless contains within it the idea that God experiences his life at one single moment, which violates principle (a). Further, if God creates the

31. Ibid.
32. Ibid., 205.
33. Ibid., 206.
34. Ibid., 208.
35. Ibid., 211.
36. Ibid., 215.

37. Swinburne's success or failure at convincing his readers that each of these principles is true is not under consideration here. What is important to note is the approach Swinburne takes insofar as it contradicts his earlier defense of the atemporal view.

universe, his creating must be prior to the effect of the creation, which also seems to rule out the atemporal view, on principle (c).

After demonstrating these conclusions about the atemporal view, Swinburne uses his principles (b) and (d) to defend against the charge of "making God time's prisoner." He suggests that on principle (b), any period of God's life prior to the creation of the laws of nature would be qualitatively indistinguishable from any other period; and therefore it would not have the effect of God's having a long, infinite history that constantly slips away from his grasp.[38] Rather, on this principle God would still be immediately aware of the whole of his history prior to creation. On principle (d), Swinburne argues that it could be said that God is ever losing knowledge as each "now" passes by. But, he argues, on principle (a), knowledge does not occur at an instant, but over a period. Therefore, God's "now" in which he is in full possession of all his knowledge can simply be thought of as the period which contains all of the "now"s posited as passing. Swinburne admits, however, that God may experience some of the things that make the temporal view unpalatable to some theologians. He argues however, that there is still good reason to reject the atemporal view and hold instead the opposite, writing, "The unwelcome features of time—the increase of events that cannot be changed, the cosmic clock ticking away as they happen, the uncertainty about the future—may indeed invade God's time; but they come by invitation, not by force [by virtue of God's having created a universe such as it is]—and they continue for such periods of time as God chooses that they shall. There is no reason for the theist to object to the view that God is everlasting on the grounds that it makes God time's prisoner; and since the rival doctrine is incoherent, the theist should adopt the view that God is everlasting."[39]

The manner in which Swinburne has reversed himself and defends the "God everlasting" view is instructive. In the comments made about the nature of creation, it seems as if Swinburne has left himself vulnerable to the charge that he holds an "open" view of God, or some variety of "open theism." Whether the concerns often raised by open theism lay behind Swinburne's reversal is not immediately obvious. However, it is important to take note of the fact that the doctrine of the Incarnation is

---

38. Swinburne, "God and Time," 220.
39. Ibid., 221–22.

not addressed in this essay; therefore it is assumed here that the doctrine did not play a significant role in Swinburne's change of mind.

Recall that the essay "The Timelessness of God, II" did address the Incarnation, and highlighted the fact that it created a problem for the atemporal view. Swinburne sets up a dilemma that faces the philosophical theologian who is considering God's relationship with time. He asserts that regardless of the position taken, whether God is seen as atemporal or temporal, a sacrifice must be made; and at least one doctrine essential to Christianity must be considered a mystery. Either God is temporal and his omnipotence and immutability are a mystery; or God is atemporal and the Incarnation is a mystery. In that essay, Swinburne states that given the choice as to which doctrine is a mystery, he would choose to allow the Incarnation to fall into that category. The most immediate response available to someone who may disagree with Swinburne is to answer by saying he has presented a false dilemma. But, more importantly, given the weight that the doctrine of the Incarnation has in defining the very essence of Christian Trinitarian theism, it seems imprudent—even if the dilemma is proper—to choose as Swinburne has suggested. Since the church councils have gone to such great lengths to establish what is meant when it is said that God is incarnate in Jesus, and if there is any theological adjustment to be made in the context of the debate on God's relationship to time, it would seem more advisable to hold fast to the creeds and adjust one's concept of omnipotence or immutability.

But it seems clear that an appeal to mystery to explain how the Incarnation fits with the idea of the timelessness of God seems to be inappropriate on at least two counts: first, mystery ought not be appealed to in areas of essential doctrine (without a clear understanding of such doctrine the Christian faith would be rendered almost meaningless); and, second, appealing to mystery wrongly implies that the Incarnation is somehow at odds with omnipotence and immutability. Swinburne comments in his essay that sometimes theologians give arguments that "God is so different from anything with which we are familiar that we must not be surprised if talk about him is completely incomprehensible."[40] But Swinburne strongly—and rightly—objects to this line, and thinks it unwise to say things such as this when attempting to explain one's concept of God. Swinburne writes that Christians "would be ill advised to take

40. Swinburne, "Timelessness of God, II," 484.

this line, for if the Christian is unable to describe in some moderately intelligible way the object of his faith, it would be irrational for him or any one else to believe in that object."[41] This same standard, however, ought to be applied to the doctrine of the Incarnation. If it cannot be explained in some intelligible way without appealing to mystery, then perhaps it should be abandoned. Since the Incarnation is essential (and therefore ought not be abandoned), then mystery ought not be appealed to in order to deal with the Incarnation and how it fits in to one's concept of God's relationship to time. Rather, the Incarnation should govern our conception of God's relationship to time, as well as other doctrines about God.

Since Swinburne has abandoned the atemporal view, he is no longer vulnerable to this particular criticism. Nevertheless, it seems as if Swinburne has pointed out accurately a serious flaw in the atemporal view. Namely, if God is atemporal, then there is no explanation for what happens in the Incarnation other than an appeal to mystery. If this is correct, then this reason alone could serve as adequate grounds for abandoning the atemporal view. However, there remain many proponents of the view, some of whom also seek to explain how the atemporal view accounts for the Incarnation. One such author is Brian Leftow, whose arguments will now be examined.

Brian Leftow

Leftow's work on the nature of time and on God's relationship to time is extensive. Chief among his publications on the topic is his 1991 *Time and Eternity*, which is exhaustive in addressing details often overlooked in the discussion of God and time. This work, while exhaustive otherwise, does not address substantially the doctrine of the Incarnation. Unlike *Time and Eternity*, Leftow's essay "A Timeless God Incarnate" is written specifically as a defense of the classical atemporal view against the charge that it is incompatible with the doctrine of the Incarnation. At the start of this essay, Leftow seeks to establish an historical linkage between the doctrine of the Incarnation and the atemporal view by arguing that those who helped develop Chalcedonian orthodoxy also were the expositors and defenders of the atemporal model of God's relationship to time. Leftow writes, "The orthodox view of the incarnation was hammered out in the theological debates culminating in the council of Chalcedon (AD 451). . . . The church

41. Ibid.

Fathers who worked out incarnational orthodoxy were those very Greeks (and Latins) whose fondness for such doctrines as God's simplicity and atemporality so many now chide."[42] The purpose of this pronouncement is presumably to anchor both the doctrines of the Incarnation and God's timelessness in Christian orthodoxy. Leftow asserts strongly, "Thus it is the simple historical fact that those who defined orthodox Christian belief about the incarnation universally held that God is non-temporal."[43] Thus Leftow establishes one of the foundational assumptions in his work: the atemporal view of God's relationship to time existed comfortably alongside the doctrine of the Incarnation in Christian theological history.

Unlike Swinburne, Leftow anchors the classical view with Augustine, not Boethius. He writes, "To see what [God's atemporality] meant for [the church Fathers] we can consult Augustine."[44] And in the essay, it is Augustine's conception of the notion of "eternity"[45] and God's relationship to time that Leftow seeks to defend. In defending this position, Leftow argues that God must be thought of as "non-temporal";[46] that is, God is neither "in" nor "outside of" time. Rather, "eternity" is to be thought of as a mode of existence and not a location with respect to time. Further, "eternity" means that all of God's life is contained within a single instant. He writes, "God lives his life in a single present, no 'part' succeeding any other. God's life simply does not have temporal parts."[47] And Leftow emphasizes what this means as he asserts, "'God is eternal' ascribes a mode of being, not a location 'in' or 'outside' time."[48] This idea of God not being "in" or "outside of" time is consistent with what Leftow has written elsewhere. Leftow argues that *things* do not occupy time, but rather *events* do. He writes, "What we primarily speak of as located at times, then, are

42. Leftow, "Timeless God Incarnate," 273.

43. Ibid.

44. Ibid., 274. Cf. Leftow, *Time and Eternity*, 73, where Leftow writes, "Augustine's thinking was the core that determined the broad outlines of all that later medieval philosophical theology made of the concept of God. So Augustine's thought about eternity is an appropriate place to begin our investigation."

45. Leftow consistently uses the word "eternity" to mean "atemporal" or "timeless" existence. As mentioned in earlier chapters, this is the very matter under debate.

46. Leftow uses "non-temporal" in the context of his discussion; but even though he makes several important clarifications of how he uses this term, it nevertheless seems to have the same usage as "atemporal."

47. Leftow, "Timeless God Incarnate," 274.

48. Ibid.

states (e.g., of existence), events, processes, and the like. I take it that these *are* what are primarily located at times, and that things involved in these states . . . are located at times because their states, etc., are."[49] In summary, then, Leftow seeks to defend the following model of God's relationship to time: God experiences all of his life at one instant, which has no temporal parts or relations, and contains no succession or sequence; and God's eternity is a mode of existence, whereby God is neither in nor outside of time, but rather is purely non-temporal. Leftow takes this dual-component model to be the same view held by those who also established Chalcedonian orthodoxy with regard to the Incarnation.[50]

Before examining Leftow's defense of God's atemporality in light of the Incarnation, it will be important to summarize his exposition of the doctrine of the Incarnation. The bulk of Leftow's essay is devoted to an exposition of the doctrine,[51] and most of this material is intended to make important clarifications and distinctions necessary to defend his atemporal view against the charge that it is incompatible with the Incarnation. In explaining the Incarnation, Leftow explains and defends a "three part" view of the union of the natures in Christ. He argues that the incarnate Christ includes God the Son, a human body (abbreviated as "B" in Leftow's essay), and a human soul (abbreviated as "S"). Therefore, Christ has two immaterial parts (God the Son and S), and one material part (B). Further, Christ has one uncreated part (God the Son) and two created parts (S and B).

Leftow understands that this "three part" view may leave him open to the charge of Nestorianism. Recalling the debate between the Antiochene and Alexandrian schools of thought, the question becomes whether Christ assumed a human person in the Incarnation, which would be the case if S + B constitute a human person. To avoid the charge, Leftow argues that while normally S + B do constitute a normal person, in the case of Christ they did not, because as soon as there was the S and B, they were united to God the Son to form the whole. He writes, "So soon as Mary's egg began to live the life that would be Jesus', the life being lived was God the Son's life."[52] Leftow employs an illustration of DNA: God the Son provides

49. Leftow, *Time and Eternity*, 18.

50. Leftow, "Timeless God Incarnate," 275.

51. Out of 26 pages in the essay in question, there are 15 pages devoted to an explanation of the Incarnation.

52. Leftow, "Timeless God Incarnate," 282.

what is like a "super-DNA," which, when united to S and B determines the identity of the life being lived and brings it about that the life is that of God the Son. He explains further, "I claim that the Son assumed S + B at conception, and so S + B live the Son's life as soon as they begin living, and this is *why* they do not on their own compose a human being."[53]

Leftow next defends his "three part" view of the Incarnation by illustrating how it is compatible with three types of personal identity theories: body-based theories, soul-based theories, and psychological continuity theories.[54] In each case, Leftow accounts for how his three-part model would fit a proposed theory of personal identity without violating any claim of orthodoxy. One key element of this discussion is important to note at this point: During his discussion of psychological continuity theories, Leftow explains a further implication of his three-part model. He argues that in the Incarnation, Christ is in possession of two minds: one the mind of God the Son, and the other the mind of S. He writes, "Now on a three-part (and eternalist) view, in the incarnate Christ are two minds, one a timeless complex of mental states in the timeless son, one a temporal series of mental states in S."[55] Immediately recognizing the need to preserve the unity in Christ, Leftow qualifies this description. He writes, "So the orthodox who also hold psychological continuity theories of personal identity cannot allow the series in S an independence that would let it constitute a new person. They must hold that the S-series branches out of the Son's mind in some way sufficient to count as a second mind, but not with such independence as to constitute a second person."[56]

Leftow summarizes his model of the Incarnation by referring to Christ as a mereological sum. He writes, "Let 'the Son' name the Trinity's second person and 'Jesus Christ' name the whole consisting of the Son + B + S. Then for the incarnation to take place is for Jesus Christ to come to be, by the joining of the Son, S, and B."[57] Leftow suggests that when statements attributing properties or actions to Christ are read mereologically, many supposed contradictions disappear. Leftow uses descriptions of an apple to illustrate the solution to the often cited "*qua* move" made by phi-

53. Ibid., 283.
54. Ibid., 284–85.
55. Ibid., 285.
56. Ibid., 285–86.
57. Ibid., 287.

losophers. He writes, "Wholes often have attributes because their parts do. Apples are red because their skins are—that is, because their parts include red skins."[58] The purpose of this illustration is to draw an analogy between describing the parts and properties of apples and describing the parts and properties of Christ. He makes the point:

> Christologists often say things like
>
> (C) Christ died *qua* human but not *qua* divine.
>
> I think the best reading of claims like (C) is mereological: we ought to read them as we just read my claims about apples. If (C) is true, I suggest, Christ did die: for a person including a human body and soul dies if his body dies and his soul is parted from it. What (C) asserts is that Christ died because his human part died, not because his divine part did. In fact, his divine part did not die. But this does not alter the fact that Christ did. So too, an apple's skin is not nutritious, but this alone does not alter the fact that the apple is.[59]

The point of this illustration is to disarm certain objections that arise when the question is considered of how predicates can be applied to Christ. We can say the apple is red because the skin is; and we can say the apple is nutritious because the flesh is. On the converse, the skin of the apple is not nutritious, but it isn't thereby concluded that the whole is not nutritious, nor is it said that the apple is both nutritious and non-nutritious because it contains both nutritious and non-nutritious parts. Deciding *which* properties belonging to parts of a mereological set apply to the whole is not easy. Leftow writes, "So the attributes of the apple's non-red and non-nutritious parts do not become attributes of the whole, and there is just no uniform rule by which to figure out which part's attributes will come to qualify its whole. Thus christologists and students of apples must work things out case by case."[60]

But working things out case-by-case does not directly solve any potential objection based on the properties of parts. Nevertheless, Leftow thinks the *methodology* sound. Even though contradictory properties are observed, and Christ is said to be A *qua* human and not-A *qua* God,

---

58. Ibid., 288. Leftow uses the word "attribute" to refer to both essential and non-essential properties.

59. Ibid., 288–89.

60. Ibid., 290.

Leftow employs the mereological reading of "*qua*" to solve the problem. He writes that the mereological analysis of the Incarnation that he proposes "explains why the incompatibility [between parts' attributes] is only apparent." In the context of the essay, of course, Leftow wants to address the fact that Jesus Christ *qua* human lived an ordinary temporal life. This would seem to indicate an incompatible set of properties, for the author would also assert that Christ *qua* God the Son is atemporal. And this leads to Leftow's attempt to defend his atemporal view against the charge that the Incarnation demonstrates an incompatible set of properties if God the Son is atemporal.

The argument from the Incarnation can be defined as the claim that the doctrine of the Incarnation is incompatible with the classical atemporal view of God's relationship to time. But in his defense of the atemporal view, Leftow does not address the argument from the Incarnation generally; rather he gives two, very narrow versions of the argument,[61] and then demonstrates why these versions fail on his view of the Incarnation (as explained above). Leftow seeks to demonstrate that the following two versions fail:

> (1) Jesus Christ existed in time.
> But (one would think)
> (2) Jesus Christ = God the Son, the second person of the Trinity.
> So it seems to follow that
> (3) God the Son existed in time.[62]

And

> In the incarnation
> (4) God the Son began to be human.
> Beginning to be human sounds like some sort of intrinsic change.
> That is, seemingly
> (5) whatever begins to be human changes intrinsically,
> So it seems to follow that in becoming incarnate,
> (6) God the Son changed intrinsically.

---

61. The two versions given are based on, but different in important respects from the argument offered by Thomas Senor, "Incarnation and Timelessness." This will be addressed more fully in chapter 4.

62. Leftow, "A Timeless God Incarnate," 276. Leftow cites by footnote Senor's essay "Incarnation and Timelessness," but it is clear that the argument presented is not Senor's argument. There are similarities between the two, and perhaps this similarity caused Leftow to refer his readers to Senor's essay.

But
(7) whatever changes intrinsically exists in time.
For to change intrinsically is to have different intrinsic attributes at different times. So it seems to follow that
(8) God the Son exists in time.[63]

Leftow uses two strategies to defeat the first argument. First, he argues that (1) can be brought into question given his mereological part/whole analysis of the Incarnation. When his methodology is employed, it is plain that (1) does not follow, simply because *part* of Jesus Christ existed in time. So Leftow offers:

(1a) Jesus Christ has a part in time[64]

This means that on a part/whole analysis of the Incarnation, Jesus Christ's S and B are in time, but God the Son is not in time. He writes that on this account, "God the Son is part of a partly temporal whole."[65] The second strategy offered deals with (2). Leftow argues that on a part/whole account of the Incarnation, (2) identifies a part of the whole—God the Son—as being equal to the whole. He writes, "For (2) appears to identify a proper part (God the Son) with its containing whole (Jesus Christ). If it does, (2) is not just false, but necessarily so."[66] Therefore he suggests the alternative:

(2a) the person who is Jesus Christ = God the Son[67]

Explaining this, Leftow writes, "Jesus Christ is just the sum of one person of the Trinity and two non-divine things. Christ's deity and personhood *are* the Son's."[68] Leftow emphasizes that Christ has a temporal part (S and B) as well as a non-temporal part (God the Son). Therefore, demonstrating the inadequacies of (2) seems to defeat the challenge of the first version of the argument from the Incarnation.

63. Ibid. Leftow again refers his readers by footnote to Senor's essay; and in this case it seems the reference is given because this argument is almost identical to one presented there.
64. Ibid., 292.
65. Ibid., 293.
66. Ibid., 294.
67. Ibid.
68. Ibid.

As with the first argument, Leftow attacks the second with two strategies. First, Leftow argues that (4) is false, pointing out that if God the Son *timelessly* has any properties because of events in time, then the property of being human could be one of those properties. If so, then God the Son never *began* to be human, for "began" speaks only of a temporal event, and does not transfer its temporal nature to the Son, who is timeless. He further explains his position:

> Let us ask just why we are supposed to accept (4). The answer, surely, is that
> (9) S + B began to exist,
> and we are supposed to accept that
> (10) before S + B existed, God the Son was not human.
> Now taken at face value, (10) just begs the question against divine timelessness. To a timeless God, there *is* no "before" S + B appear.[69]

Important to note at this point is the fact that Leftow takes it for granted that God is timeless, and if that were true, then clearly there would be no temporal "before" applying to an event in God's life, as the Incarnation. Leftow adds the important statement, "If any event in God's life (say, God's knowing that he is God) is before any other (e.g., S + B's appearing), God *ipso facto* is temporal."[70] This admission is important to my argument; and so it will be reexamined shortly.

The second strategy Leftow employs against the second version of the argument from the Incarnation challenges (5), and the strategy is fairly straightforward. Leftow argues that beginning to be human does not represent an intrinsic change, and therefore (5) is false on at least two counts: First, any ordinary human who "becomes" a human being does so at the initial moment of existence. But "change" seems to indicate that a single entity exists both before and after the change. Therefore, if there is no being prior to the existence of the human being in the mother's womb, then no change has taken place. So, becoming human is not ordinarily a measure of a change. But (5) is also false, Leftow argues, because being human is not essential to God. God could have remained God without taking on flesh. Leftow writes that the Incarnation "consists in [God the Son] beginning to have certain relations to S and B. One can begin to have

---

69. Ibid., 295.
70. Ibid.

relations without changing intrinsically."[71] So, in Leftow's model, that God the Son took on flesh in the Incarnation does not indicate an intrinsic change, and therefore does not require that God the Son be a temporal being.

Analysis of Leftow's Argument

Rather than discuss all of the strengths and weaknesses of the author's description of the Incarnation itself, it will be sufficient at this point to offer an analysis of how Leftow handles these two versions of the argument from the Incarnation. Whether the author is correct in his three-part, part/whole mereological Christology remains to be debated; but his Christological account does not seem to affect dramatically the success or failure of his argument regarding how God's relationship to time ought be viewed in light of the Incarnation. Therefore, his approach at seeking to defeat the argument from the Incarnation will be analyzed in the same order given.

The immediately apparent oddity in the argument is Leftow's offering of

(1) Jesus Christ existed in time.[72]

as the first premise in the exemplary argument from the Incarnation. In the footnotes to this argument, Leftow refers his reader to Thomas Senor's argument from the Incarnation. However, this initial premise is quite different from the one Senor offers.[73] Therefore, it must be assumed at this point that Leftow himself has constructed premise (1) as an example of what could be offered, and only refers his readers to Senor so that the two versions can be compared. But, if Leftow himself is responsible for the construction of (1), then he seems to be guilty of setting up a straw man in order to easily knock it down, for (1) fails even on Leftow's own account of time, independent of how it is applied to the Incarnation. Recall from the author's statements elsewhere that only *events* can be said to be in time, and not persons: "What we primarily speak of as located at times, then, are states (e.g., of existence), events, processes, and the like."[74] This

71. Ibid., 298.
72. Leftow, "Timeless God Incarnate," 276.
73. Senor's argument will be analyzed in chapter 4.
74. Leftow, *Time and Eternity*, 18.

analysis seems to be correct, and therefore it seems out of step for Leftow to offer the alternative:

(1a) Jesus Christ has a part in time[75]

when it seems he should have offered something like:

(1b) The events of Jesus Christ's life occurred in time,

which would have been more consistent with his own view of how beings such as God or humans can relate to time.

Unlike his dealings with (1), Leftow's analysis of (2) seems to be correct. Again, the author has referred his reader to Senor, and (2) is drawn directly from Senor's argument. Leftow is right in his correction of (2) and in offering the alternative:

(2a) the person who is Jesus Christ = God the Son.[76]

But, (2a) hardly has direct application to (1b), because (2a) speaks of persons while (1b) speaks of events. Recall that Leftow emphasizes that the life lived in Jesus Christ is the life of God the Son. He writes, "So soon as Mary's egg began to live the life that would be Jesus', the life being lived was God the Son's life."[77] Therefore what Leftow should have offered is

(2b) the life of Jesus Christ = the life of God the Son.

But then, it would be immediately apparent from (1b) and (2b) that

(3a) the events of the life of God the Son occur in time.

It is hard to see from Leftow's argument and his own commitments—with regard to how persons and events relate to time—how he could avoid (3a). But if (3a) is true, then Leftow is unable to defeat the argument from the Incarnation, because (3a) indicates that God the Son experiences temporally sequenced events in his life, which runs counter to Leftow's atemporal view.

Leftow's analysis of (4)–(8) is also instructive, and reveals elements of his atemporal view that are not immediately apparent in his discussion of the argument from the Incarnation. Recall that in his analysis, the author states, "Now taken at face value, (10) just begs the question

75. Leftow, "Timeless God Incarnate," 292.
76. Ibid., 294.
77. Ibid., 282.

against divine timelessness. To a timeless God, there *is* no 'before' S + B appear."[78] In other words, since God is atemporal, S + B are an ever present feature of his life. What is revealed in this statement is the idea of two independent perspectives on the nature of time: God has one perspective, and temporal creatures have another. This idea comes out elsewhere, as Leftow describes "eternity"[79] as a reference frame, similar to the reference frame of time in which human beings live and observe events in the universe. He writes, "We can take eternity as one more frame of reference, distinct from any temporal reference frame."[80] He explains further, "If we take eternity as one more frame of reference, then, we thus can say that a temporal event's being present and actual in eternity does not entail that it is present and actual at any particular time in any temporal reference frame (though it does follow that this event is, was, or will be actual in all temporal reference frames.)"[81] Here, Leftow's argument seems to be in defense of Boethius's man on a hill illustration. For God, as the man on the high hill, the temporal event of S + B coming into existence is observed in a single eternal instant with every other temporal event. Therefore, from this high vantage point, there is no "before" (S + B)'s coming about.

It could be countered that on Leftow's account, if there is no "before" the existence of S and B, then S and B are co-eternal with God the Son. Anticipating this, Leftow states that this is not the case. He writes, "There were times when S + B did not exist, and during those times, it was true to say that God timelessly exists. But the import of the 'taking on' claim on God's side is modal, not temporal. That God took on flesh does not entail that he changed. . . . Here I simply put the ball back onto the temporalist's side of the net: why *isn't* this enough to make orthodox sense of the claim that God the Son [timelessly] took on flesh?"[82] But, it could be further countered that Leftow is himself engaging in question begging; for in the

---

78. Ibid., 295.

79. Again, Leftow uses this word to mean *timeless* eternity.

80. Leftow, *Time and Eternity*, 234. Leftow seems to be borrowing from Relativity Theory for his use of the term "reference frame." If this is the case, he has misused the term; because it is doubtful that Leftow is saying that God occupies a physical reference frame.

81. Ibid.

82. Ibid., 299. Leftow does not specify the kind of change to which he is objecting. Based on the context of the discussion, however, it seems that Leftow holds to a Thomistic account of immutability, according to which it is not possible for any kind of variation in states of affairs in God's life.

defining "taking on" he has assumed the desired conclusion. In order to fit Leftow's model, all such terms as "taking on" or "becoming" or "made" describing Christ's assuming human nature and flesh must be emptied of their normal temporal senses. Indeed, it would seem that the Nicene statement that Christ "came down from heaven, and was incarnate by the Holy Spirit of the Virgin Mary" must be taken as "modal" and not a description of an actual sequence of events.

Clearly this discussion demonstrates the propensity for authors on both sides of the debate to "talk past" one another in the construction of their arguments. When Leftow rules out *a priori* the notion of "before" in the life of God, he is no longer open to *any* argument that may demonstrate that God's life is composed of temporally sequenced events. For Leftow, no evidence from the Incarnation will ever be admissible as an indication of temporality in the divine life. Additionally, the part/whole mereological account of the Incarnation provides Leftow a dividing line that can separate any supposed temporal aspects of the life of Christ from God the Son; thereby insulating the divine from the appearance of temporal passage. But, it remains to be seen whether Leftow can employ this scheme without resorting to circular reasoning: Leftow identifies an atemporal "part" of Christ; this part is known to be atemporal because it is divine; and how is it known that the divine part is also atemporal? Answer: Because it is divine. Under this analysis, Leftow's defense of his position amounts to little more than an *assertion* of his position. Nevertheless, there remains on Leftow some burden of proof. If he is willing to admit to

(2a) the person who is Jesus Christ = God the Son[83]

it would also seem that he would be obligated to account for how a single person can live a temporal life in Jesus Christ and still remain *essentially* timeless as God the Son. Such an account is absent in Leftow's work. It would seem then that Leftow must hold either that God the Son is eternally incarnate (on the fact that the whole of God the Son's life—including, as it does, the Incarnation—is possessed by him in one timelessly eternal instant); or else (2a)—and along with it, Chalcedon—is false.

One final element of Leftow's presentation must be addressed. Recall that Leftow summarized the "Chalcedonian age" as being one in which the church Fathers developed both the orthodox statements

83. Leftow, "Timeless God Incarnate," 294.

on the Incarnation as well as the classical atemporal view of God's relationship to time.[84] Leftow comments that the argument from the
Incarnation against the classical view "implies that those who worked out
Chalcedonian Christology somehow overlooked a glaring contradiction
at the heart of their thinking."[85] Thus, he urges his readers, out of defer-
ence to the church Fathers, to reject out of hand the suggestion that there
might be a contradiction between the Chalcedonian statement and the
atemporal view of God's relationship to time. But it seems that in describing the "Chalcedonian age," Leftow has painted with a very broad
brush. Augustine, on whose view of eternity much of Leftow's argument
is based, died some 20 years before the Chalcedonian statement of 451
AD, and wasn't converted to Christianity until approximately 5 years after
the statement at Constantinople. Boethius, whose definition of eternity
is said to be the *locus classicus* of the atemporal view, didn't publish his
Consolation until approximately 73 years after Chalcedon. Clearly, then,
although Augustine can be counted among the Fathers, it would be inappropriate to suggest that the same *individual men* crafted both the classical atemporal view and the foundational statements on the Incarnation.
Leftow's description of the Chalcedonian "age" would be akin to asserting
that there could be no contradiction between the U.S. Constitution and
laws passed in the year 1900 because the "same" congress passed both
documents during the same "age."

PAUL HELM

Like Leftow, Paul Helm's work on God's relationship to time is extensive,
and he is considered to be at the forefront of defending the classical atemporal view. Helm has published a book-length work on the topic, *Eternal
God: A Study of God Without Time* and he contributed to *God and Time:
Four Views*, in which his essay "Divine Timeless Eternity" is offered as
a defense of the classical view.[86] In that essay, Helm defines the classical
atemporal view as "eternalism,"[87] and he argues that the Boethian concep-

84. Ibid., 275.

85. Ibid.

86. The whole of the content of the 1988 edition of *Eternal God* is included (un-
changed) in the 2010 edition, which includes four additional chapters, the majority of the
content of which has appeared in other published works. "Divine Timeless Eternity" is a
more recently written work in which Helm describes his views on the topic.

87. Helm, "Divine Timeless Eternity," 28.

tion of the possession of fullness of life is at the heart of this view. He writes, "There are a number [of reasons to accept the classical view], but they all may be said to rest . . . on an intuition that has had an enormous appeal to many thinkers and still has to some. It is the idea of the divine fullness or self-sufficiency."[88] Helm argues that if God did experience something like temporal sequence, as humans do, then there would be segments of God's life: he would have a past, a present, and a future. But, Helm argues, this is in direct conflict with the idea that God is in complete possession of the fullness of his life. He writes, "There never was a time when God was not. It follows [if God were temporal] that there are segments of his life—those segments that existed before the present moment—which together constitute a part of God's life that is over and done with. And the eternalist will say that such an idea is incompatible with God's fullness and self-sufficiency."[89]

This objection, then, is the core of Helm's perspective. Despite other arguments against the temporalist perspective that may be offered, Helm claims that it is in conflict with some basic assumptions that Christians have about God. He writes that the temporal view "flouts the basic theistic intuition that God's fullness is such that he possesses the whole of his life *together*."[90] Thus, it is an appeal to intuition. He continues, "To many, the idea that God is subject to the vicissitudes of temporal passage, with more and more of his life irretrievably over and done with is incompatible with divine sovereignty, with divine perfection and with that fullness of being that is essential to God. The temporalist view may be intelligible, but it does not do justice to the nature of God's being."[91]

Having laid the foundation of his atemporal view, Helm goes on to explain and defend it. The first element of his defense is to establish the source of the "eternalism" perspective. Helm cites two sources of data on which the atemporal view is based: Scriptural statements about God, and *a priori* reflection on the concept of God.[92] For Scriptural statements, Helm cites passages such as Isa 57:15, which emphasizes God's transcendence; Heb 1:10–12, which points to God's being everlasting and changeless; and

88. Ibid., 29.
89. Ibid.,
90. Ibid., 30.
91. Ibid., 30–31.
92. Ibid., 34.

Ps 90:2, which indicates God's existence before the world. Helm admits, however, that the Scriptural statements "are not sufficiently precise so as to provide a definitive resolution of the issue one way or the other."[93] He continues, "So it would be unwise for the eternalist to claim that divine timeless eternity is *entailed* by the language of Scripture."[94] With regard to the philosophical reflection on the concept of God, Helm points his readers to the idea that the atemporal view sufficiently allows for a distinction between Creator and creation. He writes, "Not only do eternalists believe that this position is consistent with the biblical data about God and time, but they hold that by employing the idea of timelessness it is possible to articulate the distinction between Creator and creature, and to make clear that divine creation is a unique metaphysical action, the bringing into being of the whole temporal order, not a creation of the universe by One who is already subject to time."[95] To back this claim, Helm points his readers to the work of Augustine, Anselm, and Boethius; with specific reference to statements made by these figures that emphasize God's immutability and his possession at once of the whole of his life.[96]

While Helm spends much of the beginning of his essay focusing on the Boethian concept of the fullness of God's life, it is important to focus briefly on the connection of this concept to the idea of immutability found in another of Helm's publications. In *Eternal God*, Helm's main argument with regard to immutability is that it is impossible for an immutable being to have temporal relations to creatures. To explain what he means, he writes, "This does not mean that there are no relations at all between the eternal God and his creation, only no temporal relations."[97] Helm draws the connection between immutability and the Boethian conception of eternity by emphasizing Augustine's assertion that God *cannot* change (call it strong immutability). Helm argues that action within time requires change. He writes, "A God who acts, but who is immutable [in the sense that he cannot change] . . . must be timelessly eternal, since any action in time (as opposed to an action the effect of which is in time) presupposes a time before the act, and a time when the act is completed,

---

93. Ibid., 31.
94. Ibid.
95. Ibid., 33.
96. Ibid., 33–34.
97. Helm, *Eternal God*, 36.

and thus presupposes real change, which rules out immutability [in the strong sense]."[98]

Returning again to the analysis of his "Divine Timeless Eternity" essay, Helm focuses on the idea of *impassibility*. Closely connecting it with immutability, Helm emphasizes that impassibility is necessary for an atemporal God. He writes, "But a timelessly eternal God is immutable and so impassible in a very strong sense; he *necessarily* cannot change, for change takes time, or is in time, and a timelessly eternal God by definition is not in time, and so his actions cannot take time, nor can he experience fits of passion or changes in mood."[99] While impassibility in a human being, Helm notes, may be considered a defect of some sort, not so with God. He writes, "Impassibility in God is not a defect but a perfection; it signals fullness, not deficiency."[100] Additionally, Helm notes that much of what is considered to be possibility is closely connected to the uniquely human status of sin and embodiment. That humans lust, or have envy, or seek vengeance, Helm argues, is the source of much of human possibility. Further, feelings such as hunger and thirst arise only because humans have a physical body; but since God is not embodied, he is exempt from any such feelings.

Having focused his case on what he believes are the most important issues—immutability and the possession of the fullness of life—Helm then gives his account for how God can stand timelessly in relation to creation. Since the Incarnation is an example of God's acting in relation to the created universe, Helm's ideas on this topic are of special concern. In one important passage, Helm summarizes how the atemporal perspective views God's action as creator:

> It is the bringing of the universe into being from a standpoint outside it. For this reason the idea that God exists (timelessly) "before" the universe cannot mean that God exists temporally before it. He exists before the universe . . . in the way . . . age comes before beauty, or duty comes before pleasure. These "befores" are not temporal . . . they are another kind of priority, betokening a constitutional or hierarchical or normative arrangement. There was no time when the Creator was not, any more than there was

---

98. Ibid., 90.
99. Helm, "Divine Timeless Eternity," 38–39.
100. Ibid., 39.

a time when the creation was not. And yet the Creator exists "before" the creation.[101]

In a formal sense, according to Helm's atemporalism, God's action with
creation is not *within* time at all, but rather it is action outside of time,
the effects of which are in time. From the act of creation, to God's acts
throughout human history, and even to those actions of God that are
considered future, all that God does is in a single timeless act. This divine
act can only be said to be "before" in the sense that all of creation is contingent and dependent on God's act. Helm emphasizes that from God's
perspective, the created order is eternal. He writes that "according to the
eternalist [atemporalist], there need be no temporal first moment of creation, and so the universe need not have begun (temporally) to exist, for
from the divine standpoint the universe is eternal, even though it exists
contingently."[102] So for Helm, God exists "before" the universe only in the
sense that the universe is logically contingent on God.

In addition to the creation, however, Helm asserts that all divine acts
relating to the created order are also to be seen as timelessly eternal acts.
In Helm's model, God's various actions are more properly thought of as
a singular timeless act. Helm defines what it means to act as "to bring
about something as a result of desiring or willing that thing, and to do
so for a purpose."[103] But obviously, if God were to will various actions in
time, then he would not be a timeless being. The solution to this, Helm
explains, is that God doesn't will at various times, but timelessly; and he
does this so that certain effects are brought about in time. To make this
clear, Helm offers an illustration: Suppose someone sets an automatic
thermostat for a heating system. That one act of setting the timer has
various effects throughout the day as the furnace fires and heats the house
at the appointed times. So it is with God's will: it is one act with various
effects in time. He writes, "The correct way to think of God's eternally
willing something in time is to think of one eternal act of will with nu-
merous temporally scattered effects."[104] This is also the case, Helm argues,
even if God's actions are in response to something that happens in time.
Since God knows what will be the case, an element of his eternal will can

101. Helm, "Divine Timeless Eternity," 51–52.

102. Ibid., 49.

103. Ibid., 53.

104. Ibid.

contain a response to what creatures will do at specific times. Helm illustrates, "Thus God may eternally will the burning bush and his temporally subsequent utterances to Moses, eternally knowing that Moses' attention will be attracted by the burning bush."[105]

Following that idea, Helm asserts that the Incarnation is also a timeless act of God. In fact, Helm admits that "[t]he Incarnation is a unique case of God's acting in time."[106] Although human beings see the Incarnation as if it were within time, God sees Christ as being eternally incarnate. There is no "time" when God the Son was not embodied in Jesus of Nazareth. Helm writes that "there is no time in [Christ's] existence when he was not incarnate."[107] Helm makes the point more emphatic as he writes, "There is therefore no sense in talking of the eternal Son of God apart from the incarnation. . . ."[108] It is worth repeating Helm's position, for he also repeats it often. He writes "there is no preexistent Christ with a life history independent of and prior to the incarnation."[109]

Even though these statements alone seem to say enough, it is important to get a better idea of the significance of Helm's claims about the eternal nature of the Incarnation. In order to do so, the explanation in his essay "Eternal Creation"[110] can be examined, in which he briefly addresses the topic of the Incarnation. Helm argues in this essay that Nicene orthodoxy actually *requires* the doctrine of divine timelessness.[111] To make this point, Helm specifically draws on the statement of Nicaea that was crafted as a response to Arian Christology. Helm interprets the Arian claim to be that there once was a time when the Incarnate Christ did not exist. Therefore, Helm reads the Nicene response to the Arian error was to assert that the Incarnation itself is eternal. Nicaea addressed Arianism by saying "As for those who say that 'there was when he was not,' and 'before

105. Ibid., 54.

106. Ibid.

107. Ibid.

108. Ibid.

109. Ibid. This idea is presented somewhat less emphatically in Stump and Kretzmann, "Eternity," 452–53; in which the authors claim that arguing along these lines is a "Boethian account of the compatibility of divine eternality and the Incarnation."

110. Helm, "Eternal Creation," 321–38.

111. In this statement, Helm is at odds with other defenders of the classical atemporal view, such as Leftow, "Timeless God Incarnate," 273, who argues that the atemporal view is not essential to Christianity.

being born he was not,' and 'he came into existence out of nothing,' . . . the catholic and apostolic church condemns these."[112] Helm thinks that the "he" addressed in this statement is Christ Incarnate in Jesus of Nazareth (again, in Leftow's scheme, God the Son + S + B). So he interprets Nicaea as anathematizing the belief that "there was when the *Incarnate Christ* was not." He writes, "On [the temporalist view] there was *time* when the Son was not. That is, it is difficult to see how a temporalist could hold to the classical Nicene position that the Son came into existence before time; that there was no time when he was not."[113] He concludes, then, that any form of the temporalist view is heretical because "if there was such a time, and the Son was begotten at a time, then this would seem to strongly favour, if not actually entail, some form of Arianism."[114] So on Helm's reading of Nicaea, orthodoxy requires that God the Son is eternally incarnate in Jesus of Nazareth.

Before offering an analysis and evaluation of this position, one more element of Helm's understanding of God's relationship to time is important to note. Helm puts forward what he refers to as "the doctrine of two standpoints."[115] In explaining this, Helm attempts to describe the difference between God's perspective on the world and the human perspective on the world. He argues that God has a unique perspective in that his timeless existence is one that allows him to "see" all of the events and occurrences within creation at once, including the Incarnation. Helm writes, "From the Creator's standpoint his creation is a timeless whole, including, as it does, the incarnation."[116] This idea of two opposing, or contrary, standpoints is implicit in Boethius's description of eternity. Recall that Boethius himself uses a spatial illustration to explain God's relationship to time. God is like a man standing on high hill observing a wagon train going by below him; and a human (or other temporal creature) is like an observer at the base of the hill, who is able only to see the wagon going by his position. With regard to the Incarnation, Helm writes, "If God is timelessly eternal then this is necessarily so, and he could not occupy any temporal standpoint, though in Christ he is united to a nature that nec-

112. In McGrath, *Christian Theology*, 21.

113. Helm, "Eternal Creation," 336.

114. Ibid.

115. This is found in Helm, "Divine Timeless Eternity," 55–59; as well as in Helm, "Eternal Creation," 29–46.

116. Helm, "Divine Timeless Eternity," 55.

essarily does have some temporal standpoint."[117] Helm further explains, "God has a unique perspective on the world, a perspective necessarily free of temporal and spatial indexicals."[118] Being consistent with other claims, Helm adds, "And so, saving the case of the incarnation, he does not take up the cognitive standpoint of any one of his creatures more than that of any other."[119] So Helm understands that the two standpoints are completely isolated from one another, creatures unable to see the world timelessly, and the Creator unable to see the world from the cognitive standpoint of a temporal creature.

Analysis of Helm's Argument

The weakest part of Helm's argument is one of the first elements he presents: his attempt to demonstrate consistency between the atemporal view and statements of Scripture. Each passage Helm mentions in support of his atemporal view can easily be given a temporal reading, such that it could be concluded just as easily that his view is inconsistent with the passages noted. Helm realizes this weakness as he writes, "These verses are consistent with eternalism [the atemporal view] in that they can fairly be interpreted in an eternalist way. Whether the authors intended by their words to teach eternalism is a more difficult question, for the statements can equally well be interpreted in a temporalist way."[120] What makes this admission noteworthy is that Helm relies on the statements in Scripture as one of the two sources for his atemporal argument.[121] But, if the statements in Scripture do not actually support his view—other than the fact that they could be given a reading that may be "consistent" with his view—then the statements could hardly be said to be a "source" of the view. On the contrary, in order to read these passages in an atemporal way, Helm admits, the atemporal view must first be assumed, so that it guides the interpretation of the passages.

Further, Helm admits that most of the language of Scripture, especially that in which God is said to dialogue with a human being, seems to

117. Ibid., 56.
118. Ibid., 58.
119. Ibid.
120. Ibid., 31.
121. Ibid., 34.

indicate that God is temporal.[122] His solution for this problem is divine accommodation. Dialogue presented in Scripture between God and humans is only the *appearance* of dialogue. He writes that "it is a logically necessary condition that each of the partners in the dialogue should appear to act and react in time."[123] In other words, dialogue between God and creatures is affected by God's immutability. God, being outside of time, must accommodate his actions to the level of the human participant in order for dialogue to take place. Helm explains, "If dialogue between God and humankind is to be real and not make-believe, then God cannot represent himself (in his role as dialogue partner) as wholly immutable, for then dialogue, real dialogue, would be impossible."[124] But, it might be argued, if God represents himself as other than immutable, then he is *mis*representing himself, and not simply accommodating his language. Helm writes, "If a timelessly eternal God is to communicate to embodied intelligent creatures who exist in space and time . . . then he must do so by representing himself to them in ways that are not literally true."[125] While this solution provides a way to read the passages in question in a manner (that may be) consistent with the atemporal view, Helm does not provide a justification for such a method of accommodation.

Also important to note is how Helm handles the doctrine of God's immutability. Helm defines his view of immutability as "strong immutability," and ties this concept very closely to the atemporal view. He writes, "But a timelessly eternal God is immutable and so impassible in a very strong sense; he *necessarily* cannot change, for change takes time, or is in time, and a timelessly eternal God by definition is not in time, and so his actions cannot take time, nor can he experience fits of passion or changes in mood."[126] What Helm seems to be saying here is that the reason God is immutable is because he is timeless; or, said another way, God's timelessness is the cause of his immutability. This view puts Helm at odds with the classical defenders of the atemporal view, who most commonly argued that God's immutability was the reason that he is timeless. Aquinas, for example, argues that the notion of time arises from change; but since God

122. Ibid., 42–44. Helm at this point relies on Aquinas and Calvin.
123. Ibid., 45.
124. Ibid.
125. Ibid.
126. Helm, "Divine Timeless Eternity," 38–39.

is completely free of change, then God is atemporal. He writes that "just as numbering the antecedent and the consequent in change produces the notion of time, awareness of invariability in something altogether free from change produces the notion of eternity."[127] Aquinas further concludes, "Eternity, in the true and proper sense, belongs only to God, for eternity follows upon unchangeableness, as I have made clear. And, as I have also shown, God alone is altogether unchangeable.[128] So for Aquinas, the root of God's atemporality is his immutability, while Helm places God's atemporality at the root of his immutability.

In discussing the notion of impassibility, Helm is led directly into his attempt to account for the Incarnation. Recall first that Helm begins with the premise that God's existence is timelessly eternal, and that God is in no way in time. Further, Helm argues that God is completely impassible, and is eternally so. This means that Helm would seem to be committed to

(11) God is timelessly eternal

and

(12) God is eternally impassible.

But also, Helm argues that passibility arises (among other things) from being embodied. He writes that when considering the divine nature, "we must rule out feelings or affections that require . . . the possession of a body; hunger or thirst or tiredness."[129] In other words, Helm seems to commit himself here to the idea that

(13) Passibility arises necessarily from embodiment.

Helm would presumably affirm the basic creedal statements about Jesus, namely that God the Son was embodied in Jesus of Nazareth, and experienced many such things as hunger, thirst, and tiredness. But Helm has also asserted that God the Son is *eternally* Incarnate. This means, for Helm, that there is no period of the life of God the Son in which it would make sense to refer to him as anything other than Incarnate in the man Jesus Christ. Further, since God must be in full possession of the whole of his life at once, then God the Son is in full possession at once of the whole of his incarnate life. His life and his incarnate life are one and the same.

127. Aquinas, *Summa Theologiae*, 1a.10.1 (93).
128. Ibid., 1a.10.3 (96).
129. Helm, "Divine Timeless Eternity," 39.

So, following Leftow's scheme, Helm believes that God the Son is eternally united with S and B in Jesus Christ. But since Christ's embodiment caused him to experience many things such as thirst and hunger, it would be difficult, then, to see how Helm could avoid the unwieldy conclusion:

> (14) God the Son is eternally impassible and God the Son is eternally experiencing thirst and hunger.

Whether or not Helm could account for this in his model and thus avoid the appearance of a contradiction remains to be seen. Helm does not address the Incarnation in sufficient detail to account for the notion of impassibility as he has defined it.

In addition to discussing the Incarnation and impassibility, Helm also discusses it with regard to his "two standpoints" doctrine. Recall that because of the two standpoints, Helm is committed to the idea that it is impossible for God to take the cognitive standpoint of a creature. In his discussion of the two standpoints, Helm mentions the Incarnation only as a side note or a qualifier to the statement of his position. He writes, "If God is timelessly eternal then he is necessarily so, and he could not occupy any temporal standpoint, though in Christ he is united to a nature that necessarily does have some temporal standpoint;"[130] and so, "saving the case of the incarnation, he does not take up the cognitive standpoint of any one of his creatures more than that of any other."[131] In other words, Helm seems to be committed to

> (15) God necessarily cannot occupy a particular temporal standpoint.

But, in Helm's view, the Incarnation seems to be a special case to consider. When he uses the phrase, "saving the case of the Incarnation," Helm seems to be indicating that it is an example in which God does take the cognitive standpoint of a creature. Helm asserts that God the Son is "united to a nature" that does indeed have a temporal standpoint. So, Helm would be committed to

> (16) In the Incarnation, God takes the cognitive standpoint of a creature.

But then, Helm is left with another difficult conclusion, namely that

130. Ibid., 56.
131. Ibid.

(17) God cannot occupy a temporal standpoint, and yet eternally does so in Christ.

As with impassibility, whether Helm could avoid the appearance of a contradiction with a more detailed explanation is not immediately obvious. Nevertheless, Helm seems to be aware of the tension created with the atemporal view when it is made to account for the Incarnation.

Finally, it is important to note how Helm deals with the Nicene statements concerning the Incarnation. Helm asserts that what the council at Nicaea meant to condemn was the very notion that there is temporal sequence in the life of God. He writes, "On [the temporalist view] there was *time* when the Son was not. That is, it is difficult to see how a temporalist could hold to the classical Nicene position that the Son came into existence before time; that there was no time when he was not."[132] Further, Helm asserts that those who do not hold to the classical atemporal view are guilty of the Arian heresy. He writes that the temporalist perspective "would seem to strongly favour, if not actually entail, some form of Arianism."[133] While no doubt some temporalists may hold to the idea that there was a time when *the Son* was not, my position is that there was indeed a time when *the man Jesus* did not exist—and this I take to be perfectly consistent with Nicene orthodox Christology. As I have previously indicated, it seems that the Nicene position is *not* asserting the eternality of Jesus, or of the Incarnation; but it seems clear that it *is* asserting that God the Son existed prior to the Incarnation. So Helm's accusation of heresy seems to be founded on a confusion between *God the Son* and *the man Jesus*. It seems clear that what Nicaea sought to condemn was the idea that God the Son came into existence at the birth of Jesus. In Helm's view all of God the Son's life (including the Incarnation) is experienced by God the Son in one timelessly eternal instant. So the basis for Helm's accusation seems to be merely a case of assuming the atemporal view *a priori* and then giving the Nicene formula an atemporal reading.

IMPLICATIONS OF THE ATEMPORAL VIEW

Having considered three examples of the classical atemporal view of God's relationship to time, and how these views account for the Incarnation, several important theological and philosophical implications of the view

132. Helm, "Eternal Creation," 336.

133. Ibid.

must be noted. The first of these implications is that the classical view requires understanding God's immutability in a particular sense. Normally, to say that God is immutable is to say that he does not change. Scripture testifies that God does not change; and in fact God proclaims of himself, "For I am the Lord, I do not change."[134] Contrasting many things that change, the Psalmist writes, "But You [God] are the same, and Your years will have no end."[135] The author of Hebrews even applies this immutability to the incarnate Christ, "Jesus Christ is the same yesterday, today, and forever."[136] But defenders of the atemporal view mean to say much more than this. They argue that it is logically impossible for God to change; and they argue that this logical impossibility is not based on the essential nature of God or on his maximal perfection. Rather, atemporalists derive their notion of God's immutability from the concept of his timelessness. Just as it does not make sense to think the number two could change—for it is a timeless concept—so also it does not make sense that God could change. This is stated explicitly in Helm's argument, is entailed by Swinburne's "ordering principle" theory, and is implicit in Leftow's analysis of the Incarnation. However, it could be countered against this atemporal understanding of immutability that God is immutable in that he does not change *through time*. In fact, this is exactly what the Hebrews passage says (quoted above). Changelessness is something that is recognized as time passes: many things change as time passes, but the unchanging God remains the same through time. So it seems that defenders of the atemporal view are only willing to admit a technical concept of immutability, based on philosophical reflection on other beliefs about God's nature, and not on biblical passages such as Heb 13:8 that give actual description of God's changelessness.

The second implication of the classical atemporal view of God's relationship to time is that it rules out any kind of sequence in God's life. This is related to the concept of immutability as described above. Just as God's timelessness rules out change in God, so also it requires that there is no sequence of events or succession of any kind in the life of God. This idea is incipient in Boethius (the complete possession *at once* of the fullness of life); but is perhaps made most prominent in Aquinas, who

134. Mal 3:6.
135. Ps 102:27.
136. Heb 13:8.

draws as a direct consequence of God's immobility and immutability the absence of succession in the divine life. Aquinas writes, "There is, therefore, no *before* and *after* in Him . . . nor can any succession be found in His being."[137] He concludes that since God is immutable, "His existence is simultaneously whole."[138] Swinburne's version of the argument assents to this fact in his acceptance of the Boethian position. Leftow agrees. Helm goes to great lengths to prove the point. The absence of succession in the divine life is a logical consequence of timelessness in the Boethian and Thomistic sense; and in the atemporal view, it makes no sense of speaking of *events* in God's life, because the whole of his life is a singular, durationless, timeless event.

The lack of succession in God's life leads directly to the third important implication for the classical atemporal view. If God is timeless in the sense described, then time itself is static, and all temporally sequenced events occur simultaneously within God's life. This fact becomes clear when Helm's doctrine of the two standpoints (derived from Boethius) is examined.[139] Recall the illustration found in Boethius of God's view of the created order being likened to a man standing on a high hill, observing a long train of events before him. So, for the atemporalist, a creature has the standpoint like someone standing on the street corner watching a wagon train go by, while God is like a man on a hill who is able from his vantage point to see the whole train. But in the illustration, it is not the case that the man on the ground "sees" only the part of the train that is passing by his location. Rather, he believes that his part of the train *is all that exists*. The part of the train that has already passed by is thought to be in the past, over and done with. The part not yet arrived is thought to *not yet exist*. But this is a skewed, and inaccurate vision of reality. The man on the high hill has much more than just a different perspective; he has access to information that the people below do not have. Therefore, the man on the hill believes that there is actually a long wagon train moving before him. And what this man believes is actually the case—his belief corresponds to

137. Aquinas, *Summa Contra Gentiles*, 1.15.3 (98).

138. Aquinas, *Compendium of Theology*, 1.8 (13).

139. The same idea is presented in Leftow, "Time and Eternity," where Leftow speaks of reference frames. See also Padgett, "Eternity as Relative Timelessness," 99; where Padgett makes a similar observation to the one offered here, and argues that Leftow's use of the term "reference frame" is based on a misunderstanding of the Special Theory of Relativity.

a genuine feature of reality. Stepping out of the illustration, then, God does not merely have a "different" standpoint or perspective on the temporal events in the created order. Instead, he has a *privileged* standpoint—he sees things as they really are. Since, on the atemporal view, he sees them "all at once," in a "timelessly eternal" instant, that is how they *actually are*. Each moment of time is equally present to God, and therefore static in terms of God's relationship to those events. Therefore, the appearance of the passage of (dynamic) time to persons within the created order is illusory. Time itself is static.

But not only is time static on the atemporal view, so also the created order must be co-eternal with God. God possesses the whole of his life in one timelessly eternal instant; and a feature of that life is his relation to the created order. Since every event and moment within the created order is sustained by God and present to him at once, then it must be the case that every event, object, entity, and being in the created order *exists* with God in that one timelessly eternal instant. As Boethius argues (along the modern defenders of the classical view) God is in full possession of the whole of his life in one timelessly eternal instant. One obvious feature of God's life is his being creator and sustainer of the material universe. Therefore, one would have to conclude that the material universe (and every "temporal" feature of it) is ever present to God, an eternal feature of God's life.

One element within the material universe, of course, is Jesus of Nazareth. With regard to the Incarnation, Helm makes an emphatic point that "there is no preexistent Christ with a life history independent of and prior to the incarnation."[140] It is indeed a logical consequence of the atemporal view that the whole of the life of God the Son is concurrent (timelessly) with his being Incarnate in the man Jesus Christ. What appear to be temporal relations—even from the standpoint of Jesus Christ as he lived on earth—are not actually temporal relations. Even though the creeds and certain passages of Scripture speak of a sequence in the Incarnation, the atemporalist must either read these statements as purely analogical and symbolic or reject them outright as untrue. But even if they are said to be only analogous to temporal sequence, it may be asked: In what way are they analogous? For on the fact that the atemporalist is committed to the idea that God the Son possesses all of his life at once,

140. Helm, "Divine Timeless Eternity," 54.

including the incarnational aspects of that life, no sequence whatsoever would be admissible. And since an analogy only conveys truth insofar as it has some connecting point with reality, it would also seem that the creedal and Scriptural statements cannot be drawing an analogy. Therefore, the atemporalist means to tell us that God the Son *did not* "empty himself" and *did not* "become" anything other than what he timelessly is. This is exactly what both Leftow and Helm assert. Their view is that the Son only *appeared to have* become something, appeared to those who occupy a temporal standpoint (and are unable to see things as they really are). Thus, on the atemporalist account, the *event* of the Incarnation described in both creed and Scripture is reduced to the status of illusion; for no such event, distinct from any other aspect of God's life, has actually taken place.

TIMELESSNESS AND THE INCARNATION

The implications stated above seem to be unavoidable when considering the classical atemporal account of God's relationship to time. Yet each of them significantly shapes how the doctrine of the Incarnation is to be understood; and each is bound up with one another in their account of the incarnation. If God is timeless as described, then God is immutable (in the qualified strong sense), and therefore there is no sequence in his life. This leads to the conclusion that time itself is actually static, because God sees all of time in an instant, and (of course) he sees things as they really are. Part of what he sees is the Incarnation; but he also experiences the incarnation. This means that a feature of his life (experienced all at once, in one instant) is the fact that God the Son is incarnate in Jesus. Of course, God the Son must be *eternally* so; and no aspect of the life of God the Son is separable from the Incarnation.

This presents a kind of order in the reasoning process from immutability and timelessness to certain conclusions about the Incarnation. It seems clear, however, that this order of reasoning is exactly backwards. Each of the authors examined in this chapter (and indeed all others consulted who defend the classical atemporal view) begin with the presumption of timelessness (or derive it from philosophical reflection on the nature of God apart from special revelation); and then consider divine action in the temporal world (as exemplified in the Incarnation) as a problem or challenge to be overcome. It would seem that the Trinitarian theologian is already committed to a great deal with regard to the Incarnation, by virtue of his Trinitarian theology. Given this, it would seem pertinent for such to consider divine action in the Incarnation as the centerpiece, the starting point, and the paradigm for theological and philosophical reflection on God's relationship to time. As Leftow admits, if a contradiction is discovered between divine timelessness and the Incarnation, the former must be jettisoned. This is so, he writes, "For the incarnation lies at the core of Christian belief. Divine timelessness does not."[141]

When the Incarnation is given its proper place in the theological and philosophical discussion, quite another picture emerges of God's relationship to time. In chapter 2 I presented a three-fold paradigm for understanding God's relationship to time. The Incarnation seems to indicate a sequence in the divine life: sequence in the Incarnation event and its permanence; sequence in the life of God the Son incarnate in Jesus Christ; and sequence in the finished work of the Son in the atonement. In this chapter, I showed that defenders of the atemporal view rule out the possibility of sequence in the life of God the Son, and then are faced with the challenge of explaining the (apparent) sequential elements in the Incarnation. In each case observed, the authors seemed to be unable to give adequate account of the Incarnation. Instead, the atemporal view paints a picture of a timelessly eternal Incarnation, and suggests that the man Jesus, against all appearances otherwise, is an eternal feature of the life of God the Son. The next chapter will examine several examples of *temporal* models of God's relationship to time. These, too, will be examined for whether and how they account for the Incarnation.

---

141. Leftow, "Timeless God Incarnate," 273.

4

Analysis of Some Alternatives
to the Atemporal View

T HE PREVIOUS CHAPTER WAS devoted to an examination of three
prominent examples of arguments defending the classical atemporal
view of God's relationship to time. In this chapter, I will similarly examine some examples of authors who have defended the notion that God's
existence is in some way temporal. Nicholas Wolterstorff's[1] contribution
is included because it is one of the more prominent in the contemporary
debate, and he has given one of the most straightforward, unqualified de-
fenses of the view that God's existence is temporal. Alan Padgett,[2] whose
contribution also plays a significant role in the debate, has offered a more
nuanced version of God's relationship to time; and so a brief analysis of
his views is also included here. Additionally, a brief examination of temporal models owing their heritage to Process Theology and Open Theism
will be given, with special attention paid to whether these arguments
can account for the doctrine of the Incarnation. Before examining these,
however, I want to first examine the argument made by Thomas Senor.[3]
Senor's contribution is somewhat unique in the contemporary debate in
that he is one of very few authors who have sought to develop a model

1. Wolterstorff's contribution is found in Wolterstorff, "God Everlasting"; and
Wolterstorff, "Unqualified Divine Temporality," 187–225. The latter will be given greater
emphasis in this chapter.

2. Padgett's main contributions to the debate include Padgett, "New Doctrine of
Eternity," 559–78; Padgett, *God, Eternity, and the Nature of Time*; and Padgett, "Eternity
as Relative Timelessness," 92–128.

3. Senor, "Incarnation and Timelessness," is where the argument is initially presented,
and therefore will be the source considered in this chapter. In a later essay, Thomas Senor,
"Incarnation, Timelessness, and Leibniz's Law Problems," Senor confirms that the earlier
essay is the most complete presentation of his arguments.

of God's relationship to time based on the doctrine of the Incarnation; therefore this chapter will begin with an analysis of it. Following the pattern of the previous chapter, several philosophical and theological implications of the temporal models will also be considered. Finally, some preliminary conclusions will be given related to how temporal models of God's relationship to time are able to account for the doctrine of the Incarnation.

THOMAS SENOR

In his important essay, Thomas Senor sets out to demonstrate that the doctrine of the Incarnation is in direct conflict with the idea of divine timelessness. In this article, Senor presents two logical arguments from the Incarnation against the classical atemporal view of God's relationship to time. The two arguments seek to demonstrate that God the Son is temporal. If these arguments are successful, Senor argues, the classical model must be abandoned. He writes, "I assume that if I can show the doctrines of timelessness and the Incarnation to be fundamentally in conflict, the former will have to be surrendered."[4] In addition to presenting the arguments, Senor also anticipates, and answers, several challenges that might be leveled against his arguments. Additionally, Senor explores the idea of whether the temporality of the Son entails the temporality of the Godhead. Each of the two arguments will be summarized and explained, and some brief comments of analysis will be offered along the way.

Senor's First Argument

Senor's first argument is the more straightforward of the two:

> [A]: (P1) Jesus Christ read in the synagogue (at the start of His ministry) before He carried His cross.
> (C1) So, temporal predicates apply to Jesus Christ.
> (P2) Jesus Christ = God the Son
> (C2) So, temporal predicates apply to God the Son
> (P3) Temporal predicates don't apply to timeless beings.
> (C3) So, God the Son isn't timeless.[5]

---

4. Senor, "Incarnation and Timelessness," 150.

5. Ibid.

This first argument is a series of three premises, (P1), (P2), and (P3), each of which seem to lead to a specific conclusion with regard to time. The first premise picks out a common way of speaking about the life and activities of Jesus Christ. Senor points out that "Christians commonly use temporal predicates when speaking of Christ."[6] Indeed such statements are even common to Scripture, and the conclusion (C1) seems to follow.

The second premise/conclusion pair is an appeal to a Leibniz-type identity of indiscernibles. Christianity asserts that Christ is God the Son. Since, then, the temporal predicates apply to Christ, the predicates also apply to God the Son. Senor explains, "Yet orthodox Christianity also holds that Christ is the Second Person of the Trinity. Thus, by Leibniz's Law, the property 'one's being such that temporal predicates apply to one' is true of God the Son, from which it follows that God the Son is not timeless."[7] In other words (P2) states what Senor believes to be a basic tenet of Christian theism: that Jesus is God the Son. Therefore, (C2) follows from (C1) and (P2): temporal predicates also apply to God the Son. The final move in the argument is the addition of (P3)/(C3): since temporal predicates do not apply to timeless beings, then God the Son is not timeless.

In order to defend his first argument, Senor first sets out to distinguish his challenge to the classical atemporal view from other challenges by addressing the notion of God's action in time. Senor points out that many challenges to the classical view are formulated in terms of whether a timeless God could bring about effects in time. He explains, "Many of these objections allege that a timeless being would be unable to act in time; and since the God of the Bible is undoubtedly portrayed as Creator and Sustainer, they conclude that He is temporal."[8] Senor also points out the response by Stump and Kretzmann to this argument: that just because some of the effects of God's intentions are in time, it does not follow that God is in time.[9] But, Senor argues, the challenge presented by the Incarnation is not like the other challenges referring to the effects of God's action in time. He points out that even Stump and Kretzmann admit this, and Senor quotes the following passage from their article:[10] "The

6. Ibid.

7. Ibid.

8. Ibid., 151.

9. The argument to which Senor refers is from Stump and Kretzmann, "Eternity."

10. The quotation appears in Senor, "Incarnation and Timelessness," 151.

principle difficulty in the doctrine of the Incarnation seems intractable to considerations of the sort with which we have been trying to alleviate difficulties associated with an eternal entity's willing to bring about a temporal event, because according to the doctrine of the Incarnation an eternal entity itself entered time."[11] Since Senor has the agreement of his opponents in the debate, it would seem that he has successfully established that the argument from the Incarnation is of a different kind than other arguments based on God's action in the world.

In the remainder of the defense of his first argument, Senor considers possible reasons why any one of (P1), (P2), or (P3) might be false. Senor states simply that (P2) is essential to Christianity, and that (P3) is a conceptual truth. Therefore, he concludes that the only way to defeat the argument would be to deny (P1). On this point, Senor engages Stump and Kretzmann and their version of the "*qua* move" as a potential defeater for Senor-type arguments.[12] The "*qua* move" as it is applied to Senor's argument would argue:

> (P1´) Jesus Christ qua man read in the synagogue before Jesus Christ qua man carried His cross.[13]

Thus, the force of (P1) with respect to God the Son (P2) would be apparently removed. Since the "*qua* move" was addressed in the previous chapter in the context of analyzing Leftow's argument, that material will not be duplicated here. Although Stump and Kretzmann's version of this move is laid out somewhat differently than Leftow's, the idea behind both is the same.[14] It will suffice at this point to note that Senor relies on Thomas V. Morris's arguments against the "*qua* move."[15] The key feature

11. Stump and Kretzmann, "Eternity," 451. In the remainder of their article, they seek to solve the problem by appealing to the "*qua* move," discussed in chapter 3, above. As I have already suggested, and will discuss further in the concluding chapter, the "*qua* move" does not seem to eliminate the problem.

12. Throughout the essay, Senor repeatedly quotes portions of Stump and Kretzmann's argument from "Eternity."

13. Senor, "Incarnation and Timelessness," 152.

14. Senor defines very clearly what he understands the "*qua* move" to be: "I mean the defensive maneuver according to which two inconsistent properties can be had by Christ as long as they are not predicated via the same nature." Senor, "Incarnation and Timelessness," 162 n. 8. This is the same as Leftow's use of the term. Cf. Leftow, "Timeless God Incarnate," 288–90. Therefore, even though Senor is directly addressing Stump and Kretzmann, it is assumed that he would argue similarly against Leftow.

15. Morris's argument is in Morris, *Logic of God Incarnate*, 38, 48–55, 146–47.

of Senor's rejection of the "*qua* move" (and perhaps Morris's), is the idea that such a move overemphasizes the duality in the person of Christ at the expense of his unity. Senor writes, "Again, it would seem that those who use such a maneuver in an attempt to avoid problems with the doctrine of the Incarnation overemphasize the dual nature of Christ and fail to pay enough attention to the unity of his being."[16] So, Senor rejects any appeal to the "*qua* move" as a defeater of his argument on the basis that it violates the unity of the person of Christ.

In analyzing this argument, it will be assumed for the present discussion that the "*qua* move" fails to show how (P1) (as originally formulated in Senor's argument) could be false.[17] Rather than being open for criticism on (P1), it seems that the weakest element of the argument is (P2), which Senor states is "necessary for Christological orthodoxy."[18] Again recalling the discussion from the previous chapter regarding Leftow's argument, it would seem that Leftow has offered an account of the Incarnation whereby "Jesus Christ = God the Son" is possibly false. Leftow states that Jesus Christ is "S + B + God the Son."[19] This is at the center of Leftow's criticism of Senor's argument; and it hardly seems apparent that Leftow has departed from orthodoxy in his formulation.[20] But even if one does not accept Leftow's three-part mereological understanding of the Incarnation, Leftow's discussion of the matter reveals that Senor's pronouncement that (P2) is "necessary for Christological orthodoxy," fails to anticipate any challenge of this kind. The truth that Senor seems to be identifying in his (P2) seems to be

> (P2*) The person who is Jesus Christ is the person who is God the Son.

Modifying (P2) in this way would both convey the truth that Senor is attempting to identify (and that which is essential to orthodoxy), and at the same time avoid the challenge posed by Leftow.

One final element of Senor's defense of his first argument is worth noting. Senor states that an argument could be constructed similar to [A], but with references to Christ being *spaceless* instead of timeless. It would

16. Senor, "Incarnation and Timelessness," 154.
17. The discussion in chapter 5 will return to consideration of the "*qua* move."
18. Ibid., 156.
19. See chapter 3, above, and Leftow, "Timeless God Incarnate," 280.
20. His metaphysics of personhood may be deficient, however.

seem that if such an argument were offered, the defender of [A] would also have to be committed to something like "God the Son isn't spaceless."[21] But, Senor argues, this does not create a problem even if this conclusion is accepted. He asserts that there is an "asymmetry between spacelessness and timelessness."[22] He argues that temporal predicates are such that if they ever apply to a particular entity, they always do. He writes that "a being that exists at a particular time will always be such that it existed at that time and so temporal predicates will always apply to it. Thus, if Christ was ever temporal, temporal he remains."[23] But whether or not something exists in space does not have such restrictions. Instead, he proposes that a being could go from being spaceless to existing outside of space, and then return again to spacelessness. He writes, "Spacelessness does not share this rigidity [as timelessness]. As far as I can tell, there is nothing even apparently incoherent in the idea of an aspatial being's becoming spatial and then returning to spacelessness."[24] Therefore, he suggests that an appeal to a parallel argument based on spacelessness will not cause a problem for his argument against God's timelessness.

Senor's Second Argument

Senor's second argument is different from the first in important respects. In the second argument, Senor emphasizes that Christ took on human nature and emptied himself, as stated in Phil 2:7.[25] According to Senor, this indicates that a change took place in God the Son in the Incarnation; for otherwise "making," and "taking" language would be devoid of meaning. But, if the Son changed, then the Son is mutable. Further, mutability entails temporal duration, which rules out the possibility that the Son is timeless. Senor constructs this formally as follows:

> [B]: (P1) God the Son eternally (and essentially) has His Divine nature.
> (P2) The human (accidental) nature of God the Son is assumed (or "taken on").

21. Senor, "Incarnation and Timelessness," 155.

22. Ibid.

23. Ibid.

24. Ibid.

25. Senor refers to Phil 2:5–7 as "the most explicit scriptural basis for the orthodox doctrine of the two-natures view of Christ." Ibid., 156.

(P3) X's assuming (or "taking on") a nature involves a change in X's intrinsic properties.

(C1) So, the assumption of the human nature brings about a change in the intrinsic (though non-essential) properties of God the Son.

(C2) So, the Son is mutable.

(P4) Mutability entails temporal duration.

(C3) So the Son is not timeless.[26]

Senor notes that if [B] were to fail, it would be on either (P2) or (P3); and so his defense of this argument focuses on defending these two premises. Senor starts his defense by pointing out, "Clearly, one way of rejecting [B] is to deny that Christ 'assumed' his human nature; that is, someone might maintain that a human nature was not 'taken on' by Christ since He has it eternally."[27] At this point in his discussion, Senor again turns to Stump and Kretzmann and their statement to this effect. Stump and Kretzmann write, "The divine nature of the second person of the Trinity, like the divine nature of either of the other persons of the Trinity, cannot become temporal; nor could the second person at some time acquire a human nature he does not eternally have."[28] Senor quotes this passage, and then offers two possible interpretations for what they mean in this statement: either, it could be that they mean that the Son has the human nature eternally (a straightforward denial of [P2]); or they might be intending to claim that the Son did not assume the human nature *at some time*.[29]

But each one of these alternatives, Senor argues, creates a problem for Stump and Kretzmann. If interpreted in the second sense, Senor argues, Stump and Kretzmann's statement means that the Son took on the human nature timelessly; and hence did so without a change in his intrinsic properties (a denial of [P3]). But, Senor points out, this would require that Christ's human nature—the nature that the Son timelessly assumed—also is timelessly eternal. According to Senor, this creates a problem with either the truthfulness of the atemporal account of the assumption of the nature, or an equivocation on the meaning of the word "nature," or perhaps both.

---

26. Ibid., 157.

27. Ibid.

28. Stump and Kretzmann, "Eternity," 453.

29. Senor, "Incarnation and Timelessness," 157–58.

The first sense in which the statement can be taken, Senor argues, is unorthodox; and so he does not offer substantive comment on it, assuming instead that Stump and Kretzmann have not intended their statement to be taken this way.[30] But Senor is too quick to give them the benefit of the doubt; for the very next sentence in their essay—which Senor does not quote—indicates that they did intend the statement in this sense. They write that "the second person eternally has two natures. . . ."[31] So the most straightforward reading of their statement is the way in which they intend it to be taken. They claim (on the Boethian model of eternity) that God the Son eternally has his human nature. This, of course, is quite similar to Helm's argument to that effect.[32] Nevertheless, Senor does not address this. Instead he simply states that a denial of (P2) is a rejection of orthodoxy with respect to the Incarnation. He writes, "Now if they intend this passage in [the first sense], they've avoided [B]'s intended sting. Timelessness will be spared, but not without cost; for they will have denied a part of the traditional Christian claim about the Incarnation."[33] Whether or not Senor is correct—that is, whether or not a Stump/Kretzmann-type denial of (P2) is Christologically unorthodox— is an important question. But at this point, Senor's charge of unorthodoxy could perhaps devolve into a debate about the charge and not about the substance of the matter. It will be sufficient at this point to say only that Senor's argument [B]—and especially (P2)—seems to be in line with the most straightforward reading of both Scriptural and creedal statements about the Son taking on human nature. A conclusion to the debate over this issue will be offered in the next chapter.

The final step in Senor's argument from the Incarnation is his drawing a conclusion of God's temporality from that of the Son. Senor writes, "The idea is that the unity of the Godhead requires its members to have the same relation to time."[34] Therefore, if either or both of [A] and [B] are successful in demonstrating that the Son is not timeless, then this would be *prima facie* evidence that the Godhead is not timeless. Or, it could

30. In laying out the alternatives, Senor gives the first and then comments, "However, it could be that Stump and Kretzmann do not intend anything this unorthodox." See ibid., 157.

31. Stump and Kretzmann, "Eternity," 453.

32. See chapter 3, above.

33. Senor, "Incarnation and Timelessness," 158.

34. Ibid., 159.

be said that if the Son is not timeless, then the other members of the Trinity are not timeless. Either way, it seems that Senor's desired conclusion obtains upon the success of either [A] or [B]: God is not timeless as indicated by the classical atemporal model of God's relationship to time.

NICHOLAS WOLTERSTORFF

The essay "Unqualified Divine Temporality" is the most recent contribution Wolterstorff has made to the debate on God's relationship to time, and it represents a succinct summary of his views on the matter, as well as a refinement of ideas presented in previous work on the topic. Unlike Senor's work, Wolterstorff does not devote the bulk of his material to addressing the doctrine of the Incarnation. Instead, in his essay Wolterstorff argues that the most important factor in considering God's relationship to time is the question of whether or not God has a history. This question, in turn, is dependent on the question of whether there is change in God. Thus, Wolterstorff asserts, "Change in God is what is really at issue."[35] In this statement, he is in agreement with the classical position as it has been developed. Adherents to the atemporal view have consistently charged that God's atemporality and his immutability mutually entail one another: if God is immutable, then he is timeless; if he is timeless, then he is immutable. Wolterstorff concludes, however, that God does change in some way. This is true, he argues, because God has a history, and only temporal entities can have a history.

To begin his argument, Wolterstorff first sets up the debate with an assertion that the plain presentation of the Bible is that God is an active and dynamic agent, acting within human history. The Bible, he argues, presents the reader with a narrative of God's actions in the world and responses to human actions. He writes, "The God of Scripture is One of whom a narrative can be told; we know that not because Scripture tells us that but because it offers such a narrative. I hold that an implication of this is that God is in time."[36] So, Wolterstorff looks to the Bible for the solution to the debate on God's relationship to time; but he does not look to engage in linguistic analysis or word studies. Instead, he is arguing that Scripture presents the history of God's actions, and it would not be able to do so unless God himself had a history.

35. Wolterstorff, "Unqualified Divine Temporality," 211.
36. Ibid., 188.

From this simple statement, Wolterstorff argues that the normal pattern of biblical interpretation is to take Scriptural accounts of God at face value, unless there is some reason to think of it as something other than a literal description of God. He writes, "And now let me articulate a methodological principle that on this occasion I will affirm without defending: an implication of one's accepting Scripture as canonical is that one will affirm as literally true Scripture's representation of God unless one has good reason not to do so."[37] Given this principle of interpretation, he asserts that since Scripture presents God as temporal, those who hold that God is atemporal bear the burden of proof. He writes, "[T]he burden of proof lies on those who hold that the biblical representation of God, as One who has a history that can be narrated, is not be taken as the literal truth of the matter."[38]

In his argument, Wolterstorff seeks to demonstrate that the defender of the classical atemporal view does not enjoy the support of Scriptural statements about God regarding either timelessness or change. To begin, Wolterstorff addresses the three passages of Scripture he thinks have the strongest statements that an atemporalist might use as demonstration that God is timeless: Ps 90:1–4; 2 Pet 3:8; and John 8:58. Wolterstorff points out that while these passages are used by those who hold to the atemporal view, they do not support such a view. Rather, the passages uniformly used temporal language and speak of God existing "before" the physical world and his being "everlasting" (Ps 90:1–2), of his experience of temporal duration (2 Pet 3:8, even though the experience is not identical to human experience of time), and of Jesus' existence "before" Abraham (John 8:58). The point here seems to be that these passages use temporal language to refer to God's life and experiences. He writes, "The conclusion is inescapable: the scriptural passages traditionally cited as supporting divine timelessness provide no such support whatsoever."[39] The conclusion, in his estimation, is that the defender of the classical atemporal view of God's relationship to time is not able to prove his position with statements of Scripture.

37. Ibid.

38. Ibid., 189.

39. Ibid., 190.

Next, Wolterstorff addresses the question of God's immutability by referring to what he calls God's "ontological immutability."[40] As in his treatment of the passages examined regarding God's having a history, Wolterstorff examines several passages in Scripture that present strong statements of what could be taken as God's ontological immutability: Mal 3:6; Ps 102:27; and Jas 1:17.[41] Wolterstorff argues that when Mal 3:6, which states, "For I am the Lord, I do not change," is examined in context, it should be seen as a statement of God's covenantal fidelity and not a statement relating to his ontological immutability.[42] Similarly, when Ps 102:27 is examined in context, the passage does not speak directly to ontological immutability. Wolterstorff writes, "What the writer says is not that God is ontologically immutable but that God is everlasting; God endures."[43] Finally, with Jas 1:17, which states that "with [God] there is no variation or shadow of turning," Wolterstorff argues that the passage speaks to God's unchanging moral character. He writes that the passage is "saying that God is unchangeable in that God is never the source of evil, only and always of good—which falls far short of affirming ontological immutability."[44] Wolterstorff then concludes that as with viewing God as being atemporal, those who hold that God is ontologically immutable cannot support their position directly with statements of Scripture. He writes, "I conclude that the situation for God's ontological immutability is like that for God's timelessness: there are no passages in Scripture which can be cited as supporting the doctrine."[45]

Having argued against the two main elements of the classical atemporal view (timelessness and immutability) using Scripture, Wolterstorff then moves on in his essay to present a positive case for his view for God's unqualified temporality. To accomplish this, the author uses a three-fold strategy: he first comments on the nature of time; second, he considers what it is for something to be outside of time; and third, he argues based on the results of the first two steps that God could not be outside of time.

40. Ibid., 191. See the analysis of Wolterstorff's argument, below, for comment on his choice of words here.

41. Interestingly, these are the same passages quoted in Feinberg, *No One Like Him*, 265, as the exemplary strong statements of God's immutability in Scripture.

42. Wolterstorff, "Unqualified Divine Temporality," 191.

43. Ibid., 192.

44. Ibid., 193.

45. Ibid.

To begin his comments on the nature of time, Wolterstorff briefly outlines McTaggart's distinctions and the rival conceptions of the tensed (dynamic, or A-theory) notion of time and the tenseless (static, B-theory) view of time. Wolterstorff then argues that the tenseless view of time is untenable based on the necessity of tense for human action. To argue this, he points out that for the B-theorist, all events are only ordered temporally as earlier than, simultaneous with, or later than all other events; and that there is no special ontological status given to any event in the temporal array. Describing this, he argues that "no event in the series differs from another in ontological status, nor does any event ever change its ontological status."[46] But, he argues, it is essential in the operation of a temporally indexed system for an agent to be aware of what is happening "now." Using the example of turning on the radio to hear the one o'clock news,[47] Wolterstorff argues that in order to make the determination on when to turn on the radio, he must be aware of when the present event is if its becoming one o'clock is happening "now." He writes, "The tenseless theorist, for whom all dates and events have exactly the same ontological status, has no way of accounting for how we make that determination. If all the events of its becoming one o'clock, and all acts of my turning on this radio, have exactly the same ontological status, how do I get started in implementing my decision that my *present* act of turning on this radio shall coincide with this *present* event of its becoming one o'clock?"[48] He concludes his rejection of the tenseless view of time by writing, "Knowing which events occur simultaneously with which falls short of knowing which ones *are occurring now*."[49]

For the second element of his strategy, Wolterstorff considers what it would mean for something to be outside of time. He begins by pointing out that events are obviously within time. But, he argues, in considering other things such as human beings, animals, and numbers, the problem becomes more complex. The determining factor, Wolterstorff argues, in deciding whether or not such things are in time is whether or not such things have a history, a story that can be told about them.[50] He gives

46. Ibid., 197.
47. Ibid., 201.
48. Ibid.
49. Ibid.
50. Ibid., 202.

two examples: numbers and his cat. His cat, he argues, has a life full of events that happen in time, and therefore the history of his cat can be narrated. But numbers, on the other hand, do not come to be or go out of existence; they do not have events, nor do they change. Wolterstorff concludes, "When it comes to nonevents, I propose that we take whether or not something has a history as the determinate of whether or not it is in time."[51]

This leads to the third element of Wolterstorff strategy: he attempts to demonstrate that God does have a history. He writes, "The question comes down to whether there's a history of God's actions and responses, and of the knowledge that lies behind those."[52] In order to answer the question, Wolterstorff again turns to a discussion of the atemporalist account by describing the distinction between that view and his own:

> Those who hold that God is timeless agree, of course, that Scripture offers us this narrative [of God's actions and responses]. They deny, nevertheless, that God has a history. Not only does God not come into or go out of existence, there are also no changes in God: no alterations in action, response or knowledge. The Biblical narrative is not to be interpreted as presenting items in God's history; it's to be interpreted as presenting items in human history. The analogue to numbers is helpful: what appears at first sight to be a history of numbers is in fact a history of human beings dealing with numbers.[53]

Wolterstorff points out that defenders of the classical view follow Aquinas, making a distinction between God's action and the temporal results of God's action. This means that while God's action has resulting events that have a history, God's action itself does not occur in time and does not have a history. To counter this view, Wolterstorff offers the notion of God's response to human actions, and God's knowledge of tensed facts. Recalling the first element of his strategy, Wolterstorff argues that tensed facts are necessary for human actions. Further, God must have knowledge of tensed facts; he must know when "now" is. Therefore, God's knowledge has a history; and so God has a history. Additionally, Scripture presents God as responding to human action. Since God has knowledge

51. Ibid., 203.
52. Ibid.
53. Ibid., 203–4.

of the tensed facts about human action, then God is able to respond to that action.

It is in the context of this discussion of God's knowledge of tensed facts and his response to human action that Wolterstorff addresses the implications of the doctrine of the Incarnation on the debate. He points out that the classical atemporal view of God's relationship to time understands God's action as a single, timeless, eternal act, that has its effects borne out and experienced by human beings in the temporal array. Considering the interaction between Moses and God, for example, he writes, "God's speaking to Moses consists of timelessly bringing about the event consisting of those sounds emerging at that precise time from the unburned flaming bush."[54] But, he argues, this picture of God's action seems to run afoul of the Incarnation. He writes, "The actions of Jesus were not simply human actions brought about by God, plus human actions freely performed by Jesus in situations brought about by God; they were God's actions. In the life and deeds of Jesus it was God who dwelt among us. The narrative of the history of Jesus is not just a narrative concerning events in the history of the relationship of a human being to God; it's a narrative about God. God does have a history; the doctrine of the incarnation implies that the history of Jesus is the history of God."[55] These brief comments are all that Wolterstorff offers concerning the Incarnation, and he spends the remainder of his discussion on the question of God's immutability.

Analysis of Wolterstorff's Argument

Wolterstorff's argument seems to be open to at least three criticisms; the first of which offered here concerns his consideration of the question of God's immutability. In his essay, Wolterstorff has suggested that immutability as it is often defined by defenders of the classical atemporal view of God's relationship to time is not compatible with the scriptural accounts of God's life. In this discussion, he has chosen to use the word "ontological" to describe this kind of change, and it is for selecting this descriptor that leaves him open to criticism on the point.

54. Ibid., 209.
55. Ibid., 209–10.

The use of the term "ontological immutability" in this essay appears to be a carry over from his earlier essay, "God Everlasting."[56] In that essay, he writes, "God's ontological immutability is not part of the explicit teaching of the biblical writers."[57] But earlier in that same essay, Wolterstorff hints at what he might want to include in the category of "ontological" change in his description of God's actions in the world. He writes, "And from the manner in which [God's] acts are described [in Scripture], it seems obvious that many of them have beginnings and endings, that accordingly they stand in succession relations to each other, and that these successive acts are of such a sort that their presence or absence on God's time-strand constitutes changes thereon."[58] So what Wolterstorff seems to be objecting to is the kind of Thomistic immutability that rules out succession of any kind in God, including succession in God's relations, actions, or knowledge.[59]

One further element of clarification is included in the earlier essay that sheds light on why Wolterstorff has chosen the term "ontological" in his discussion. In that essay, Wolterstorff makes the comment that fundamental to God is his being the Redeemer.[60] Further, Wolterstorff argues that God cannot be Redeemer unless there is some variation or change among his aspects. Wolterstorff writes, "Yet, *ontologically*, God cannot be a redeeming God without there being changeful variation among his states."[61] So, it seems that what Wolterstorff is arguing is not that God changes ontologically (which would be the straightforward understanding of his chosen terminology); rather he is saying that there is some fundamental aspect of God's being—God's ontology—which requires that there be change in God's states or relations. Since God is fundamentally Redeemer, then there must be change in some of God's states or relations in his actions as Redeemer. So, "ontological change" for Wolterstorff is to

---

56. Wolterstorff, "God Everlasting," 96–97 appears to be the source material for what appears in the later essay. In this section, he addresses the same three passages of Scripture and argues for the same conclusion.

57. Ibid., 97.

58. Ibid., 88.

59. In both essays, Wolterstorff quotes Aquinas, although not from the passages that emphasize the absence of succession in God. See Wolterstorff, "Unqualified Divine Temporality," 204; cf. Wolterstorff, "God Everlasting," 89.

60. Wolterstorff, "God Everlasting," 78.

61. Ibid.

be interpreted as changes in relations or states *required by* something essential to God's being, not *changes in* something essential to God's being.

But in using the term "ontological" when arguing that God does change in some way, Wolterstorff has left himself open to the charge that he holds that God changes *in his very being* or in some way relative to properties *essential to his being God*, and not in the sense described above. While it seems that he is only arguing for change in relation to the created order, specifically in his actions as Redeemer, the terminology itself does not indicate this. Further, the clarification in the earlier essay related to why he chose the term "ontological" is absent in the later essay. Without this explanation, the reader is left to judge the meaning of the term. It would seem, then, that Wolterstorff's choice of words (at least in the later essay under examination here) hinders the defense of his model of God's relationship to time.

The second criticism offered also involves terminology that Wolterstorff has used in making his argument. Recall that the second element of Wolterstorff's strategy was to consider what it would be for something to be "in" or "outside" of time. The beginning element of this strategy seems to be exactly correct: Wolterstorff argues, "Events are obviously within time."[62] This statement is consistent with statements he has made elsewhere. He has, for example, explained that "events" are those things that bear the temporal ordering relationships of precedence, succession, or simultaneity to other things.[63] But then he writes, "When it comes to nonevents I propose that we take whether or not something has a history as the determinant of whether or not it is in time."[64] But it seems as if Wolterstorff has here inadvertently allowed a fundamental assumption of the classical atemporal view into his model. The classical model assumes that time is of such a nature that it is possible for beings to be "in" or "outside of" it. But if God is everlasting in the way Wolterstorff is arguing, then *only events* can be "in" time. It would seem a better strategy would be to concede that God is not in time, and then affirm that no entities are in time in the way that the atemporalist wants to argue, but only events in the life of those (living) entities are. God, human beings, and numbers all represent entities—events concerning which are in time. Further,

---

62. Wolterstorff, "Unqualified Divine Temporality," 202.

63. Wolterstorff, "God Everlasting," 80.

64. Wolterstorff, "Unqualified Divine Temporality," 203.

God, human beings, and other living entities have lives, events of which they experience in time. But on Wolterstorff's own model of the nature of time, it would not seem appropriate to allow into the discussion the question of whether or not such entities themselves are "in" time. To do so would be to concede an important point regarding the atemporalist's model of the nature of time.

One final criticism can be noted concerning Wolterstorff's argument: the majority of his essay can be defeated rather simply by a deterministic account of events in the world. A fundamental underlying assumption within Wolterstorff's argument is that *apparent* creaturely freedom of action is *genuine* freedom of action. Nearly all the elements of Wolterstorff's analysis—his reasons for accepting an A-theory of time as well as his reasons for why God must be in time—all required genuine freedom of human action if the conclusion is to obtain. Wolterstorff places heavy emphasis, for example, on God's response to human action. The defender of the classical atemporal view, however, has available to her the option of appealing to determinism: if God has determined all human actions then there is no problem created by divine-human interaction that has to be solved. Indeed, it seems that the only element of Wolterstorff's argument that cannot be defeated by an appeal to determinism is his comments regarding the Incarnation. As I have already suggested, the Incarnation requires succession—or sequence—in the divine life and therefore is not dependent on whether nor not human actions are genuinely free.

Despite these areas of criticism, Wolterstorff's argument enjoys many strengths. The strongest element of his argument is that it is centered on a reading of Scripture that does not require a nuanced explanation for why the text seems to be saying the opposite of what is concluded from the text. It does seem that the atemporalist bears the burden of proof: an answer must be given as to why important passages of Scripture describing God's relation to time require a symbolic or metaphorical interpretation.[65] Wolterstorff's inclusion of an analysis of several key passages is critical to his argument's strength. Another important strength of the argument is the discussion of whether or not God changes. While the criticisms regarding Wolterstorff's discussion have been noted, the fact that he includes this in his discussion is important. As I will argue in the conclud-

---

65. Paul Helm, for example, admits that such passages need to be interpreted symbolically. This matter will be discussed further in the final chapter of this work.

ing chapter, Thomistic immutability seems to be incompatible with an orthodox understanding of the Incarnation.

Wolterstorff is correct in his assertion that change is the real issue. Of course the most important strength of Wolterstorff's presentation is his emphasis on the theological priority of the Incarnation. While his comments concerning the Incarnation are brief, he makes an important point regarding the issue at stake. He writes, "The most important question for the Christian to consider, in reflecting on this understanding of divine action, is whether it is compatible with an orthodox understanding of what happens in the incarnation."[66] This, in fact, is the main thrust of my argument. In what follows, a few other examples of temporal arguments will be examined for how well they account for this essential feature of Christian theology.

ALAN PADGETT

Padgett has contributed to the debate through the development of his model of God's relationship to time, which he refers to as "relative timelessness." While Wolterstorff suggests that God's life is temporal, with no qualifications needed to describe the relationship, Padgett has sought to develop a more nuanced view that takes into consideration some important theological concepts. In this view, Padgett rejects the classical model based on its dependence on the static (or, B-theory) view of time; and based on the fact that (as he argues) the static theory of time is false. In the process of developing his argument, Padgett argues that God does experience real change in his life; but Padgett also attempts to account for the intuition that God must transcend time in some manner. God's eternity is relatively timeless, he argues, in that God is the creator of the physical time that we experience, that God's eternity is infinite, and that God's time is dependent on his being.

In his discussion, Padgett addresses two competing models for God's relationship to time and attempts to reject both of them: the "everlasting" model, and the "timeless" model. First, Padgett argues that the main problem with thinking of eternity as "everlasting" lies in the area of theological adequacy. He argues that the ideas that God is temporally everlasting runs counter to the idea of God's greatness. Padgett writes, "The main problem with the everlasting model is not logical consistency

---

66. Wolterstorff, "Unqualified Divine Temporality," 209.

but theological inadequacy. Given our notion of God as an infinite, personal Creator, we would expect God to transcend time in some way."[67] So Padgett is appealing (at least in part) to the strong intuition concerning God's transcendence: If God is who Christians claim him to be, he must transcend the created order. In Padgett's understanding, time as we know it is part of the created order. He writes, "Space-time as we know it has a beginning—but God does not. . . . Thus God must be beyond time as we know it, in some sense."[68]

While Padgett's rejection of the everlasting model begins with his assessment of its ability to account for God's transcendence, his rejection of the classical atemporal model is based on a philosophical-theological argument. He argues that the atemporal model is "self-consistent," but that even ideas that are self-consistent ought to be rejected because they are incompatible with other truths. He writes, "The main objection I have to the timeless model is simply stated: It is true only if the stasis theory of time is true."[69] Noting the alternatives in the debate about the nature of time that have come from McTaggart's contribution, Padgett argues that the classical atemporal model is dependent on the static[70] view of the nature of time. He asserts, however, that the tenseless view of time is false, and therefore cannot be used in developing a model of God's relationship to time. He writes, "Since I believe the stasis theory of time is false, I cannot use it in theology."[71] So Padgett rejects the classical atemporal model of God's relationship to time based on its dependence on the stasis theory of time, and on the falsity of the stasis view.

In arguing for this two-part defeat of the classical model, Padgett begins with the doctrine that God sustains the universe. This doctrine, he asserts, "is so essential to theism that it is simply more important than the timeless model of eternity."[72] He points out that on the atemporal model, God cannot change in any way. Further, on the doctrine that God sustains the universe, God "is responsible directly for the being of all things, at all

67. Padgett, "Eternity as Relative Timelessness," 93.

68. Ibid.

69. Ibid., 95.

70. Padgett uses the term "stasis view" to refer to what I have called the "static," "B-theory," and "tenseless," view of time. Padgett writes, "Thus I will call the 'tenseless' theory of time 'the stasis theory.'" See ibid. Cf. Padgett, *God, Eternity*, 82–121.

71. Padgett, "Eternity as Relative Timelessness," 95.

72. Ibid., 96.

times."[73] Furthermore, Padgett points out, that on the process[74] view of time, when God creates something, that represents a change in God; and likewise, as God sustains something through time, this also represents a change in God. This is true, he asserts, because on the process view of time, the only things that exist are those that exist at the present moment. Since God is changeless (on the atemporal view), then the atemporalist is in need of a solution to the apparent incompatibility between immutability and the sustaining of *processes* in the universe. Padgett suggests that the only available option is to reject process theories of time in favor of the stasis view; because only the stasis view allows for things to exist all at once in a way that would allow God's action of creation and sustaining to be timeless. He explains, "Since the stasis theory of time allows every event to 'exist' (using this word without tense) at the time it 'occurs' (again, tenseless) in the spread of space-time, this theory and only this theory makes atemporal eternity compatible with God's creating and sustaining all things."[75] So, in this argument, Padgett has demonstrated that the stasis theory of time is essential to the classical atemporal model.

In order to highlight the incompatibility between the dynamic view of time and the atemporal model, Padgett uses the illustration adopted by defenders of the classical view as first given by Boethius: God is like a person on a high hill, observing the whole of events of time before him at once. As was indicated in the previous chapter, Padgett points out that the problem with this is that (on the process view of time) the whole line of events does not exist, but only that which is at the present moment. Padgett writes, "This is a picture of God, high and lifted up, seeing all of time at once, in the way an observer on a high hill can see the whole of the road at once. The problem here is that only one step of the road exists, even for the observer."[76] So, Padgett is pointing out that defenders of the classical view rely on this abstract conception of time, making it like space so the whole temporal spread is thought to exist at once. On this view of God's relationship to the created order, the process view of time cannot be true; and the stasis view is therefore essential to the classical atemporal model of God's relationship to time.

73. Ibid., 97.

74. This term is equivalent to "dynamic" or "A-theory," and is not to be confused with any thesis of process philosophy.

75. Ibid.

76. Ibid., 99.

Having established the necessity of the stasis view of time for the classical atemporal model of God's relationship to time, Padgett then lists several reasons for rejecting the stasis view as untrue.[77] The first reason he gives is that stasis models of the nature of time rely heavily on logical and symbolic abstractions, which seem to lead to conclusions that are contradictory with our normal human experience. Second, Padgett argues that stasis theories of time cannot account for what he refers to as "process facts" about the world, such as facts about what date it is, or what is past or future. He argues that such facts are part of our common experience, and yet "stasis theories give us dubious explanations of these facts."[78] Third, he asserts that the relationships among events of past, present, and future are evident to the senses; and therefore stasis theories are wrong to reject these relationships as real. Padgett concludes based on these objections that stasis theories of time ought to be rejected.[79]

As Padgett moves from a rejection of the "everlasting" model and the classical atemporal model to a presentation of his view of God's relationship to time, it is important to note that Padgett places emphasis on the witness of Scripture. However, he admits that the Bible does not provide a clear-cut answer to the philosophical problem of God's relationship to time. He writes, "As the Bible is not meant to be a book of philosophy or dogmatics, our philosophical and dogmatic questions (like the nature of eternity) will not be directly answered."[80] Padgett has offered an analysis of many important passages in both Old and New Testaments that relate to the concept of eternity; and in doing so, he defends the thesis "that the Bible knows nothing of an absolute timeless divine eternity."[81]

77. See ibid., 102–4. In chapter 5 of Padgett, *God, Eternity*, 82–121, the author gives a detailed account of how those who hold stasis theories defend their view of the nature of time. He lists arguments from both science—including arguments from the Theory of Special Relativity—and philosophy. In each case, Padgett presents a case for rejecting the arguments in favor of stasis theories. Such a detailed approach, while important to the philosophical question of the nature of time, is only secondary to what I am presenting in this work. Therefore, only the most important elements of Padgett's argument relative to Christian theism are included, and the philosophical argument discussed here is only a summary of Padgett's view.

78. Padgett, "Eternity as Relative Timelessness," 104.

79. As noted above, it is assumed that Padgett has other reasons for rejecting stasis theories of time, some of which are given in chapter 5 of his *God, Eternity*.

80. Padgett, *God, Eternity*, 23.

81. Ibid., 35.

Nevertheless, Padgett allows for the possibility that defenders of the atemporal view might be able to demonstrate that their view is compatible with the biblical data. The point behind this, Padgett argues, is that the Bible simply does not engage in the kind of philosophical-theological discussion that might be necessary to solve the debate. He writes, "The Bible alone may not help us decide between two definitions of divine eternity. . . . The biblical authors were not interested in philosophical speculation about eternity, and thus the intellectual context for discussing this matter may simply not have existed at that time."[82] So for Padgett, the Bible alone may not be able to solve the debate.

But, Padgett argues, the Bible does "hint at a particular direction."[83] Citing Ps 90:4, and the parallel passage 2 Pe 3:8, Padgett argues that the biblical text itself gives hints of one particular kind. That is, it gives direction to philosophical theologians that will lead them to the conclusion of what Padgett calls "relative timelessness." He writes, "Exactly which notion of eternity one develops from Scripture will depend as much on our philosophical theology as on our exegesis. Nevertheless, Scripture does seem to this exegete to point in the direction of relative timelessness."[84] So Padgett is not arguing that the statements of Scripture entail his position; rather he is arguing that his view seems to fit the biblical data more readily than the classical atemporal model.

The material surveyed thus far provides important context and background for what kind of model Padgett develops. Padgett is persuaded that neither the "everlasting" model (as in Wolterstorff), nor the classical atemporal view adequately account for other important theological and philosophical issues. While Padgett has rejected the everlasting model out of hand based on what he believes to be its theological inadequacy, he has spent the bulk of his argument attempting to defeat the classical atemporal view. This is so, perhaps, because his view of "relative timelessness," perhaps despite its name, shares much more in common with Wolterstorff's view than with the classical model.

---

82. Ibid., 36. In the context of making this point, Padgett quotes from Barr, *Biblical Words for Time*, 138, and draws his conclusions, in part, from Barr's discussion. See chapter 1, above, which addresses the nature of the debate as philosophical-theological and includes a brief discussion of Barr's ideas, especially in his criticism of Cullmann.

83. Padgett, *God, Eternity*, 37.

84. Ibid.

Padgett's "relative timelessness"[85] is so named because he argues that God is timeless *relative to* the physical time in the created order. He seeks to retain a high view of God's transcendence; therefore, in his view God is the creator of time as we know it; and therefore God is not limited or contained by time in any way. Padgett writes, "In this way, relative time-lessness attends to the intuition that God cannot be 'contained' within any created category."[86] But, Padgett argues, God is not absolutely timeless: God has his own time. Padgett explains, "Because God does really change in order to sustain a dynamic, changing world (assuming the process theory), there must be some sense in which God is temporal."[87] But this time must be different from our own; it is a pure duration that is relatively timeless compared to the created, physical time in the world.

Physical time, Padgett argues, is both measurable and relative to reference frames. He argues that in measuring physical time, metrics employed are relative to inertial frames of reference and change with gravity and velocity. He argues that this kind of measurement is not applicable to God in any way. He writes, "There is no reason to assume that such metrics apply to God."[88] Instead, Padgett proposes, God has a time that is pure duration, and that depends on God's being. He explains that "God's being is *conceptually prior* (in terms of ontological dependence) to eternity, even though God's life is not temporally prior to God's time."[89] This allows God to remain outside of physical time, and to be Lord of both physical time and his own, relatively timeless, eternity. He states that "even God's own time, eternity, exists only because God exists (and not the other way around)."[90] So Padgett conceives of God's relationship to time to be one in which God is thought of as being in some sense temporal, and therefore able to create and sustain the temporally dynamic world. Yet God also transcends the physical time of the created order—that which is measured by clocks and planetary orbits—and remains Lord over all time.

---

85. The view is developed and defended in chapter 6 of Padgett, *God, Eternity*, 122–46; and in Padgett, "Eternity as Relative Timelessness," 104–10. The former is concerned with defending against various philosophical arguments that have come about in the context of the larger work. The latter presents a succinct summary.

86. Padgett, "Eternity as Relative Timelessness," 105.

87. Ibid.

88. Ibid.

89. Ibid.

90. Ibid., 107.

In summarizing his position, Padgett offers three "theological points"[91] to lay out some of the implications of his model of God's relationship to time. The first is that God is not in any way limited by time: time does not in any way interfere with or limit God's actions or the accomplishment of his works. Padgett explains, "God could accomplish any series of events in any amount of [physical] time, no matter how small."[92] Second, just as God is not limited by time in his activity, neither does time limit God's life in any way. Normal aspects of human experience, such as fear of growing old or of dying, do not affect God, for he "is the ever-living Fountain of being itself."[93] Further, Padgett argues that time does not affect God's life because God is immutable, "unchanging in basic powers and attributes, living for ever and ever."[94] The final theological point Padgett makes is that God is the Lord of time because God has a plan, by which he is aware of all future possibilities and actualities. Padgett explains, "Time brings nothing outside the will and purposes of God. Even human free will, so often abused, is the gift of God and exists because God wills it to be so."[95]

Analysis of Padgett's Model

While Padgett does not specifically take the doctrine of the Incarnation into account, his argument represents a strong case against the classical atemporal model; and his model does seem to be compatible with the Incarnation. The primary strength of Padgett's argument is that he successfully demonstrates that the classical atemporal model of God's relationship to time requires (and is dependent on) the static, or stasis, view of the nature of time. Some of the implications of the static model of time for the doctrine of the Incarnation were discussed briefly in the previous chapter, and I'll explore them more fully in the concluding chapter. But Padgett has established a point critical to the thesis I am defending in this work: if God is atemporal as the classical model indicates, then time must be static and the temporal relations of past, present, and future have no basis in reality. This means (among other things) that for the defender of

91. Ibid., 107–8. The three points along with the explanation are summarized here.
92. Ibid., 107.
93. Ibid.
94. Ibid., 108.
95. Ibid.

the classical model the event of the Incarnation "occurs" (tenseless) at a specific time, but it is not past, present, or future. It simply "exists" (tenseless) as a single feature of God's atemporal simultaneous life, coincident with every other feature of God's life. This seems to rule out (or relegate to pure metaphor) several essential elements of both biblical and creedal descriptions of the Incarnation. Padgett's model, on the other hand, allows for temporal sequence in the divine life, and therefore would be compatible with the sequence indicated in the doctrine of the Incarnation.

Another important component in Padgett's argument is that he answers the concerns raised by atemporalists concerning God's transcendence. Padgett speaks of the intuition that "[g]iven our notion of God as an infinite, personal Creator, we would expect God to transcend time in some way."[96] Clearly, the idea that God must stand outside of his creation is more than an intuition or an expectation. It must be the case that God is not identical to, or contained within, that which he has created. In response to this concern, Padgett emphasizes that even if God is only "relatively" timeless, he is still "the Lord of time."[97] Indeed, it must be the case that both time and eternity are ontologically dependent on God, and not the other way around. Because God is the creator of the material world, then time must be grounded in God's very being. Padgett writes, "God's eternity is thus similar to other divine attributes that are always part of God's existence, but are not logically essential to the divine Being. Thus, God remains the Lord of time and the creator of our (measured) time."[98] Additionally, Padgett emphasizes that God "is the metaphysical precondition for the existence of eternity."[99] So, it seems that Padgett's model of God's relationship to time does give an adequate account for how God transcends the created order. Although it almost certainly is not detailed enough to satisfy the defenders of the classical atemporal view, it does eliminate any concerns of thinking of God being "subject to the vicissitudes" of time, or being "time's prisoner."

Despite its strengths, Padgett's model does have at least one important weakness: Padgett does not seem to address adequately the nature of time itself. The closest we get to an understanding of the nature of

96. Ibid., 93.
97. Ibid., 107.
98. Ibid.
99. Ibid., 106.

time in Padgett's work are statements such as, "God's choice, then, to live a certain kind of life—to be dynamic, active, changing—is the ground of the temporality of the universe. I have suggested that we understand time to be the dimension of the possibility of change. This dimension, like space, is a creation of God's."[100] And, "Time as we know it—that is, time with change and measure—did not take place before creation. We can, if we like, consider all of the infinite past before the first change as a single 'moment' of eternity."[101] So, Padgett is proposing that there are two kinds of time, one that is changeless and in which God exists, and one that was created with the material world and is observed through the measurements of change in material objects. According to Padgett, the time of the material world is within God's time: "Our time takes place within (and only because of the prior existence of) God's own time."[102] This seems to be, *prima facie*, correct.

But the problem, of course, is that Padgett has not offered an analysis of time, without which it is not clear what "relative timelessness" amounts to. When Padgett speaks of time as a "dimension of the possibility of change . . . [which is] like space, a creation of God's"[103] he seems to be open to the charge that he conceives of time as a dimension of space-time; which of course is a criticism he has leveled at the defenders of the classical view. But Padgett himself has also said that time is "the measure of change," and has seemed to endorse the Aristotelian model.[104] But how can time be both a system of measurement *and* the dimension within which exist the things being measured? This would be akin to saying that the inch is identical to the ruler. So it seems that Padgett's view of time as the dimension of potential change and the measurement of such change is internally inconsistent, or perhaps not worked out in sufficient detail.[105] But this is only a mild criticism of Padgett's work, for developing an adequate model of the nature of time has proven elusive.[106] It would seem that one possible solution to the problem in Padgett's model of the na-

100. Padgett, "New Doctrine of Eternity," 561.

101. Padgett, "Eternity as Relative Timelessness," 109.

102. Ibid., 107.

103. Padgett, "New Doctrine of Eternity," 561.

104. Ibid., 105.

105. Paul Helm also criticizes this aspect of Padgett's model, but emphasizes different reasons for his criticism. See Helm, "Response to Alan G. Padgett," 111–14.

106. See the discussion on this topic in chapter 1.

ture of time would be to say that time is composed of non-simultaneous events, and time is measured in the interval between those events. This idea will be further explored in the concluding chapter.

OPEN THEISM

Before moving on to address some important implications that arise from temporal models of God's relationship to time, it will be important to consider Open Theism. While (in my view) there are many reasons to reject Open Theism, the connections between some of the key points of debate and the topic of God's relation to time are obvious. There are a wide range of theological and philosophical concepts that are important to consider in a detailed analysis of Open Theism, including the nature and scope of human freedom, divine omniscience and providence, and the so-called problem of evil. But here, I'll focus my analysis on how these issues pertain to God and time.

Open Theism, broadly construed, is a perspective on both the nature of God and the nature of the universe. It shares many of the same concerns as process philosophy and process theology;[107] and is primarily driven by the desire to preserve a libertarian conception of human freedom in the face of a supposed conflict between that freedom and the traditional conception of God's omniscience. Gregory Boyd, for example, defines the classical conception of omniscience as he writes, "Most evangelical Christians take it for granted that God knows everything that is ever going to take place. They have been taught that the future is completely settled in God's mind and has been so from all eternity."[108] This, however, is unacceptable to Open Theists, who place great value on human freedom. Boyd continues, "If you think about the matter deeply, the classical view raises a number of thorny questions. For example, if every choice you've ever made was certain an eternity before you made it, were you really free when you made each choice?"[109] While the Open view of

107. See, e.g., Loomer, "Christian Faith and Process Philosophy," 70–98; and Cobb, "Whiteheadian Doctrine of God," 215–43. Both Sanders, "Historical Considerations," 93; and Hasker, "Philosophical Perspective," 139–40 are critical of Process Theology. Hasker admits that the Open view "seeks to preserve the strengths of . . . process theism."

108. Boyd, *God of the Possible*, 10.

109. Ibid., 10.

God is not as simple as a statement about omniscience and freedom, it seems that this is the starting point.[110]

While Open Theists may be driven by a desire to preserve a high view of human freedom, the matter quickly turns to important implications on the nature of creation and God's interaction with the created universe. Specifically, Boyd writes that Open Theists wish to engage their counterparts in "a debate about the nature of the future."[111] Boyd argues that Open Theists do not deny God's omniscience; but that they deny the future can be known. He explains, "Though open theists are often accused of denying God's omniscience because they deny the classical view of foreknowledge, this criticism is unfounded. Open theists affirm God's omniscience as emphatically as anybody does. The issue is not whether God's knowledge is perfect. It is. The issue is about the nature of the reality that God perfectly knows. More specifically, what is the content of the reality of the future? Whatever it is, we all agree that God perfectly knows it."[112]

Clark H. Pinnock agrees with this perspective. He argues that since future events are shaped by the free choices of creatures, the future is not determined, and cannot exist. He writes, "The future does not yet exist and therefore cannot be infallibly anticipated, even by God. Future decisions cannot in every way be foreknown, because they have not yet been made. God knows everything that can be known—but God's foreknowledge does not include the undecided."[113] So the Open view contains within it the conviction that the future does not yet exist, and this is why God cannot know certain elements of it.

This idea, of course, has immediately obvious implications for God's relationship to time. A denial of the classical atemporal model is entailed by these important core values in Open Theism. If God does not know the future (or some aspects of the future) because it does not yet exist, then obviously God cannot be in full possession of the whole of his life at once. God must wait for the future to come to pass before he can know it.

---

110. Frame, for example, argues that the idea of libertarian freedom "is the engine that drives open theism." Frame, *No Other God*, 119.

111. Boyd, *Possible*, 15.

112. Ibid., 15–16.

113. Pinnock, "Systematic Theology," 123.

In the context of defending Open Theism, Hasker presents an argument designed to refute the classical model of God's relationship to time.[114] In the first step of his argument, Hasker points out that "the doctrine of divine timelessness is not taught in the Bible."[115] Further, Hasker notes that "the biblical writers undeniably do present God as living, acting and reacting in time. . . ."[116] In making this statement, Hasker is in agreement with many others who have rejected the atemporal view, but who are not Open Theists.[117] Additionally, Hasker attempts to make the point that the idea of "timelessness," and what it would be for God to be timeless is not easily defined. He writes, "But even if divine timelessness is not incoherent and not in conflict with other key beliefs, it seems we have at best only a tenuous grasp on the conception of God as a timeless being."[118] Hasker suggests that even if he is correct in his assessment of divine timelessness, it may be that Christians would have to accept it if there were clear and compelling reasons to do so. However, he contends, there are no such reasons. Hasker concludes that "divine timelessness is strongly dependent for its justification on neo-Platonic metaphysics, and in particular on the doctrine of divine simplicity (whose intelligibility has also been strongly challenged). Once this metaphysical taproot has been severed, the prospects for divine timelessness are not bright—nor, I think, should they be."[119] It seems, then, that Hasker's argument with regard to God's relationship to time is similar to portions of Wolterstorff's: the Bible seems to describe God as doing many things he couldn't do if he were atemporal; therefore the burden of proof is on the atemporalist to prove why divine timelessness must be accepted; but no proof is available; so the classical view must be rejected.

There are two important points to make with regard to Open Theism in the context of developing a model of God's relation to time. First, while the Open view happens to agree that the classical atemporal model of God's relationship to time is wrong—that is, God is not atemporal in the

114. The argument is in Hasker, "Philosophical Perspective," 128–29. See also Hasker, *God, Time, and Knowledge*.

115. Hasker, "Philosophical Perspective," 128.

116. Ibid.

117. See, e.g., the previous discussion of Padgett and Wolterstorff. Hasker refers to the work of each.

118. Hasker, "Philosophical Perspective," 129.

119. Ibid.

classical sense—the failure of the atemporal model does not entail Open Theism. The Open Theist is committed to the idea that God does not have foreknowledge, as foreknowledge is classically defined. This demands that God must be temporal. But Open Theism is obviously not the only alternative available to the classical atemporal model of God's relationship to time.

The second important point to make is this: The Open view fails to account for the Incarnation irrespective of its model of God's relationship to time. Open Theists agree with Boethius that God's exhaustive foreknowledge and significant human freedom are incompatible. Unlike Boethius, the Open Theists place the higher priority on creaturely freedom and deny that God can know the future actions of free creatures. But when the Incarnation is considered, it would seem that God must have comprehensive knowledge about many details of free human action in order to enact his plan in a way that would achieve the desired results. God must have known that there would be one like John the Baptist to prepare the way, that Joseph would heed the advice of the angel and not put Mary away, that the disciples would follow Jesus, that the owner of the donkey would provide it for Jesus' use, that the Roman authorities would agree to crucify Jesus in spite of the fact that he committed no crime. But since the Open Theist would deny that God could know *free* decisions, then the only option is that God directly caused these decisions and actions of his creatures. If the Open Theist allows that God did directly cause these actions, then why is there a complaint that foreknowledge is incompatible with freedom? An equally viable solution to the problem (if exhaustive foreknowledge and freedom are incompatible) would be that human beings are not free. So regarding the essential elements of the Incarnation, including the details of Jesus' life foretold by prophecy and necessary for the accomplishing salvation, the Open Theist must hold one of these two positions: either that the Incarnation was merely a chance happening, and even God did not know if it was going to turn out as planned; or that every element surrounding Jesus' life was directly caused by God. The former violates the notion of biblical prophecy and fulfillment; the latter is contrary to the central claims of Open Theism. The conclusion is that the Open Theism perspective does not have an adequate account for the Incarnation, regardless of its view of time.

SOME PHILOSOPHICAL-THEOLOGICAL IMPLICATIONS
OF TEMPORAL MODELS

Based on the above brief survey of the various forms of temporal arguments, one immediately obvious implication is that such models are not compatible with Thomistic-type "strong" immutability. If God is temporal in any of the ways examined, there is some change in God. Clearly God cannot change in any essential attribute, but on temporal accounts of God's existence, he does undergo relational changes to creatures and other aspects of the created order. Additionally, temporal models require that there is temporal succession or sequence in God's life. Succession in God's life is specifically denied by Thomistic immutability. Therefore, if *any* version of the temporal model is correct, then God is not immutable in this strong, Thomistic sense. More specifically, Senor has argued that the incarnation event itself is an example of a change in God: God the Son changed in his intrinsic (though not essential) qualities in the assumption of a human nature. It seems that, if successful, arguments such as Senor's will rule out Thomistic immutability specifically from what is meant in the doctrine that the Son took on human nature. In place of Thomistic immutability, the defender of the temporal perspective can offer that God does not change fundamentally *through time*. In the following chapter, a proposal will be made for how immutability should be understood as it relates to the Incarnation and God's relationship to time.

Perhaps equally as obvious as the implication concerning immutability is the necessity of a dynamic theory of time in temporal models. In the previous chapter it was argued that the static or stasis theory of time is essential to the classical atemporal model of God's relationship to time. This is the case, it was argued, based on the fact that if God is timelessly eternal, then his perspective on the created order is the correct one. If God sees all moments of time as one static feature of his life, then this is how the created order actually is—God's atemporality entails that the stasis theory of time is true. But it would also seem that the reverse is true. If the human experience of dynamic time is simply a phenomena internal to the human mind with no basis in reality—if the stasis view of time is correct—this entails that God is atemporal; he would transcend the flow of time and see it all at once. This, of course, sounds very much like what the defenders of the atemporal view assert. But if the stasis theory of time entails that God is atemporal, there is but one alternative left for those who deny that God is timeless: the dynamic theory of time is true. The relationships of past, present, and future reflect an actual feature of reality.

One final implication for temporal models must be noted; one that goes to one of the historical motivations for the origin of the debate on God's relationship to time. Recall that Boethius developed his model of divine timeless eternity out of a concern to preserve the notion of human freedom in the face of absolute divine foreknowledge. The ironic twist is that nearly 1,600 years later, those who invoke Boethius[120] have developed intricate arguments which, when taken to their logical conclusions, seem to rule out that which Boethius sought to preserve.[121] If time is static and the future is fixed, and if all events past, present, and future share equal ontological status, then it would seem difficult to construct a theological model that would preserve any meaningful notion of human freedom. On this point, some defenders of the classical atemporal model are in perfect agreement with their Open Theist counterparts. Both parties agree that there is a conflict between absolute divine foreknowledge and significant human freedom. And while the classical view seeks to preserve foreknowledge, Open Theism seeks to preserve freedom. But the obvious alternative to this dilemma is to deny that there is a conflict between absolute divine foreknowledge and significant human freedom. It is important to offer this alternative because some defenders of the classical atemporal view may misunderstand the arguments I am presenting here and assume that I am offering just another argument in favor of the "Open" view of God. It will be sufficient to (once again) state it clearly: there is no conflict between absolute divine foreknowledge and significant human freedom. Of course I'll have to leave the details of this assertion (and an adequate defense of it) for another project. The important point to make here is that arguments against the classical view of God's relationship to time, and in favor of temporal alternatives to the classical view, are not necessarily committed to a denial of God's absolute foreknowledge.

TEMPORAL MODELS AND THE INCARNATION

In chapter 2, I presented a three-fold paradigm for understanding God's relationship to time. The Incarnation seems to indicate a sequence in the

---

120. See Helm, "Divine Timeless Eternity," and also Frame, *No Other God*.

121. This tendency perhaps follows naturally from some forms of Calvinism, and certainly from all forms of theistic determinism.

divine life: sequence in the Incarnation event and its permanence; sequence in the life of God the Son incarnate in Jesus Christ; and sequence in the finished work of the Son in the atonement. In chapter 3, I argued that the classical atemporal view of God's relationship to time is inadequate in accounting for this sequence. In this chapter, I showed that temporal arguments for God's relationship to time are able to account for this sequence. Indeed, it was shown that Thomas Senor uses the Incarnation as the very basis of his argument. Senor's essay is an admirable attempt to give proper weight to this essential doctrine at the heart of Christianity. Senor's argument is not without its weaknesses, but it represents a good step in the right direction. While I hope to offer some important modifications to his approach (given the weaknesses discovered), the argument in the following chapter begins as Senor's: with the priority given to the Incarnation as the basis for understanding God's relation to time.

Nicholas Wolterstorff has also presented a forceful argument against the classical atemporal view, and has done so with at least some concern for the Incarnation. While the Incarnation does not seem to be the driving force behind Wolterstorff's position, he does take it into account and challenge defenders of the classical view for their inability to account for the doctrine. Alan Padgett does not deal directly with the Incarnation, but there was nothing discovered in his essay that would create problems for the doctrine. While his view has weaknesses, it is assumed here that none of them have serious negative implications for the Incarnation. The only alternative conception surveyed in this chapter that could not account for the Incarnation was that of Open Theism. But the Open view fails on its denial of God's foreknowledge, not on its view of God's relationship to time.

It seems clear that for the theist who wishes to preserve a robust doctrine of the Incarnation, the classical atemporal model must be abandoned. The following chapter will continue this idea and present a proposal for an alternative to the classical atemporal view.

5

An Argument from the Incarnation

B ASED ON THE MATERIAL surveyed in the previous chapters, I will now offer some conclusions; and I will attempt to present some insights into God's relation to time based on these conclusions. This chapter will focus on Incarnation as the priority for philosophical theology; and it will show that when this doctrine is given priority, the classical atemporal model becomes far less tenable. I will also include a brief discussion on the nature of time and offer some tentative conclusions, as well as a modest proposal for the manner in which the debate should be framed in contemporary philosophical theology.

It was evident in the survey in chapters 3 and 4 that the notion of properties in the person of Christ resulting from the unity of natures is the center of much controversy. Therefore, I will address these concerns briefly, and will comment on the suitability of the "*qua* move" in the context of the debate. Once these outstanding issues have been addressed, I will focus again on the three-fold paradigm first proposed in chapter 2. This paradigm will be re-traced in light of the intervening discussion and will be formulated as a modest proposal for how the Incarnation should impact the debate on God's relation to time. Specifically, the model will be used to suggest that God does experience temporal sequence in his existence. Finally, I will offer a brief defense of this proposal that responds to several possible challenges that have been suggested. It will be argued that the proposal offered here is the best option available for preserving a robust doctrine of the Incarnation—one that best fits both Scriptural data and historic statements of the church.

METHODOLOGY AND THE PRIORITY OF THE INCARNATION

I suggested in chapter 1 that two primary theological concerns have determined the trajectory for the development of models of God's relation to time: God's immutability; and the apparent incompatibility between human freedom and God's foreknowledge. Augustine argued that time itself was an aspect of the created order, and therefore God stood outside of time, as he cannot be contained within creation. Augustine sought to preserve a high view of God's transcendence: God must be wholly other than his created order, which is characterized by movement and change. God, as creator, stands above and outside of the material realm of movement and change. Augustine was, no doubt, informed by a neo-Platonic perspective on reality; and brought certain of its tenets to bear as he worked out the philosophical elements of his biblical worldview. In contrast to the dynamic, changing physical realm, God's eternity was seen as the dimension of changelessness.

Writing more than 100 years after Augustine, Boethius shared some of Augustine's concerns; but his model of God's relation to time was borne directly out of a desire to preserve a high view of human freedom in the face of its apparent incompatibility with absolute divine foreknowledge. The two enduring features of Boethius's work—perhaps inchoate in Augustine, and certainly seen vividly in contemporary defenders of the atemporal view—are his definition of eternity and his "man on the hill" illustration. Boethius approached the question of God's relation to time by way of *definition*: he writes, "So what does rightly claim the title of eternal is that which grasps and possesses simultaneously the entire fullness of life without end; no part of the future is lacking to it, and no part of the past has escaped it."[1] This resulted in the spatializing of time: God is like a man sitting on a high hill, observing the passage of events below him, each event equally present to his vision. So Boethius resolved his dilemma through a modification of terminology: God does not have *fore*knowledge, he just has direct immediate knowledge of all temporal moments in a durationless present.

Chapter 1 also demonstrated that the philosophical developments regarding both the nature of time and God's relation to it have taken place largely outside the context of biblical theology. The Bible universally uses temporal language to describe God's life and activity. In developing and

1. Boethius, *Consolation*, 5.6 (111).

refining their arguments, defenders of the classical atemporal view of God's relation to time do not have the luxury of appealing to Scriptural evidence. This fact became clearer in chapters 3 and 4, as authors on all sides of the debate seem to be in agreement that the Bible nowhere describes nor gives direct evidence for a divine timeless eternity or an atemporal divine life. Rather than depend on biblical theology, models of God's relation to time have traditionally been the task of philosophical theology.[2]

Informed by the history of the debate, contemporary defenders of the classical atemporal model have employed the tools of philosophical theology to refine, develop, and expand upon the ideas first laid down by Augustine and Boethius. Additionally, they have incorporated and built upon the work of Thomas Aquinas, primarily as their work has been related to the concept of God's immutability. Contemporary contributors have taken for granted the fact that the Augustinian/Boethian model entails a Thomistic sense of immutability: if God is atemporally eternal, there can be no sequence or succession of any kind in God's being or his life. Clearly, if God possesses the fullness of his life *at once*, it is nonsensical to attempt to refer to "before" or "after" as it pertains to any action or decision of God.[3] Those categories simply do not apply to God. Every feature of his life is instantaneously coterminous with every other.

This model of God's mode of being was affirmed by all those defenders of the classical view that have been surveyed in the course of this work; and is found almost universally in the broader range of literature written from the perspective of classical theism. It is from this premise that the defenders of the atemporal view have then attempted to account for the Incarnation. Swinburne began with the classical view; and then he appealed to "mystery"[4] as a solution to the apparent incompatibility between the atemporal view and the Incarnation. Likewise, Leftow began with the atemporal view and then created a defense, arguing that

2. This point was discussed in detail in chapter 1.

3. Some may argue that God's actions can be ordered "logically," thus maintaining a sequence without a temporal aspect. In spite of this argument, the atemporal view nevertheless asserts that all of God's actions and decisions occur at once, with no temporal relation whatsoever to any other event, decision, or action.

4. Swinburne, "Timelessness of God, II," 486. Here (as in chapter 2) I am focusing on Swinburne's early efforts to defend the classical atemporal view. All of this is notwithstanding his change of mind and abandonment of the atemporal view in later works.

since the church fathers believed in both God's timelessness and the Incarnation, there must be no conflict.[5] Finally, Helm was shown to have placed the theological priority on a Thomistic sense of immutability and the Boethian sense of "divine fullness."[6] And by Helm's own admission, the Incarnation is an exception to his doctrine of the "two standpoints," to which it does not apply.[7] Virtually all authors writing on the topic from the classical atemporal perspective employ a methodology by which the Augustinian and Boethian models, along with a Thomistic view of immutability, are *assumed* and laid down as the foundation. The details of the defense of the classical view in the face of various challenges are then built on that foundation.

In the context of Christian Trinitarian theism, this methodology is unwise at best. It is not sufficient for Christian philosophical theology to assume a particular model of God's relation to time (for whatever reason), and then attempt to construct models of that relation that are in accord with the most essential doctrines of Christianity. To do so would be to put the philosophical cart before the theological horse, if for no other reason than that the Incarnation is essential to Christian theism, and divine timelessness is not—a fact that is even admitted by some defenders of the classical atemporal model.[8] The primary distinguishing feature of Christianity as compared to other forms of theism is the worship of Jesus Christ of Nazareth as the Incarnate Son of God. Therefore, a methodological approach that does proper justice to this necessary and essential doctrine will utilize the Incarnation as the theological starting point—the center—for the development of all manner of philosophical-theological concerns, including the question of God's relation to time. Additionally, the Incarnation must serve as the standard by which proposed models of God's relation to time should be evaluated. In short, the doctrine of the Incarnation must be given the status of "control belief" over the debate on God's relation to time.

The source data of the doctrine of the Incarnation are the biblical statements about the person of Christ; and chapter 2 detailed specific passages that have been considered as such. That chapter also pointed out

5. Leftow, "Timeless God Incarnate," 273.

6. See Helm, "Divine Timeless Eternity," 29–35. Helm does not mention Aquinas, but the description given is in accord with Aquinas's exposition of immutability.

7. See ibid., 54, 58.

8. See, e.g., Leftow, "Timeless God Incarnate," 273.

how the creedal statements of Nicaea and Chalcedon ultimately were systematized formulae based on the councils' understanding of the teaching of many of those passages of Scripture. One of the most obvious elements of the doctrine is that it depends on a literal interpretation of the passages in question. It is clear from the creedal statements that the councils believed that God himself literally became a first-person participant in the created order by taking on human nature and human flesh in the person of Jesus of Nazareth. The remarkable feature of this doctrine (for the present topic) is that the biblical statements also universally use the language of time and change to describe the Incarnation. The passages in question describe a state of affairs in which God the Son—the Word—existed in a state un-joined to human nature and human flesh; and then there was a specific action taken by the Son to assume human nature and a specific human body; which resulted in a new state of affairs which is God the Son living in the Incarnate state in perpetuity. The temporal implications of the statements in these passages are unavoidable.

It could be—however difficult it would be in figuring out *how* it could be—that the passages forming the foundation for the doctrine of the Incarnation are only *partially* literally true: the fact of the Incarnation is true, but the temporal aspects describing it are not literally true, and should therefore be interpreted symbolically, metaphorically, or analogically. This is, of course, what defenders of the classical atemporal view claim about all passages of Scripture that utilize the language of time and change with regard to the Divine life. This was seen in the authors surveyed in chapter 3; and it is clear that the atemporal view depends logically on a metaphorical interpretation of temporal language in Scripture. Helm, for example, writes, "On the eternalist [atemporal] view, in revealing his will God must accommodate himself to human spatiotemporal conditions by the use of sensory, figurative, anthropomorphic language about himself, particularly by using the language of change."[9] But if the doctrine of the Incarnation is to be the theological center, and if this doctrine depends on the literal truth of the biblical statements, then the defender of the classical view must demonstrate that there is another doctrine—at least equally important to Christian theism as is the Incarnation—that demands that the passages concerning the Incarnation be taken as figurative. As Wolterstorff has argued,[10] the defender of the atemporal view

9. Helm, "Response to Critics," 79.

10. See, e.g., Wolterstorff, "Unqualified Divine Temporality," 189.

bears the burden of proof—and this is especially applicable in the case of the biblical passages describing the Incarnation.

But what have the defenders of the atemporal view offered that could be taken as a good reason to take such passages in a figurative or metaphorical sense? Owing its dependence on Boethius, the classical atemporal view claims to arise on the intuition[11] that God must possess "fullness of life;" that God is utterly immutable (in the Thomistic sense),[12] and therefore could not have any succession of states of affairs in his life. But this model was not borne out of a concern for a particular doctrine of Christian theism. Rather, it was intended to solve a philosophical puzzle (how humans can be free if God foreknows all they will do).[13] If one looks to Augustine, the additional factor is that time is assumed to be an aspect only of the created order; which lends itself nicely to the Boethian illustration of the man on the hill. Once this model of the nature of time—and of God's relation to it—is assumed, the concepts of fullness of life (as described by the atemporalist) and Thomistic-type immutability logically follow. But, if the divine fullness of life and immutability are entailed by the atemporal model in the first place, these can hardly be appealed to as evidence for the atemporal model. And so in the end, the classical atemporal model offers no reason to take the biblical statements about the Incarnation as figurative or metaphorical with respect to the temporal language in those passages. Rather, the atemporal view is a model that is self-consistent, but at odds with a straightforward reading of the Bible, including biblical passages that describe the Incarnation.

If the classical model of God's relation to time is true, then the biblical statements describing what took place in the Incarnation simply cannot be taken to mean what they might be interpreted to mean on a straightforward reading of the text. But a literal interpretation of these passages seems essential for the doctrine, at least as it was developed by the councils at Nicaea and Chalcedon. If the Incarnation is to serve as a control belief in the debate about God's relation to time, then the atem-

---

11. Helm uses the idea of intuition in Helm, "Divine Timeless Eternity," 29.

12. Below I will offer an alternative description of immutability will be offered. Recall from chapter 1 that "Thomistic" immutability is that which rules out any sequence or succession of any kind in God.

13. This was at the heart of Boethius's work, which is now cited by many as the *locus classicus* of the classical atemporal model of God's relation to time.

poral model becomes far less tenable than first seemed when considering notions of divine fullness and immutability.

THE NATURE OF TIME AND ETERNITY

In addition to the methodological concerns, the nature of time itself is an unavoidable question. But on this question, philosophers and theologians have been sharply divided, and have offered a myriad of proposals regarding the nature of time and eternity. This fact was seen clearly in chapter 1. Although there were familiar strains in each figure examined, each was different in significant ways. Beginning with the ancients, Plato put forth the idea of time being the "moving image of eternity."[14] Eternity was changeless and motionless; while time was the image of eternity in the changing, moving physical world. Highlighting the contrast between himself and Plato, Aristotle proposed that time was the measurement of the motion of physical bodies.[15] In Newton's study of the motion of bodies in the physical world, he made a distinction between *absolute* time (metaphysical time, composed of uniformly flowing duration) and *relative* time (marked by the motion of clocks and planetary objects).[16] Einstein jettisoned the metaphysical aspect of this model and argued that time was *only* that which clocks measured;[17] and therefore only *relative* time was real time. In modern philosophy, the debate took an interesting turn when McTaggart made the claim that time was not an actual feature of the real universe at all.

It is from this heritage of secular philosophy and natural science that Christians have developed their own philosophical models. Augustine accepted the Platonic premise that time was a feature only of the physical universe; and therefore he concluded that time was created with the material world. From that point forward (until very recently) that premise has gone unchallenged. The influence of modern science on contemporary theology has bolstered the status of the initial premise through the introduction of Special Relativity into the debate. Time and space have been so tightly joined that both theologians and philosophers alike speak of the "spatiotemporal" universe, and of "space-time." What is missed in

14. Plato, *Timaeus*, 37 (2:530).
15. Aristotle, *Physics*, 4.11 (1:371).
16. Newton, *The Principia*, 408.
17. See, e.g., Davies, *About Time*, 32.

this move, however, is the fact that there is a particular standpoint regarding the metaphysical questions that comes along with this kind of account of Relativity. Specifically, the philosophy behind the conclusions about the nature of time places undue emphasis on the idea that time is only a feature of the material world, and that nothing exists "outside" of space. This is not to say that Relativity theory ought to be jettisoned, for it has proven useful in the physical sciences. Rather, those who employ it in their arguments should recognize that concerning the very nature of time, Relativity is bound by its definition of time to purely physical, material terms. To illustrate the point: assume that all material bodies in the universe stood still—that is, all reference frames came to relative rest to one another—would time then cease to exist? On Relativity accounts, it would. But if under such static circumstances there could still be activity outside of the purely physical, material world—for example, in the human mind,[18] this would show that the minds could continue to think and experience temporal sequence.[19] So while physical objects are used to mark out time; physical time is not all there is to time. Time also can be described in metaphysical terms. It seems, then, that in the debate about God's relation to time, it is unwise to make the assumption that time is somehow bound to the physical, material universe.

But if time is not constrained to the material universe, then what alternative concepts of it are available? One may be tempted to say, with Augustine, "What, then, is time? If no one asks of me, I know; if I wish to explain to him who asks, I know not."[20] But while a precise definition of time may remain elusive, it seems possible to (at least) *recognize* time. If this is true, then a formal definition of time is not necessary in order to solve the debate. Rather, all that would be necessary would be to determine if time applies in any way to—or can be recognized in—God's life. Additionally, Callahan's guidance[21] is apropos: "[C]ommon knowledge of time is something that we must consider, and any detailed examination of time must not be out of harmony with it. Otherwise we should be ex-

18. A purely naturalistic account of time would argue that even activity in the human mind is "matter in motion." This further emphasizes the point that if theists want to maintain the concept of mind as non-material, then the naturalistic assumptions about time ought to be abandoned.

19. Augustine himself seems to suggest this in *Confessions* 11.23.29 (*NPNF*[1] 1:171).

20. Ibid., 11.14.17 (*NPNF*[1] 1:168).

21. Callahan's comments were first discussed in chapter 1.

plaining something other than that which men in general call time."[22] In other words, human beings are able to recognize time through a succession of states—and that succession is what constitutes time.

Relying on human experience to recognize time is not to suggest that time is mind-dependent, or entirely subjective. Rather, the Bible itself gives very clear guidelines for recognizing time. Beginning with the creation account in Genesis,[23] the movement of planetary objects serve as "signs" or indicators of time: "Let there be lights in the firmament of the heavens to divine the day from the night; and let them be for signs and seasons, and for days and years."[24] This, of course, does not indicate that time is either created with or constituted in the movement of these objects. Rather, the movement of the bodies serves as indication of time's succession and as measurement devices for certain intervals of time. The measurement devices are useful because they relate to one another through events (the revolution of the earth around the sun, the revolution of the moon around the earth, etc.). Great practical utility is derived from this: farmers know when to plant and know that their crops will thrive during a particular interval between certain events; businessmen know when to open the doors of their shops; and customers know when the shop doors will be open. The passage of time is marked out and recognizable in the movement of, among other things, planetary objects. These objects are useful in marking out temporal intervals because their motions are related to one another through specific events, such as the earth moving about the sun in orbit.

If time can be marked out by these factors (even though it is not constituted by them) then a more formal (yet modest) proposal can be made with regard to the nature of time: the concept of time itself consists in the succession of states of affairs. If events punctuate (or serve as transitions for) successive states of affairs, then whenever it is the case that there is a series of events, then the passage of time is recognized. Although not spelled out, this idea seems to be contained within Leftow's description of events and time; as he says that the primary "occupants of time" are

22. Callahan, *Four Views of Time in Ancient Philosophy*, 97.

23. It is important to note that nowhere in the creation account are any indications given that time itself was created. Rather, the account focuses on God's creation of the material universe; and the act of creation is said to have spanned a period of six days.

24. Gen 1:14.

events and states, and not things.[25] He writes, "What we primarily speak of as located at times, then, are states (e.g., of existence), events, processes, and the like. I take it that these *are* what are primarily located at times, and that things involved in these states . . . are located at times because their states, etc., are."[26] This idea is also seen in Wolterstorff's discussion as he writes, "Events are obviously within time. They are that by virtue of occurring within a period (or moment) of time, hence of beginning at a time and of ending at a time. . . ."[27]

If this is the case, then some important conclusions can be offered regarding the manner in which the debate on God's relation to time should be framed. First, time is not a material entity, nor is it bound by material entities. Second, material objects were given by God in the physical universe, the motion of which can serve as an indicator of time and for measurement of temporal intervals. Time, then, is not the measurement or the movement of objects. Time itself does not have an intrinsic metric, but can be marked out by any regular physical process. This, of course, means that time can continue to flow even when there is no motion of material objects. If these conclusions are correct, then it does not seem to make sense to think of a material object being "contained within" time, as if time were a material vessel of some kind. When one makes reference to a year, it is not the case that the earth, while moving around the sun, is contained within the year; rather the physical event in question *marks out the year*. Therefore, it makes no sense to speak of anything other than events to be "in" or "outside of" time.

If correct, the above discussion has immediately obvious application for how the present debate ought to be framed. Perhaps one reason that the debate has engendered such a high degree of controversy is because the language used is often imprecise. To speak of God as if he could be "in" or "outside of" time conjures up images of God being subject to or contained within some feature of the material universe.[28] Clearly the concerns expressed by the defenders of the atemporal view over God's transcendence become important at this point. But such language not only stirs controversy, it also seems to distract from the issue most central to

25. Leftow, *Time and Eternity*, 18.

26. Ibid.

27. Wolterstorff, "Unqualified Divine Temporality," 202.

28. As in, for example, Helm, "Divine Timeless Eternity," 30–31, in which Helm refers to the possibility of God being "subject to the vicissitudes of temporal passage."

the debate. The important issue does not seem to be whether God is "in" or "outside" of time, as if the participants in the debate were attempting to ascertain God's "temporal location." Rather it seems as if the question at the heart of the debate is whether God experiences the coming-to-be and passing-away of states of affairs. Simply put, the debate on God's relation to time can be boiled down to this question: Does God experience genuine temporal passage of successive states of affairs, or does he experience his life as one singular atemporal whole? If there are temporally ordered events in God's life, whereby states of affairs come into and pass out of existence, then God experiences those events in that order. If there are not events so ordered in God's life, then he does not have such an experience. The classical atemporal view holds that there is no such series of events in God's life; and I am arguing here that the Incarnation indicates that there is such a series.

One final point must be made regarding the nature of time before moving on in the discussion. Chapter 3 highlighted the fact that the classical atemporal model requires a static theory of time. Recall that Padgett's strategy for defeating the classical view was to demonstrate that the static view of time is false. Padgett writes, "The main objection I have to the timeless model is simply stated: It is true only if the stasis theory of time is true. Since the stasis theory of time is false, we should reject the timeless view. . . ."[29] On this conclusion, Padgett seems to be correct on at least two counts. First, the stasis theory of time is essential to the classical model. This is made clear even in Boethius's use of the man on the hill illustration. While time appears to be dynamic to participants within the temporal order, it is actually static, and therefore existing and visible to God all at once. The static theory of time by itself rules out any possibility of a sequence of events in God's life. It also has important implications for how the life and work of Christ in the Incarnation are to be understood. Second, Padgett is also correct in that the static model is false. Important conclusions will be made in the following sections about the dynamic nature of time; but it will be sufficient at this point to say this: just as the Incarnation indicates a sequence of events in God's life, so also does it indicate that time is dynamic. Before offering final conclusions on this idea, however, it will be important to address the topic of God's properties. This

---

29. Padgett, "Eternity as Relative Timelessness," 95.

topic was shown in chapters 2, 3, and 4 to be a matter of debate, especially with regard to the Incarnation.

TWO NATURES, DIVINE PROPERTIES, AND THE INCARNATION

The debate about God's relation to time has highlighted specific concerns about divine attributes[30] in the person of Jesus Christ. Chapter 2 highlighted what has been the firm and straightforward affirmation of Christian theology since the first council was called to address the matter: in the Person of Jesus Christ, the Son of God is united to human nature and human flesh, so that in the one person are two natures: divine and human. There are two important emphases in this Chalcedonian statement with respect to the two natures of Christ. First, the creed emphasizes that in Christ are both natures, and that both natures are fully present. The creed states that Christ is "perfect in divinity, and perfect in humanity," that he is "manifested in two natures," and that, "the properties of each [nature] are kept." This fullness of both natures is reflected in contemporary references to Christ as being truly God and truly man. Second, the creed emphasizes that the natures are united into a single person. The union does not produce any "confusion, change, division, or separation;" and "they are not divided into two persons, but belong to the one Only-begotten Son, the Word of God, the Lord Jesus Christ." This dual emphasis of *two natures* in *one person* is captured in the biblical statements of the Christ as "Immanuel . . . God with us."[31] This idea is reflected in statements such as that made by Anselm: "For there is not in Christ one who is God, another one who is the human being . . . rather, the very same one who is also the human being is God. For the 'Word made flesh' (John 1:14) assumed another nature, not another person."[32] Furthermore, the Incarnation is said to be revelatory: it reveals God to mankind. As Col 2:9 says of Christ, "In Him dwells all the fullness of the Godhead bodily." What is established by orthodoxy with respect to the Incarnation is that Christ is human in the

---

30. The authors surveyed in this book have, for the most part, used the terms "property" and "attribute" interchangeably; and "property" is used more often. To describe accidental properties, the terminology typically employed is "non-essential property." Therefore in this chapter, as in the previous two, "attribute" and "property" are used interchangeably; and the term "non-essential property" will be used to refer to accidental properties.

31. Matt 1:23.

32. Anselm, *On the Incarnation of the Word*, 11 (252–53).

same way and to the same extent as other human beings;[33] and he is God in the same way and to the same extent as the Father.

This emphasis of Jesus being truly God and truly man has direct implications for the debate on God's relation to time. One vital idea implied in the Chalcedonian statement is that there can be no contradiction in the union of the two natures in the one person of Christ. That is, there is no incompatibility between the human nature and the divine nature that could prevent them from being jointly possessed by a single person. Oftentimes, however, theologians are hesitant to make such affirmations; and the presence of two natures in Christ is often spoken of as a *paradox*, as if there were some contradiction that must nevertheless be affirmed. For example, Pannenberg writes, "Jesus now appears as a being bearing and uniting two *opposed* substances in himself. From this conception all the insoluble problems of the doctrine of the two natures result."[34] It seems clear, however, that characterizing the Incarnation as a paradox is based on the faulty presumption that humanity and divinity are opposed substances.[35] If there was an incompatibility or contradiction in the union of the two natures, it is hard to see how the early church could have affirmed that there was such a union. As Gunton states, it must be asked "why . . . the members of the council of Chalcedon were *able* to juxtapose (if that is the correct word) the human and the divine in the 'one and the same Christ.'"[36]

But it seems that the classical atemporal model of God's relation to time *introduces* a paradox into the doctrine of the Incarnation. That Jesus lived an ordinary temporal life is undeniable. But, the classical model asserts that God the Son is timelessly eternal. So it seems that in Christ there is both atemporal eternity and ordinary temporal sequence, which is clearly a contradiction. Gunton explains this difficulty as he writes, "If time is the moving image, the implication appears to be that eternity is unmoving. And if eternity is by definition motionless, what is it do-

33. It is here assumed that the presence of sin is an example of what is common to man, but not essential to being human. Therefore, Christ is human in that he possesses all of those elements essential to human nature. See, e.g., Morris, *Logic of God Incarnate*, 40.

34. Pannenberg, *Jesus: God and Man*, 284. Emphasis added.

35. The point here is made more vivid in the biblical descriptions of man being made in God's image.

36. Gunton, *Yesterday and Today*, 105.

ing in the very temporal figure of Jesus of Nazareth?"[37] The conclusion seems obvious: it is the atemporal model of God's relation that creates the paradox in the first place. Again, as Gunton concludes, "Against this background it is possible to see orthodox Christology as not the slave but the critic of Hellenistic philosophy."[38] In other words, when the concept of divine timeless eternity is removed, the apparent paradoxical aspects of the Incarnation disappear.

The struggle over this apparent paradox was revealed in both chapters 3 and 4, as was seen in the utilization of the "*qua* move" as a suggested solution. Recall that this maneuver is simply the construction of a reduplicative set of propositions as:

> Christ *qua* human is temporal; Christ *qua* divine is atemporal.[39]

This form of reduplication of contradicting predicates could presumably be applied to all manner of apparent contradiction or paradox when a property essential to one nature seems to contradict a property essential to the other. Ultimately, however, a Christian who desires to preserve an orthodox view of the Incarnation should find this response to such apparent paradoxes to be rather unsatisfying.[40] In the words of Morris, this maneuver "accomplishes nothing except for muddying the waters."[41] Clearly the framers of the Chalcedonian statement had in mind possible objections to the doctrinal statement based on apparently incompatible properties in Christ. The council, however, has specifically ruled out this maneuver. In a statement that is almost prophetic in its anticipation of the *qua* move, the council wrote, "The union does not destroy the difference of the two natures, but on the contrary the properties of each are kept, and both are joined in one person and *hypostasis*."[42] In other words, all essential properties belonging to each nature are simultaneously present in the one person of Jesus Christ.

---

37. Ibid.

38. Ibid.

39. See Senor, "Incarnation and Timelessness," 152; and the discussion concerning his argument in chapter 4.

40. Cf. Morris, *Logic of God Incarnate*, 55, who writes, "Accepting the apparent contradictions and trying to defuse them with reduplicative statement is in general not sufficiently convincing."

41. Ibid., 49.

42. In Gonzales, *Story of Christianity*, 1:257.

Rather than resort to the *qua* move to solve any apparent conflict, it should be instead assumed that the Chalcedonian statement *means* that there do not exist any set of mutually exclusive properties in Christ. The statement indicates that in Christ are all properties essential to divinity and all properties essential to humanity, and that there is no contradiction in the union. This is the idea that Morris conveys as he writes, "It is the claim of orthodoxy that Jesus had all the kind-essential properties of humanity, and all the kind-essential properties of divinity, and thus existed (and continues to exist) in two natures."[43] The Chalcedonian statement should not be interpreted to mean that there is a way out of the contradiction; but rather that there *is no contradiction* in saying that Christ is fully human and fully God. The person who is God the Son, incarnate in Jesus Christ, is not in possession of a set of mutually exclusive properties. For any possible property *A*, it is not the case that the person who is God the Son incarnate in Jesus Christ is both *A* and not-*A*.

The *qua* move as an explanation for how the classical atemporal model accounts for the Incarnation is not an acceptable option for anyone desiring to preserve both Chalcedonian orthodoxy and the law of non-contradiction. If atemporality is essential to divinity, there is a contradiction in the Incarnation; and this is because Jesus lives an ordinary temporal life.[44] To divide the person of Christ into his human and divine constituent parts in attempt to solve this contradiction obviously runs afoul of the Chalcedonian formula. This leaves the alternative that atemporality is not a kind-essential property for a divine person. And if atemporality is not a kind-essential property for a divine person, then the underlying structure of the classical atemporal model of God's relation to time fails.

GOD, TIME, AND INCARNATION

The above discussion has provided three key components of an alternative to the classical atemporal model. First, the Incarnation is to be taken as the "control belief" in the debate. Working out how God's relation to time is to be understood—for Christians—must be governed by this essential doctrine. Second, while virtually no participant in the debate has exactly

---

43. Morris, *Logic of God Incarnate*, 40.

44. This fact is admitted by all those authors (surveyed here) who hold to the classical atemporal model.

the same concept and definition of time as any other, common ground can still be achieved by a corrective in the language employed in framing the debate. It makes little sense to speak of God being either "in" or "outside of time;" and to do so is only to distract from the central issues. To solve the debate, it is only necessary to determine whether God's life has events ordered in sequence or succession. Finally, in order to preserve a robust Chalcedonian view of the Incarnation,[45] it must be admitted that there do not exist in Christ any set of mutually exclusive properties from the two natures. The two natures are not only joined in Christ, but they are also united without conflict or contradiction. With these elements in place, I can return once again to the paradigm I first offered in chapter 2. This paradigm will make more explicit several key ideas that are implied in the discussion above; and it will be offered as a way to work out the remaining details of how the Incarnation can solve the debate on God's relation to time.

The Boethian model of God's eternal life argues that God is in the possession of the fullness of his life at once—that is, Boethius argues that every feature of God's life is instantaneously simultaneous with every other feature of his life. The term "simultaneous" is employed in this model to rule out the notion of temporal sequence in the divine life. Aquinas's model and definition of immutability is a direct descendant of Boethius's model. I showed in chapter 1 that Aquinas viewed immutability as ruling out the possibility of any kind of succession in God's life. Aquinas writes, "There is, therefore, no *before* and *after* in Him . . . nor can any succession be found in His being."[46] I suggested in chapter 2 that there are at least three elements essential to the doctrine of the Incarnation that indicate that the classical atemporal view is incorrect: (1) The Incarnation event itself indicates sequence in the Divine life, both in its occurrence and its permanence. (2) The earthly life of Christ demonstrates temporal sequence in the life of God the Son. (3) The purpose of the Incarnation—that is, the work of the incarnate Christ—indicates the sequence in God's life. These aspects of the Incarnation indicate that—contrary to the classical atemporal model—God does indeed experience temporal sequence in his

---

45. This is in addition to a desire to preserve the law of non-contradiction. Christ cannot be both *A* and not-*A*; and reduplicative predicates cannot be employed to avoid this.

46. Aquinas, *Summa Contra Gentiles*, 1.15.3.

existence. This paradigm was given preliminary consideration in chapter 2, and will now be re-examined in light of the intervening discussion.

Temporal Sequence and the Incarnation Event

The language of Scripture clearly refers to the Incarnation as an event, as John 1:14 states, "the Word became flesh and dwelt among us;" and Phil 2:7, Christ "made himself of no reputation, taking the form of a bondservant, and coming in the likeness of men." These passages and others[47] uniformly use the language of *process* and *sequence* in their characterization of what took place in the Incarnation. With this in mind, the Bible seems to indicate that the Incarnation is an *event* (as defined in the discussion above). Additionally, the statements of both Nicaea and Chalcedon contain similar descriptions of the Incarnation. The creed of 381 states that in the Incarnation, the Son of God "came down from heaven, and was incarnate by the Holy Spirit of the Virgin Mary, and was made man."[48] Similarly, the Chalcedonian formula states that the Son of God was "begotten in the latter days, in his humanity, of Mary the virgin bearer of God."[49] This idea is also communicated clearly in the theological controversy that served as the catalyst for the Nicene creed. The main argument was over the pre-existence of the Son of God—that is, it was a question of whether Christ *existed before* the Incarnation. The results of this controversy, along with the other descriptions of the Incarnation, both biblical and creedal, indicate that the Incarnation was an event in the life of God the Son. There was a state of affairs that was God the Son existing being un-joined to human nature and flesh; and there was then an event in the life of God the Son at which time he took on humanity to himself and became Incarnate in Jesus of Nazareth. Therefore it must be the case that there is sequence—a temporally ordered succession of events—in the life of God the Son.

This argument is similar to, but different in important respects from, Senor's second argument. Recall that Senor's second argument focuses on the idea of the Incarnation representing a change in God the Son. He argues that "the assumption of the human nature brings about a change

---

47. See, e.g., Heb 5:5.

48. In Grudem, *Systematic Theology*, 1169.

49. In Gonzales, *Story of Christianity*, 1:257.

in the intrinsic (though non-essential) properties of God the Son."[50] From this, Senor concludes then that the Son must be mutable, and therefore temporal.[51] The weakness in this argument is that it addresses a point specific to Thomistic immutability. It has already been demonstrated that such immutability and the Boethian model of eternity mutually entail one another. Since the focus on the debate is on God's relation to time, however, it seems unnecessarily cumbersome for Senor's argument to address the question of immutability. The most important idea communicated in Senor's argument is not the issue of change, but that of temporal sequence indicated by an event.

Temporal sequence in the Incarnation is precisely what some defenders of the classical view have sought to deny. Helm, for example, emphasized—with great fervor and repetition—his belief that the Incarnation was not at all an event. He argues that although the Incarnation is experienced by humans as if it were within time, from God's perspective, God is atemporally incarnate in Christ. Helm writes that "there is no time in [Christ's] existence when he was not incarnate."[52] He makes the point more emphatic as he writes, "There is therefore no sense in talking of the eternal Son of God apart from the incarnation. . . ."[53] and, "there is no preexistent Christ with a life history independent of and prior to the incarnation."[54] Leftow seems to be in agreement with Helm on this point; and argues that the "taking on" was not temporal. He writes, "But the import of the 'taking on' claim on God's side is modal, not temporal. . . . why *isn't* this enough to make orthodox sense of the claim that God the Son [timelessly] took on flesh?"[55] Of course the atemporal model of God's relation to time logically entails that Christ's taking on flesh was time-

50. Senor, "Incarnation and Timelessness," 157.

51. Ibid.

52. Ibid.

53. Ibid.

54. Ibid. This idea is presented somewhat less emphatically in Stump and Kretzmann, "Eternity," 452–53; in which the authors claim that arguing along these lines is a "Boethian account of the compatibility of divine eternality and the Incarnation."

55. Leftow, "A Timeless God Incarnate," 299. However, in Leftow, *Time and Eternity*, 236, Leftow argues that "being temporal and being eternal [are] mutually exclusive modal properties." Therefore, in the Incarnation there exists the modal property of eternity (God the Son) and the modal property of temporality (Jesus). But then there are mutually exclusive properties in Christ. It seems that the introduction of the concept of "modal property" does not help Leftow solve the apparent contradiction.

less. On this account, there can be no "before" or "after" the Incarnation event. The life of God the Son must be simultaneously whole; and the Incarnation, being a single feature in the life of God the Son, must be timelessly eternal and simultaneous with all other features of his life.

Helm takes this one step further, however, and argues that the creedal statements about Christ actually *require* divine timelessness. Helm asserts that what the council at Nicaea meant to condemn was the very notion that there is temporal sequence in the life of God. He writes, "On [the temporalist view] there was a *time* when the Son was not. That is, it is difficult to see how a temporalist could hold to the classical Nicene position that the Son came into existence before time; that there was no time when he was not."[56] Further, Helm asserts that those who do not hold to the classical atemporal view are guilty of the Arian heresy. He writes that the temporalist perspective "would seem to strongly favour, if not actually entail, some form of Arianism."[57]

Clearly Helm is mistaken in his analysis on at least two counts. First, the emphasis in Arian controversy was whether God the Son existed before the Incarnation, not on whether Jesus existed before his own birth. The Arians were wrong in their assertion that there once was a time when the Son did not exist. But there was certainly a time when the man Jesus did not exist. What Nicaea sought to condemn was the idea that the Son was not co-eternal with the Father. The Nicene Creed is simply saying that God the Son existed prior to the Incarnation. Second, Helm's interpretation of Nicaea is specifically ruled out by the later statement at Chalcedon. The Chalcedonian Creed states that the Son was "begotten of the Father before all time in his divinity, and also begotten in the latter days, in his humanity, of Mary the virgin bearer of God."[58] In other words, the Son being begotten of the Father is atemporal; but the Incarnation itself is "in the latter days." Since the Chalcedonian statement claims to be an affirmation of Nicaea, Helm's assertion that orthodoxy with respect to the Incarnation requires the atemporal model is in error. If the framers of the creeds intended to say that the Incarnation was atemporal, the language was clearly available for them to do so unambiguously: they could have said that the *Incarnation* was "before all time," but instead they

56. Helm, "Eternal Creation," 336.
57. Ibid.
58. In Gonzales, *Story of Christianity*, 1:257.

made a distinction by saying it was "in the latter days." Therefore, Helm's interpretation is ruled out. Chalcedon's distinction between the atemporal existence of the Son and the temporal becoming of his humanity is a strong positive statement in favor of the conclusion that the Incarnation was a temporal event.

In addition to the occurrence of the Incarnation, the *permanence* of the Incarnation is a further indicator of sequence in the Divine life. The Nicene Creed specifically highlights the crucifixion, resurrection, and ascension of Christ at the end of his life on earth. Additionally, it states that having ascended into heaven, he sat at the right hand of the Father; and while he awaits the full inauguration of his kingdom, he sits in session before God, interceding on behalf of those who are his redeemed. Highlighting the significance of this fact, Gregory of Nazianzus wrote, "If any assert that He has now put off His holy flesh, and that His Godhead is stripped of the body, and deny that He is now with His body and will come again with it, let him not see the glory of His Coming. For where is His body now, if not with Him Who assumed it?"[59] Christ, then, is even now in full possession of his humanity, including his resurrected body, and continues to live a temporal life in his session before the Father. The creed states that Christ will continue his existence as the God-man, and will rule over his kingdom, which will never come to an end.

One remarkable discovery in the survey of contributions to the debate in chapters 3 and 4 was the fact that none of those authors place significance on the permanence of the Incarnation. But the fact that Christ continues his incarnate existence forever has at least two direct applications for the debate. First, it means that defenders of the classical atemporal view are not able to avoid the force of the argument from the Incarnation by appealing to it as an example of God's temporary condescension. Paul Helm, for example, on developing his doctrine of the two standpoints, leaves an exception for the case of the Incarnation. He writes, "God has a unique perspective on the world, a perspective necessarily free from either temporal or spatial indexicals. And so, saving the case of the Incarnation, he does not take up the cognitive standpoint of any one of his creatures more than that of any other."[60] While not stated explicitly, Helm seems to be suggesting that the Incarnation was a temporary in-

---

59. Gregory of Nazianzus, "To Cledonius the Priest Against Appolinarius," letter 101 (*NPNF*², 7:440).

60. Helm, "Divine Timeless Eternity," 58.

stance of God assuming the cognitive standpoint of a creature, including, as it does, temporal indexicals. But the Incarnation is permanent; and this leads to the conclusion that even if Helm is right about God's standpoint prior to the Incarnation, from the moment of the Incarnation, God *permanently* has such a cognitive standpoint. Further, on the atemporal account, whatever standpoint God has at any one time, he has eternally; which means (when combined with Helm's exception) that God eternally has the temporal standpoint of a creature. This creates a contradiction: God is *atemporally* in possession of a *temporal* standpoint. The only available solution to this problem is that God does not have an atemporal standpoint—that God is not atemporal as the classical view asserts.

Second, the permanence of the Incarnation also seems to rule out the static model of time. The classical atemporal model requires a static conception of time (an idea for which Padgett argues forcefully). The static model of time is illustrated clearly in Boethius—both in his definition of eternity and his "man on the hill" illustration—and is readily employed by most contemporary defenders of the model. Implied in this model is the idea that time has both a beginning and an end; and that God has each moment of the finite temporal spectrum immediately present to himself at once. But if the Incarnation continues as Christ reigns over his kingdom, which "shall have no end," then time does not have a future ending point. Taken at face value, the statement of the creeds is that Christ—God the Son Incarnate, living a temporal human existence—will reign over his kingdom for an unending length of time. But if the atemporal model is correct, then the conclusion is that God is in complete possession at once of an actual infinite series of temporal events. This clearly creates a contradiction for which no solution that preserves the atemporal model is readily apparent. The conclusion seems unavoidable: the Incarnation, both in its occurrence and its permanence, indicates that God the Son experiences temporal sequence in his existence.

Temporal Sequence and the Life of Christ

The fact of the Incarnation clearly indicates temporal sequence in the life of God the Son; but temporal sequence is also indicated in the earthly life of Christ. Chapter 2 noted an important concept implied by the Chalcedonian Creed and stated explicitly in Scripture: Jesus Christ is a full and complete revelation of God to mankind. This idea is also stated succinctly in McGrath, as he writes, "A central element of Christian theology centers upon the idea of a *revelatory presence of God* in Christ. . . . Jesus Christ is regarded as making God known in a particular and specific manner, distinctive to Christianity."[61] When one desires to know what God is like, he only has to look to Jesus Christ. Or, in the words of Erickson, "Whereas the prophets came bearing a message from God, Jesus was God. If we would know what the love of God, the holiness of God, the power of God are like, we need only look at Christ."[62] Jesus was indeed a perfect revelation of God.

The fact that Jesus revealed God is a direct consequence of the divine nature, as was discussed above. But here it is taken one step further: Jesus was in possession of the divine nature, with all of its kind-essential properties; and it is equally important to note that because the two natures are united in *one person*, the life of that one person is the life of God the Son. As Chalcedon states, "[The two natures] are not divided into two persons, but belong to the one Only-begotten Son, the Word of God, the Lord Jesus Christ."[63] The conclusion from this is that, in Jesus, God himself entered into human existence as a first-person participant in the created order. Concerning this fact, Torrance writes, "Thus it is the faith and understanding of the Christian church that in Jesus Christ God Himself in His own Being has come into our world and is actively present as personal Agent within our physical and historical existence."[64] In this sense, the ordinary temporal life of Jesus is also the life of God.

Although Senor does not address the issue exactly as Torrance or McGrath have, this idea seems to be behind his first argument. Senor argues that because Jesus lived an ordinary temporal life, then temporal predicates can be applied to him. Senor then argues that since Jesus is God the Son, then temporal predicates can also be applied to God the Son; and this seems to be evidence that God the Son is not timeless. The strength of Senor's argument is that it begins with the life of Jesus Christ as an indicator for whether or not God experiences temporal sequence. Clearly Senor's argument is based on the orthodox conviction that the life of Jesus is revelatory—it tells us something about God's life. But the force

61. McGrath, *Christian Theology*, 349.

62. Erickson, *Christian Theology*, 703.

63. In Gonzales, *Story of Christianity*, 1:257.

64. Torrance, *Space, Time, and Incarnation*, 52.

of this seems to get lost in focusing the argument on the application of predicates. Senor's argument would be made stronger if he removed the focus on predicates and focused instead on the fact that the life of Jesus was the life of God the Son. This seems to be the conclusion that follows logically from the statements of both Chalcedon and Nicaea.

In chapter 3 I showed that even Leftow (who defends the atemporal view) also admitted that the life of Jesus was the life of God the Son. He writes, "So soon as Mary's egg began to live the life that would be Jesus', the life being lived was God the Son's life."[65] Recall that in Leftow's analysis of Senor's argument, Leftow has offered the corrective by asserting that "the person who is Jesus Christ = God the Son."[66] Perhaps the most prominent feature of Leftow's attempt to account for the Incarnation is his model of Christ as a mereological sum. Leftow asserts that Christ is "God the Son + S + B."[67] He develops from this model the idea that the life of Christ had only "a part in time."[68] While Leftow's mereological account of the Incarnation may be helpful in certain contexts, it seems as if his use of it here does injustice to the Chalcedonian conviction that the two natures were united in a single person. On Leftow's account, that which lives the temporal life in Christ is his human "part"—that is, his human nature. But it seems difficult to understand how a nature could live a life. On the contrary, it only makes sense to say that the *person* of Christ lived the life that was Jesus' life. If the person who is God the Son lived the life that was Jesus' life, then Leftow's mereological analysis does little to explain how (on the atemporal model) there can be a single person living both an ordinary temporal and an atemporal life.

It seems far more reasonable to eliminate the apparent contradiction by jettisoning the atemporal model. It seems plain from an orthodox account of the Incarnation that the life of Jesus was the life of God the Son. And since the events in the life of Jesus indicate temporal sequence in his life; then those events also indicate temporal sequence in the life of God the Son. This conclusion is only possible if both natures are united in one single person, and that the person who is God the Son lived the life that includes his Incarnation in Jesus.

65. Leftow, "Timeless God Incarnate," 282.
66. Ibid., 294.
67. Ibid., 280.
68. Ibid., 292.

Temporal Sequence and the Work of Christ

The final element of the paradigm is an appeal to the theological significance of the *purpose* of God the Son becoming Incarnate in Jesus Christ.
The Nicene Creed states explicitly that God the Son "for us men and for
our salvation, came down from heaven," and that he "was crucified . . .
suffered and was buried; and the third day he rose again, according to
the Scriptures."[69] A central element in an orthodox understanding of the
Incarnation is its soteriological purposes. Additionally, Christ's role as
Savior extends to his session at the Father's throne. Having completed the
work necessary for salvation through his death, burial, and bodily resurrection; Christ took his place "on the right hand of the Father," both as an
indicator that his work on earth was finished, and he now has moved on
in his intercessory role before the Father on behalf of those who are saved.
This idea has at its root passages such as Luke 19:10, "for the Son of Man
has come to seek and to save that which was lost;" and Heb 7:24–25, "But
[Christ], because He continues forever, has an unchangeable priesthood.
Therefore He is also able to save to the uttermost those who come to God
through Him, since He always lives to make intercession for them."[70] This
idea is only rarely mentioned in the context of the debate on God's relation to time;[71] but it does seem to have direct application in that the work
of the atonement is *complete*, and the completion of something indicates
temporal sequence.

That the work accomplished in Jesus' earthly life is completed is an
essential element of the theological context of the Incarnation. Important
passages of Scripture such as Heb 10:12–14 highlight the fact that Christ's
earthly mission was accomplished and is now finished: "But this Man,
after He had offered one sacrifice for sins forever, sat down at the right
hand of God, from that time waiting till His enemies are made His foot-
stool. For by one offering He has perfected forever those who are being
sanctified." That Christ's work is finished and complete is stated literally
in the phrase "one sacrifice for sins forever," which idea was first conveyed

69. In Grudem, *Systematic Theology*, 1169.

70. See also 1 John 2:1–2.

71. The authors I have surveyed make only passing comments related to the ideas
being presented here. In response to Helm, Craig makes mention of this objection, but
does not himself incorporate the idea as a prominent feature in his own argument. See
Craig, "Response to Paul Helm."

in the very words of Christ as he hung on the cross, "It is finished."[72] It is also made clear in the imagery of Jesus sitting down at the right hand of the Father, signifying that he needed perform no other work to accomplish the goal of salvation. Additionally, the completion is seen in the scriptural accounts of the transformed state of the redeemed man. It is found in Ps 103:12, which states, "As far as the east is from the west, So far has He removed our transgressions from us;" and 2 Cor 5:17, which says "Therefore, if anyone is in Christ, he is a new creation; old things have passed away; behold, all things have become new." These passages and others indicate a finality: a transformation achieved through the work of Christ that brings about a new standing before God. The very notion of a completed work indicates a sequence of events in the Divine life: There existed a state of affairs that was sin having not been paid for and sinners standing under God's righteous judgment. Christ's completed work made atonement for man's sins; and now individual human beings are transformed permanently in their standing before God. Christ has put away sin in his atoning work on the cross.

It seems, however, that the classical atemporal model cannot account for the completed work of Christ in salvation. In the atemporal model, every moment of God's life is simultaneous to every other. All temporal events, past, present, and future, are equally real and present before God. But if this is so, then the important work of atonement has never been fully accomplished. Sin *has not been* removed; and Christ hanging on the cross is an ever-present feature of God's life. In one criticism of the atemporal model, Craig also highlights this fact. He writes, "In a sense, Christ permanently hangs on the cross. . . . The victory of the resurrection becomes a hollow triumph, for the spatiotemporal parts of Jesus that were crucified and buried remain dying and dead and are never raised to new life. It is unclear how we can say, 'Death has been swallowed up in victory' (1 Cor 15:54) when death is never really done away with on a static theory of time."[73]

In other words, it is not possible that Christ's work of atonement ever be completed; for the sin and death are ever before God. In defense of the atemporal model, Leftow attempts to put a positive spin on this fact. He writes, "For if [the atemporal model] is true, then the Crucifixion is

72. John 19:30.
73. Craig, "Response to Paul Helm," 67. Craig limits his comments on the topic, and does not develop the idea further in his own account of God's relation to time.

not an episode God went through once and now relives only in memory. Rather, God's love for the world is so great that He is willing to be eternally crucified for its sakes, and all of His dealings with the world are commingled with His present undergoing of that pain."[74] While the ardent defender of the classical atemporal model may not be swayed by an appeal to the atonement; it seems that, taken at face value, the atonement requires completion and the actual doing away with sin. This, of course, is sufficient to demonstrate sequence in the Divine life.

In addition to offering the above three-fold paradigm, an additional step might be necessary. Clearly the Incarnation demonstrates temporal sequence in God the Son. But the question remains: Does the Incarnation indicate temporal sequence for the Godhead, or the other persons of the Trinity? Senor briefly mentions this question in his argument, and writes, "The idea is that the unity of the Godhead requires its members to have the same relation to time. Thus, if it can be shown that one Person of the Trinity is temporal, it will follow that the Godhead is temporal as well."[75] However, the model being presented here is more modest than the outright claim that "God is temporal." Instead, what I am arguing is that God is not atemporal. In other words, the classical atemporal model of God's relation to time cannot adequately account for the Incarnation; and therefore it should be rejected. But if the atemporal model is rejected, then the additional step of demonstrating the temporality of the Godhead from the temporality of the Son becomes unnecessary. Instead, beginning with the Incarnation as both an indicator of sequence and a revelation of God, it follows that God—that is, the Godhead—experiences temporal sequence in his existence.

DEFENSE AGAINST SOME POSSIBLE CHALLENGES

Despite the overwhelming theological importance of the Incarnation for Christian philosophical theology, some defenders of the classical atemporal view will no doubt find the presentation in this book less than satisfying. They will reject arguments from the Incarnation leveled against the classical view for a variety of reasons. In addition to the more serious challenges to this kind of argument that I explored throughout the course

---

74. Leftow, *Time and Eternity*, 245.

75. Senor, "Incarnation and Timelessness," 159.

of this book, for the sake of a comprehensive treatment of the subject I will address three other minor objections to my model.

First, it is important to address another aspect of the discussion related to God's immutability. Recall that the classical atemporal view understands God as being immutable in the logical sense—it is not possible that God could change because he is timeless. This is often characterized as "strong" immutability because it rules out any kind of change whatsoever; and the priority in this view is placed on timelessness, of which immutability is a logical entailment. But this seems to take away the religious significance of God's being faithful and enduring, unchanging in his nature, character, will, and plans. So with regard specifically to the *theological import* of the doctrine, it could be argued that the logical entailment from timelessness results in God only being *trivially* immutable: God just happens to be immutable because he is timeless. In contrast to this perspective, a model of God's relation with time that allows for God's experience of temporally sequenced events seems to do a greater justice to the idea of immutability. In spite of the change and flux in the material universe, God remains the same. It does seem, after all, that to call something "immutable" implies that the entity in question does not change *through time*. This undoubtedly will remain a point of contention on all sides of the debate, and calls for additional exploration.

Second, some will reject arguments from the Incarnation based on a misunderstanding of some of the central claims presented here. One example of this type of rejection is found in Norman Geisler's *Systematic Theology*. Geisler first states that the argument from the Incarnation seems plausibly true; but then he objects: "As persuasive as this argument may seem, it is based on an unorthodox assumption, namely, that the divine nature became human in the Incarnation."[76] Geisler then charges that arguments from the Incarnation are based on heresy. He writes, "As a matter of fact, this is the monophysite heresy condemned at the council of Chalcedon in A.D. 454: It is a confusion of the two natures of Christ."[77] While there are probably some who may offer an argument from the Incarnation based on monophysitism, the model offered in this work does not fit Geisler's caricature. Quite to the contrary, the model offered here depends on the preservation of the two natures in Christ,

76. Geisler, *Systematic Theology*, vol. 2, 109.
77. Ibid., 109–10.

without confusion, change, division, or separation. The argument here is not that the divine *nature* became human, but that the divine *person* became human.[78] Once this misunderstanding is cleared up, my argument retains it persuasive force. The simple conclusion being made is that the temporal events in the life of Christ are events in the life of God the Son.[79] Temporally ordered events—events that separate and distinguish states of affairs—clearly indicate temporal sequence.

Finally, despite the discussion above about the nature of time, many will remain convinced (with Augustine) that time itself is merely a created feature of the material universe. Those who hold fast to this view will cite the decay and tumult, and all the apparent vicissitudes associated with temporal passage; and conclude that since God could certainly not be subject to such things, he must be completely atemporal. They may look to Einstein and other developments in physical sciences for confirmation that time is *what clocks measure*, and therefore must be confined to the material universe. If these assumptions are held, then no argument is forthcoming that could convince these defenders of the classical view that the atemporal model is inadequate. By way of response, however, it is important to emphasize a point first made in the introduction to this work. I am suggesting here that the decay and tumult, and all the vicissitudes of temporal passage that the world currently sees are not a result of *time*, but rather of *sin*. Humans perceive growing old as a weakness, an imperfection, only because all we know of growing old is our growing nearer to death. But this is only a feature of common temporal experience insofar as we live in a world that is suffering under the curse of sin. Remove the elements of decay leading to death, and "growing old" loses its sting. Furthermore, it is at least possible that time itself is ontologically dependent on God, and yet God still experiences temporal passage. If a parallel is drawn with the *moral law* this idea may become clearer. God could never violate the moral law: he could never do evil. But it would be inappropriate to conclude from this that God is "subject to" the moral law. Quite the contrary, the moral law comes from God's character and his very being. It is likewise possible that the flow of time owes similar dependence on God's life and being. This would fit with the argument I am

---

78. A fact that Geisler admits. See ibid., 110.

79. This argument was detailed earlier in this chapter, as well as in the analysis of Leftow's argument in chapter 3.

offering: God experiences temporal sequence in his existence by virtue of his own nature.

CONCLUSION

It is likely that additional challenges will be proposed that attempt to defeat the argument presented in this book. Despite these challenges, the presentation here has revealed some of the inadequacies in the atemporal model, especially that the model is unable to account for the temporal sequence in the Incarnation. Chapter 1 described the philosophical and theological context out of which the contemporary debate on God's relation to time has been formed. As was shown in chapter 3, contemporary defenders of the classical atemporal model have followed Augustine, Boethius, Aquinas, and others in placing God's immutability and the Platonic premise of an absolutely changeless eternity as the foundation of their arguments. This presents a picture of the Divine life in which any sequence or succession whatsoever is inadmissible. Chapter 2 surveyed the doctrine of the Incarnation—the most fundamental and essential doctrine distinguishing Christianity from other forms of theism—and presented an argument that the doctrine indicates the presence of sequence in the Divine life. This contradicts the conclusions formed from the classical atemporal model of God's relation to time. Because the Incarnation is an essential doctrine to Christianity, the classical atemporal model of God's relation to time should be abandoned. When the doctrine of the Incarnation is given theological priority in the context of the debate on God's relation to time, it does serve as an indicator of temporal sequence in God's life.

Bibliography

Achtner, Wolfgang. *Dimensions of Time: The Structures of Time of Humans, of the World, and of God*. Grand Rapids: Eerdmans, 2002.

Allen, Diogenes. *Philosophy for Understanding Theology*. Atlanta: Westminster/John Knox, 1985.

Anselm. *Anselm of Canterbury: The Major Works*. Edited and with an introduction by Brian Davies and G. R. Evans. Oxford World's Classics. Oxford: Oxford University Press, 1998.

Aristotle. *Physics*. In vol. 1 of *The Complete Works of Aristotle*. Edited by Jonathan Barnes. Princeton: Princeton University Press, 1984.

Athanasius. *Defense of the Nicene Definition*. In vol. 4 of *The Nicene and Post-Nicene Fathers*, Series 2. Edited by Philip Schaff and Henry Wace. 1890. 14 vols. Reprint, Peabody: MA: Hendrickson, 1994.

Aquinas, Thomas. *Compendium of Theology*. Translated by Cyril Vollert. St. Louis: Herder, 1952.

———. *On the Truth of the Catholic Faith: Summa Contra Gentiles*. 4 Vols. Translated with an introduction and notes by Anton C. Pegis. Garden City, NY: Hanover House, 1955.

———. *Philosophical Texts*. Selected and translated with notes by Thomas Gilby. Durham, NC: Labyrinth, 1982.

———. *Summa Theologiae: Questions on God*. Edited by Brian Davies and Brian Leftow. Cambridge: Cambridge University Press, 2006.

Audi, Robert, ed. *The Cambridge Dictionary of Philosophy*. Cambridge: Cambridge University Press, 1996.

Augustine, *Confessions*. In vol. 1 of *The Nicene and Post-Nicene Fathers*, Series 1. Edited by Philip Schaff. 1886–1889. 14 vols. Reprint Peabody, MA: Hendrickson, 1994.

———. *The Works of Saint Augustine: A Translation for the 21st Century*. Edited by John E. Rotelle. Translated by Edmund Hill. Vol. 5, *The Trinity*. New York: New City, 1991.

Barbour, Ian G. *Religion in an Age of Science*. The Gifford Lectures 1989–1991, vol. 1. San Francisco: Harper & Row, 1990.

Barr, James. *Biblical Words for Time*. 2d Revised Edition. London: SCM, 1962.

Barth, Karl. *Church Dogmatics*. Vol. 1, Part 1 *The Doctrine of the Word of God*. Translated by G. T. Thompson. Edinburgh: T. & T. Clark, 1936.

Beilby, James K. and Paul R. Eddy, eds. *Divine Foreknowledge: Four Views*. Downers Grove: InterVarsity, 2001.

Bloesch, Donald G. *Jesus Christ: Savior & Lord*. Christian Foundations. Downers Grove: InterVarsity, 1997.

Blount, Douglas K. "On the Incarnation of a Timeless God." In *God and Time: Essays on the Divine Nature*, ed. Gregory E. Ganssle and David M. Woodruff, 236–48. Oxford: Oxford University Press, 2002.

Boethius. *The Consolation of Philosophy*. Translated with introduction by P. G. Walsh. Oxford World's Classics. Oxford: Oxford University Press, 1999.

Bowman, Jr., Robert M. and J. Ed Komoszewski. *Putting Jesus in His Place: The Case for the Deity of Christ*. Grand Rapids: Kregel, 2007.

Boyd, Gregory A. *God of the Possible: A Biblical Introduction to the Open View of God*. Grand Rapids: Baker, 2000.

Brabant, Frank Herbert. *Time and Eternity in Christian Thought*. London: Longmans & Green, 1937.

Bray, Gerald. *The Doctrine of God*. Contours of Christian Theology. Edited by Gerald Bray. Downers Grove, IL: InterVarsity, 1993.

Breck, John. "Reflections on the 'Problem' of Chalcedonian Christology." *St. Vladimir's Theological Quarterly* 33.2 (1989) 147–57.

Brown, Delwin, Ralph E. James, Jr., and Gene Reeves, eds. *Process Philosophy and Christian Thought*. Indianapolis: Bobbs-Merrill, 1971.

Campbell, J. McLeod. *The Nature of the Atonement*. New Edition with an Introduction by James B. Torrance. Grand Rapids: Eerdmans, 1996.

Callahan, John F. *Four Views of Time in Ancient Philosophy*. Revised Edition. Westport, CT: Greenwood, 1979.

Chemnitz, Martin. *The Two Natures in Christ*. Translated by J. A. O. Preus. St. Louis: Concordia, 1971.

Clark, Gordon H. *The Incarnation*. Jefferson, MD: The Trinity Foundation, 1988.

———. *The Trinity*. Jefferson, MD: The Trinity Foundation, 1985.

Coakley, Sarah. "What Does Chalcedon Solve and What Does it Not? Some Reflections on the Status and Meaning of the Chalcedonian 'Definition.'" In *The Incarnation: An Interdisciplinary Symposium on the Incarnation of the Son of God*, ed. by Stephen T. Davis, Daniel Kendall, and Gerald O'Collins, 143–63. Oxford: Oxford University Press, 2002.

Cobb, John B., Jr. *The Process Perspective: Frequently Asked Questions About Process Theology*. St. Louis: Chalice, 2003.

———. "A Whitheadian Christology." In *Process Philosophy and Christian Thought*, ed. by Delwin Brown, Ralph E. James, and Gene Reeves, 382–98. Indianapolis: Bobbs-Merrill, 1971.

———. "A Whiteheadian Doctrine of God." In *Process Philosophy and Christian Thought*, ed. Delwin Brown, Ralph E. James, and Gene Reeves, 215–43. Indianapolis: Bobbs-Merrill, 1971.

Cobb, John B., Jr., and David Ray Griffin. *Process Theology: An Introductory Exposition*. Philadelphia: Westminster, 1976.

Craig, William Lane. "Boethius on Theological Fatalism." *Ephemerides Theologicae Lovanienses* 64 (1988) 324–47.

———. "Divine Timelessness and Necessary Existence." *International Philosophical Quarterly* 37 (June 1997) 217–24.

———. "The Elimination of Absolute Time by the Special Theory of Relativity." In *God and Time: Essays on the Divine Nature*, ed. by Gregory E. Ganssle and David M. Woodruff. Oxford: Oxford University Press, 2002.

———. "God and Real Time." *Religious Studies* 26 (Sept 1990) 335–47.

―――. "On the Argument for Divine Timelessness from the Incompleteness of Temporal Life." *The Heythrop Journal* 38 (1997) 165–71.

―――. *The Only Wise God: The Compatibility of Divine Foreknowledge and Human Freedom.* Eugene: Wipf & Stock, 2000.

―――. *The Problem of Divine Foreknowledge and Future Contingents From Aristotle to Suarez.* Brill's Studies in Intellectual History, ed. A.J. Vanderjagt. New York: Brill, 1988

―――. "Response to Paul Helm," In *God and Time: Four Views*, ed. with introduction by Gregory E. Ganssle, 63–68. Downers Grove: InterVarsity, 2001.

―――. Review of *Eternal God: A Study of God Without Time*, by Paul Helm. *JETS* 36 (June 1993) 254–55.

―――. *Time and Eternity: Exploring God's Relationship to Time.* Wheaton: Crossway, 2001.

―――. "Timelessness and Omnitemporality." In *God and Time: Four Views*, ed. with introduction by Gregory E. Ganssle, 129–86. Downers Grove: InterVarsity, 2001.

―――. "Was Thomas Aquinas a B-Theorist of Time?" *The New Scholasticism* 59.4 (Autumn 1985) 475–83.

Crisp, Oliver D. *Divinity and Humanity: The Incarnation Reconsidered.* Current Issues in Theology, ed. Iain Torrance. Cambridge: Cambridge University Press, 2007.

Cross, Richard. *The Metaphysics of the Incarnation: Thomas Aquinas to Duns Scotus.* Oxford: Oxford University Press, 2002.

Cullmann, Oscar. *Christ and Time: The Primitive Christian Conception of Time and History.* Revised Edition. Translated by Floyd V. Filson. Philadelphia: Westminster, 1964.

―――. *The Christology of the New Testament.* Translated by Shirley C. Guthrie and Charles A. M. Hall. Philadelphia: Westminster, 1959.

Davenport, S. F. *Immanence & Incarnation.* The Norrisian Prize Essay in the University of Cambridge for the Year 1924. Cambridge: Cambridge University Press, 1925.

Davies, Paul. *About Time: Einstein's Unfinished Revolution.* London: Penguin Books, 1995.

―――. *God and the New Physics.* New York: Simon & Schuster, 1983.

―――. *The Mind of God: The Scientific Basis for a Rational World.* New York: Simon & Schuster, 1992.

DeWeese, Garrett. "Atemporal, Sempiternal, or Omnitemporal: God's Temporal Mode of Being." In *God and Time: Essays on the Divine Nature*, ed. Gregory E. Ganssle and David M. Woodruff, 49–61. Oxford: Oxford University Press, 2002.

―――. *God and the Nature of Time.* Ashgate Philosophy of Religion Series. Burlington, VT: Ashgate, 2004.

―――. "Timeless God, Tenseless Time." *Philosophia Christi* 2.1 (2000) 53–59.

Elwell, Walter A., ed. *Evangelical Dictionary of Theology.* Grand Rapids: Baker, 1984.

Enns, Paul. *The Moody Handbook of Theology.* Chicago: Moody Press, 1989.

Erickson, Millard J. *Christian Theology.* Grand Rapids: Baker, 1995.

―――. *The Word Became Flesh: A Contemporary Incarnational Christology.* Grand Rapids: Baker, 1991.

Everitt, Nicholas. "Interpretations of God's Eternity." *Religious Studies* 34.1 (March 1998) 25–32.

Fagg, Lawrence W. *The Becoming of Time: Integrating Physical and Religious Time.* Atlanta: Scholars, 1995.

Feinberg, Charles Lee. "The Hypostatic Union." *Bibliotheca Sacra* 93.368, 412–26.

Feinberg, John S. "Doctrine of God." In *New Dimensions in Evangelical Thought: Essays in Honor of Millard J. Erickson*, ed. David S. Dockery, 235–69. Downers Grove, IL: InterVarsity, 1998.

———. *No One Like Him: The Doctrine of God*. Foundations of Evangelical Theology. Wheaton: Crossway, 2001.

Ferrier, Francis. *What is the Incarnation?* Translated by Edward Sillem. Vol. 24 of *The Twentieth Century Encyclopedia of Catholicism*, ed. Henri Daniel-Rops. New York: Hawthorn, 1962.

Freeman, Eugene, and Wilfrid Sellars, eds. *Basic Issues in the Philosophy of Time*. La Salle, IL: Open Court, 1971.

Frame, John M. *No Other God: A Response to Open Theism*. Phillipsburg, NJ: Presbyterian & Reformed, 2001.

Ganssle, Gregory E., ed. *God and Time: Four Views*. Downers Grove, IL: InterVarsity, 2001.

Geisler, Norman. *Systematic Theology*. Vol. 2, *God, Creation*. Minneapolis: Bethany House, 2003.

Geisler, Norman, and Winfred Corduan. *Philosophy of Religion*. 2nd ed. Grand Rapids: Baker, 1988.

Green, Michael, ed. *The Truth of God Incarnate*. London: Hodder & Stoughton, 1977.

Gregorios, Paulos, William H. Lazareth, and Nikos A. Nissiotis, eds. *Does Chalcedon Unite or Divide?: Towards Convergence in Orthodox Christology*. Geneva: World Council of Churches, 1981.

Grudem, Wayne. *Systematic Theology: An Introduction to Biblical Doctrine*. Grand Rapids: Zondervan, 1994.

Gunton, Colin E. *The Actuality of the Atonement: A Study of Metaphor, Rationality and the Christian Tradition*. Grand Rapids: Eerdmans, 1989.

———. *A Brief Theology of Revelation*. The 1993 Warfield Lectures. Edinburgh: T. & T. Clark, 1995.

———, ed. *The Doctrine of Creation: Essays in Dogmatics, History and Philosophy*. Edinburgh: T. & T. Clark, 1997.

———, ed. *Trinity, Time, and Church: A Response to the Theology of Robert W. Jenson*. Grand Rapids: Eerdmans, 2000.

———. *Yesterday & Today: A Study of Continuities in Christology*. Grand Rapids: Eerdmans, 1983.

Hasker, William. *God, Time, and Knowledge*. Cornell Studies in Philosophy of Religion. Ithaca: Cornell University Press, 1989.

Havrilak, Gregory. "Chalcedon and Orthodox Christology Today." *St. Vladimir's Theological Quarterly* 33.2 (1989) 127–45.

Hebblethwaite, Brian. "Jesus, God Incarnate." In *The Truth of God Incarnate*, ed. by Michael Green, 101–6. London: Hodder & Stoughton, 1977.

———. *Philosophical Theology and Christian Doctrine*. Oxford: Blackwell, 2005.

Helm, Paul. "Divine Timeless Eternity." *Philosophia Christi* 2.1 (2000) 21–27.

———. "Divine Timeless Eternity." In *God and Time: Four Views*, ed. with introduction by Gregory E. Ganssle, 28–91. Downers Grove, IL: InterVarsity, 2001.

———. "Eternal Creation." *Tyndale Bulletin* 45.2 (1994) 321–38.

———. "Eternal Creation: The Doctrine of the Two Standpoints." In *The Doctrine of Creation: Essays in Dogmatics, History, and Philosophy*, ed. by Colin E. Gunton, 29–46. Edinburgh: T. & T. Clark, 1997.

———. *Eternal God: A Study of God Without Time*. 2nd ed. Oxford: Clarendon, 2010.

———. "The Problem of Dialogue." In *God and Time: Essays on the Divine Nature*, ed. Gregory E. Ganssle and David M. Woodruff, 207–19. Oxford: Oxford University Press, 2002.

———. *The Providence of God*. Contours of Christian Theology, ed. Gerald Bray. Downers Grove: InterVarsity, 1994.

———. "Response to Alan G. Padgett." In *God and Time: Four Views*, ed. with introduction by Gregory E. Ganssle, 111-14. Downers Grove, IL: InterVarsity, 2001.

Henry, Carl F. H. *God, Revelation, and Authority*. Vol. 5. Waco: Word, 1982.

Heraclitus. *Fragments*. In *The Art and Thought of Heraclitus: An Edition of the Fragments with Translation and Commentary*. Edited and Translated with Commentary by Charles H. Kahn. Cambridge: Cambridge University Press, 1979.

Heron, Alasdiar I. C. "Homoousious with the Father." In *The Incarnation: Ecumenical Studies in the Nicene-Constantinopolitan Creed A.D. 381*, ed. by Thomas F. Torrance, 58–87. Eugene: Wipf & Stock, 1998.

Hick, John. *Philosophy of Religion*. 2nd ed. Englewood Cliffs: Prentice-Hall, 1973.

Honderich, Ted, ed. *The Oxford Companion to Philosophy*, 2nd ed. Oxford: Oxford University Press, 2005.

Kelly, J. N. D. *Early Christian Creeds*, 3rd ed. New York: McKay, 1978.

———. *Early Christian Doctrines*. Rev. ed. San Francisco: Harper, 1978.

Kolak, Daniel, and Garrett Thompson. *The Longman Standard History of Philosophy*. New York: Pearson Longman, 2006.

Kennard, Douglas. *The Classical Christian God*. Toronto Studies in Theology. Lewiston, NY: Edwin Millen, 2002.

Kenny, Anthony. *The God of the Philosophers*. Oxford: Clarendon, 1979.

Kreeft, Peter. *A Summa of the Summa: The Essential Philosophical Passages of St. Thomas Aquinas'* Summa Theologica *Edited and Explained for Beginners*. San Francisco: Ignatius Press, 1990.

LaCugna, Catherine Mowry. *God for Us: The Trinity & Christian Life*. New York: Harper-Collins, 1991.

Ladd, George Eldon. *A Theology of the New Testament*. Rev ed. Grand Rapids: Eerdmans, 1993.

Ladd, Steven W. "Theological Indicators Supporting an Evangelical Conception of Eternity: A Study of God's Relation to Time in Light of the Doctrine of Creation *Ex Nihilo*." PhD diss., Southeastern Baptist Theological Seminary, 2002.

Larson, Duane H. *Times of the Trinity: A Proposal for Theistic Cosmology*. Worcester Polytechnic Institute Studies in Science, Technology, and Culture, ed. Lance Schachterle and Francis C. Lutz, no. 17. New York: Lang, 1995.

Leftow, Brian. "The Eternal Present." In *God and Time: Essays on the Divine Nature*, ed. Gregory E. Ganssle and David M. Woodruff, 21–48. Oxford: Oxford University Press, 2002.

———. "Eternity and Immutability." In *The Blackwell Guide to the Philosophy of Religion*, ed. William E. Mann, 48–77. Malden, MA: Blackwell, 2005.

———. "Eternity and Simultaneity." *Faith and Philosophy* 8 (1991) 148–79.

———. "The Roots of Eternity." *Religious Studies* 24 (1988) 189–212.

———. *Time and Eternity*. Ithaca, NY: Cornell University Press, 1991.

———. "A Timeless God Incarnate." In *The Incarnation: An Interdisciplinary Symposium on the Incarnation of the Son of God*, ed. Stephen T. Davis, Daniel Kendall, and Gerald O'Collins, 273–99. Oxford: Oxford University Press, 2002.

————. "Timelessness and Foreknowledge." *Philosophical Studies* 63 (1991) 309–25.

————. "Why Didn't God Create the World Sooner?" *Religious Studies* 27 (1991) 157–72.

Leigh, Ronald W. "Jesus: The One-natured God-man." *Christian Scholar's Review* 11.2 (1982) 124–27.

Letham, Robert. *The Holy Trinity: In Scripture, History, Theology, and Worship*. Phillipsburg: Presbyterian & Reformed, 2001.

Lewis, Delmas. "Eternity, Time and Tenselessness." *Faith and Philosophy* 5 (1988) 72–86.

Lonergan, Bernard. *The Way to Nicaea: The Dialectical Development of Trinitarian Theology*. Translated by Conn O'Donovan. Philadelphia: Westminster, 1964.

Loomer, Bernard M. "Christian Faith and Process Philosophy." In *Process Philosophy and Christian Thought*, ed. Delwin Brown, Ralph E. James, and Gene Reeves, 70–98. Indianapolis: Bobbs-Merrill, 1971.

McCabe, Herbert. *God Matters*. London: Chapman, 1987.

McDonald, H. D. *The Atonement of the Death of Christ*. Grand Rapids: Baker, 1985.

MacGregor, Geddes. *The Nicene Creed: Illuminated by Modern Thought*. Grand Rapids: Eerdmans, 1980.

McGrath, Alister E. *Christian Theology: An Introduction*, 3rd ed. Oxford: Blackwell, 2001.

————, ed. *The Christian Theology Reader*, 2nd ed. Oxford: Blackwell, 2001.

————. *What Was God Doing on the Cross?* Grand Rapids: Zondervan, 1992.

McTaggart, J. E. M. *The Nature of Existence*. Vol. 2. Cambridge: Cambridge University Press, 1927.

————. "The Unreality of Time." In *Time*, ed. with introduction by Jonathan Westphal and Carl Levenson, 94–111. Hackett Readings in Philosophy. Indianapolis: Hackett, 1993.

Marsh, John. *The Fullness of Time*. London: Nisbet, 1952.

Mellor, D. Hugh. *Real Time*. Cambridge: Cambridge University Press, 1981.

Mesle, C. Robert. *Process Theology: A Basic Introduction*. St. Louis: Chalice, 1993.

Moltmann, Jürgen. *The Crucified God: The Cross of Christ as the Foundation and Criticism of Christian Theology*. Translated by R. A. Wilson and John Bowden. New York: Harper & Row, 1974.

————. *History and the Triune God: Contributions to Trinitarian Theology*. Translated by John Bowden. New York: Crossroad, 1992.

————. *The Trinity and the Kingdom*. Translated by Margaret Kohl. San Francisco: Harper & Row, 1981.

Morris, Thomas V. *The Concept of God*. Oxford Readings in Philosophy. Oxford: Oxford University Press, 1987.

————. *The Logic of God Incarnate*. Ithaca: Cornell University Press, 1986.

————. *Our Idea of God: An Introduction to Philosophical Theology*. Vancouver: Regent College Publishing, 1991.

Muilenburg James. "The Biblical View of Time." *Harvard Theological Review* 54.4 (October 1961) 225–52.

Mullins, E. Y. *The Christian Religion in its Doctrinal Expressions*. Nashville: Broadman, 1917.

Nash, Ronald H. *The Concept of God: An Exploration of Contemporary Difficulties with the Attributes of God*. Grand Rapids: Zondervan, 1983.

Neville, Robert C. *Eternity and Time's Flow*. SUNY Series in Philosophy. Albany: State University of New York Press, 1993.

Newton, Isaac. *Newton's Philosophy of Nature: Selections from His Writings.* Edited and arranged with notes by H. S. Thayer. New York: Hafner, 1953.

———. *The Principia: Mathematical Principles of Natural Philosophy.* Translated by I. Bernard Cohen and Anne Whitman. Berkeley: University of California Press, 1999.

Oaklander, L. Nathan, and Quentin Smith, eds. *The New Theory of Time.* New Haven: Yale University Press, 1994.

O'Collins, Gerald. "The Incarnation: The Critical Issues." In *The Incarnation: An Interdisciplinary Symposium on the Incarnation of the Son of God,* ed. Stephen T. Davis, Daniel Kendall, and Gerald O'Collins, 1–27. Oxford: Oxford University Press, 2002.

Orr, James. *A Christian View of God and the World as Centring* [sic] *in the Incarnation.* The Kerr Lectures for 1890–1891. Edinburgh: Elliot, 1893.

Ottley, Robert L. *The Doctrine of the Incarnation,* 5th ed. London: Methuen, 1911.

Packer, J.I. "Incarnate Forever." *Christianity Today,* March 2004, 72.

Padgett, Alan G. "Eternity as Relative Timelessness." In *God and Time: Four Views,* ed. with introduction by Gregory E. Ganssle, 92–128. Downers Grove, IL: InterVarsity, 2001.

———. *God, Eternity, and the Nature of Time.* New York: St. Martin's Press, 1992; reprint Eugene, OR: Wipf & Stock, 2000.

———. "A New Doctrine of Eternity." In *Philosophy of Religion: An Anthology of Contemporary Views,* ed. Melville Y. Stewart, 559–78. Sudbury, MA: Jones & Bartlett, 1996.

Pannenberg, Wolfhart. "Eternity, Time, and the Trinitarian God." In *Trinity, Time, and Church: A Response to the Theology of Robert W. Jenson,* ed. Colin Gunton. Grand Rapids: Eerdmans, 2000.

———. *Jesus–God and Man,* 2nd. ed. Philadelphia: Westminster, 1977.

———. *Systematic Theology.* 3 vols. Translated by Geoffrey W. Bromiley. Grand Rapids: Eerdmans, 1991.

Peters, Ted. *God as Trinity: Relationality and Temporality in Divine Life.* Louisville: Westminster/John Knox, 1993.

Pierce, Tom. "Spatio-Temporal Relations in Divine Interactions." *Scottish Journal of Theology* 35 (1982) 1–11.

Pike, Nelson. *God and Timelessness.* New York: Schocken, 1970.

Pinnock, Clark H., Richard Rice, John Sanders, William Hasker, and David Basinger. *The Openness of God: A Biblical Challenge to the Traditional Understanding of God.* Downers Grove, IL: InterVarsity, 1994.

Pittenger, Norman. *Process Thought and Christian Faith.* New York: Macmillan, 1968.

Plantinga, Alvin. *Does God Have a Nature?* The Aquinas Lecture, 1980. Milwaukee: Marquette University Press, 1980.

———. "On Ockham's Way Out." *Faith and Philosophy* 3 (1986) 235–69.

Plato. *The Dialogues of Plato.* Translated with introductions by B. Jowett. Vol. 2. New York: Scribner's, 1907.

Plotinus. *The Enneads.* Translated by Stephen MacKenna. 2nd revised edition. New York: Pantheon, 1957.

Polkinghorn, John. *Science and Providence: God's Interaction with the World.* New Science Library. Boston: Shambhala, 1989.

Rahner, Karl. *The Trinity.* Translated by Joseph Donceel, with an introduction, index, and glossary by Catherine Mowry LaCugna. New York: Crossroad Herder, 1997.

Ramm, Bernard. *An Evangelical Christology: Ecumenic and Historic.* Vancouver: Regent College Publishing, 1999.

Rawlinson, A. E. J., ed. *Essays on the Trinity and the Incarnation.* London: Longmans & Green, 1928.

Reeves, Gene, and Delwin Brown. "The Development of Process Theology." In *Process Philosophy and Christian Thought,* ed. Delwin Brown, Ralph E. James, and Gene Reeves, 21–65. Indianapolis: Bobbs-Merrill, 1971.

Robinson, H. Wheeler. *Inspiration and Revelation in the Old Testament.* Oxford: Clarendon, 1946.

Rogers, Katherine A. "Anselm on Eternity as the Fifth Dimension." *The Saint Anselm Journal* 3.2 (Spring 2006) 1–8. Online: http://www.anselm.edu/Documents/Institute for Saint Anselm Studies/Abstracts/4.5.3.2f_32Rogers.pdf.

———. "Omniscience, Eternity and Freedom." *International Philosophical Quarterly* 36 (1996) 399–412.

Samuel, V. C. "One Incarnate Nature of God the Word." In *Does Chalcedon Unite or Divide?: Towards Convergence in Orthodox Christology,* ed. by Paulos Gregorios, William H. Lazareth, and Nikos A. Nissiotis, 76–92. Geneva: World Council of Churches, 1981.

Schaff, Philip. *The Creeds of Christendom: With a History and Critical Notes.* 6th ed. Revised by David S. Schaff. Harper & Row, 1931. Reprint, Grand Rapids: Baker, 1983.

Schleiermacher, Friedrich. *The Christian Faith.* English translation of the 2d German Edition. Edited by H. R. Mackintosh and J. S. Stewart. Edinburgh: T. & T. Clark, 1928.

Sellers, R. V. *The Council of Chalcedon: A Historical and Doctrinal Survey.* London: SPCK, 1953.

Senor, Thomas D. "Divine Temporality and Creation Ex Nihilo." *Faith and Philosophy* 10 (1993) 86–92.

———. "Incarnation and Timelessness." *Faith and Philosophy* 7 (April 1990) 149–64.

———. "Incarnation, Timelessness, and Leibniz's Law Problems." In *God and Time: Essays on the Divine Nature,* ed. Gregory E. Ganssle and David M. Woodruff, 220–35. Oxford: Oxford University Press, 2002.

Sherover, Charles M. *Are We In Time? And Other Essays on Time and Temporality.* Edited with a preface by Gregory R. Johnson. Evanston, IL: Northwestern University Press, 2003.

Smith, A. D. "God's Death." *Theology* 80.676 (July 1977) 262–68.

Sontag, Frederick. "Is God Really in History?" *Religious Studies* 15.3 (1979) 379–90.

Stace, W. T. *Time and Eternity: An Essay in the Philosophy of Religion.* Princeton: Princeton University Press, 1952.

Stump, Eleonore, and Norman Kretzmann. "Eternity." *The Journal of Philosophy* 78.8 (August 1981) 429–58.

———. "Eternity, Awareness and Action." *Faith and Philosophy* 9 (1992) 463–82.

Studer, Basil. *Trinity and Incarnation: The Faith of the Early Church.* Translated by Matthias Westerhoff. Edited by Andrew Louth. Edinburgh: T. & T. Clark, 1993.

Sturch, R. L. "The Problem of Divine Eternity." *Religious Studies* 10 (1974) 489–90.

Swinburne, Richard. *The Christian God.* Oxford: Clarendon, 1994.

———. *The Coherence of Theism.* Oxford: Clarendon, 1977.

———. *The Coherence of Theism,* rev. ed. Clarendon Library of Logic and Philosophy. Oxford: Clarendon, 1993.

———. *Faith and Reason.* Oxford: Clarendon, 1981.

————. "God and Time." In *Reasoned Faith*, ed. Eleonore Stump. Ithaca, NY: Cornell University Press, 1993.

————. *The Resurrection of God Incarnate.* New York: Oxford University Press, 2003.

————. *Space and Time*, 2nd ed. London: Macmillan, 1981.

————. "The Timelessness of God, I." *Church Quarterly Review* 166 (July–Sept 1965) 323–37.

————. "The Timelessness of God, II." *Church Quarterly Review* 166 (October–December 1965) 472–86.

Torrance, Thomas F. *Divine and Contingent Order.* Oxford: Oxford University Press, 1981.

————, ed. *The Incarnation: Ecumenical Studies in the Nicene-Constantinopolitan Creed A.D. 381.* Reprint, Eugene, OR: Wipf & Stock, 1998.

————. *Space, Time, and Incarnation.* London: Oxford University Press, 1969.

————. *Space, Time, and Resurrection.* Grand Rapids: Eerdmans, 1976.

————. *The Trinitarian Faith: The Evangelical Theology of the Ancient Catholic Church.* Edinburgh: T. & T. Clark, 1988.

Turcescu, Lucian. *Gregory of Nyssa and the Concept of Divine Persons.* Oxford: Oxford University Press, 2005.

von Orelli, Conrad. *Die hebräishen Synonyma der Zeit und Ewigkeit genetisch und sprachvergleichend dargestellt.* Leipzig: Lorentz, 1871.

Wainwright, Geoffrey. *For Our Salvation: Two Approaches to the Work of Christ.* Grand Rapids: Eerdmans, 1997.

Walgrave, J. H. "Incarnation and Atonement." In *The Incarnation: Ecumenical Studies in the Nicene-Constantinopolitan Creed A.D. 381*, ed. by Thomas F. Torrance, 148–76. Eugene: Wipf & Stock, 1998.

Ware, Bruce A. "An Evangelical Reformulation of the Doctrine of the Immutability of God." *Journal of the Evangelical Theological Society* 29.4 (December 1986) 431–46.

————. *God's Lesser Glory: The Diminished God of Open Theism.* Wheaton: Crossway, 2000.

Whitehead, Alfred North. *Process and Reality.* 2nd ed. Edited by David Ray Griffin and Donald W. Sherburne. New York: Macmillan, 1978.

Wilkinson, David. *God, Time and Stephen Hawking.* Grand Rapids: Monarch, 2001.

Williams, Arthur H., Jr. "The Trinity and Time." *Scottish Journal of Theology* 39 (1986) 68–51.

Wolterstorff, Nicholas. *Divine Discourse: Philosophical Reflections on the Claim that God Speaks.* Cambridge: Cambridge University Press, 1995.

————. "God Everlasting." In *Contemporary Philosophy of Religion*, ed. Steven M. Cahn and David Shatz. Oxford: Oxford University Press, 1982.

————. *Reason Within the Bounds of Religion*, 2nd ed. Grand Rapids: Eerdmans, 1984.

————. "Response to Critics." In *God and Time: Four Views*, ed. with introduction by Gregory E. Ganssle, 225–38. Downers Grove, IL: InterVarsity, 2001.

————. "Unqualified Divine Temporality." In *God and Time: Four Views*, ed. with introduction by Gregory E. Ganssle, 187–213. Downers Grove, IL: InterVarsity, 2001.